ASVAB
SUCCESS

ASVAB
SUCCESS

4th Edition

LEARNINGEXPRESS®

NEW YORK

Copyright © 2015 LearningExpress, LLC.

All rights reserved under International and Pan American Copyright Conventions.
Published in the United States by LearningExpress, LLC, New York.

Library of Congress Cataloging-in-Publication Data: on file

Printed in the United States of America

9 8 7 6 5 4 3 2 1

Fourth Edition

ISBN-13: 978-1-61103-000-6

For more information or to place an order, contact LearningExpress at:
   80 Broad Street
   4th Floor
   New York, NY 10004

CONTENTS

CONTRIBUTORS

CDR Bill Paisley is a former F-14 Tomcat radar intercept officer with 25 years active and reserve service. He holds two undergraduate degrees in education and a master of arts in National Security. He lives in northern Virginia and works as a modeling and simulation professional for the U.S. Navy.

Stephen A. Reiss, MBA, is the founder and owner of the *Math Magician* and the Reiss SAT Seminars test preparation centers in San Diego. Reiss has authored and coauthored several test preparation books and is a member of MENSA.

Mike Segretto has been an assessment writer for 10 years while also creating a wide assortment of informational and entertainment material for various online sites and print publications. He holds a degree in film and English from Hofstra University.

1

Preparing for the ASVAB

Every person who wants to enlist in the Army, Navy, Air Force, Marines, or Coast Guard must take the Armed Services Vocational Battery (ASVAB). If you are thinking about joining the military and have chosen this book to prepare for the ASVAB exam, you are a giant leap ahead of people who will take the ASVAB, but will not study for it.

To succeed on the ASVAB, you must prepare. Your ASVAB score not only determines if you can enlist, but also determines for which military jobs you will qualify. Make no mistake: The better you score on the ASVAB, the more job choices will be open to you.

Section 1 of *ASVAB Success, Fourth Edition* provides you with the most up-to-date information on the exam. Additionally, the exclusive nine-step LearningExpress Test Preparation System will minimize test stress and maximize your score. Finally, you will learn multiple-choice test strategies that will help you get the score you need for the career you want.

Now get started and good luck!

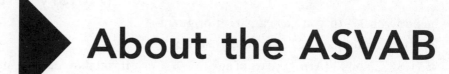

LESSON

1 ▶ About the ASVAB

The Armed Services Vocational Aptitude Battery, or ASVAB, is a multiple-aptitude test consisting of nine sub-tests on various subjects. The ASVAB is used for three main purposes:

1. As a military recruiting tool used by the U.S. Department of Defense to determine enlistment eligibility for a potential recruit.
2. As a military job-placement tool to test potential recruits and determine their developed abilities (i.e., to gauge what they already know about certain subjects); to measure their general learning ability and vocational aptitude; and to predict performance in certain academic, mechanical, and technological areas.
3. As a guide for high school and post-secondary school students, to help them decide upon career paths for which they might best be suited, whether in the military or in some other field.

There are three different ASVAB tests that are currently being used today—two are for military recruiters and the third is used by educational institutions. We will discuss the ASVAB and the differences between the various tests in much more detail later on in this lesson.

Before we get into the exam, let's review the process of joining the military and some of the jobs that are available to you there.

Basic Requirements

Certain requirements for enlistment vary with each service, so checking with a recruiter of your military service of choice is the only way to ensure you know all the service-specific qualifications. In general, you must:

- be between 17 (if you have a parent or guardian's permission) and: 27 (Air Force); 34 (Navy); 35 (USMC); or 42 (Army) years of age.
- be a U.S. citizen or legal resident.
- have a high school diploma or GED.
- be drug-free.
- have a clean arrest record.

It is important to be truthful with your recruiter about any trouble you have had in the past with drugs or with the law. While criminal history checks are conducted on applicants, some kinds of problems can be overcome, if they are really *in the past*, not current difficulties. Check with your recruiter.

Working with Your Recruiter

The recruiter is there to help you. You will have the opportunity to ask as many questions as you want and get a detailed picture of what each branch of the military has to offer. All recruiters will have brochures, videotapes, pamphlets, and years of personal experience to offer as resources. Don't be afraid to bring a parent or trusted friend to help ask questions.

You can find out about salaries, fringe benefits, postings, and educational opportunities—including financial aid for college. The recruiter will also ask you about your education, physical and mental health, and all sorts of in-depth questions about your goals, interests, hobbies, and life experience.

Your recruiter will talk to you about the benefits of enlisting: the pay, travel, experience, and training. You and your recruiter can also start to discuss the kinds of military jobs available. These jobs are mentioned later in this lesson.

Military Entrance Processing Station (MEPS)

If you show definite interest in enlisting, your recruiter will schedule you for a trip to a MEPS in your area (there's one in almost every state) for a day of computer-based and physical testing. The MEPS is where applicants for every branch of the military begin the enlistment process.

During your day at MEPS, you will go through three phases:

- **mental (aptitude) testing**—taking the ASVAB
- **medical exam**—having a routine physical by non-military doctors
- **administrative procedures**—filling out paperwork and discussing your military job options

If all three phases are successful, you will join the military and begin your Basic Training.

Military Occupational Specialties (MOS)

Joining the military does not just make you a soldier. In fact, there are numerous jobs and job types in every branch of the military. The following is a limited list of the many options available. Your score on some sections of the ASVAB *can* affect whether you are eligible to fill certain positions.

Administrative

Administrative Specialist

Cartographer
Executive Administrative Assistant
Finance Specialist
Information Systems Operator
Intelligence Analyst
Personnel Administration Specialist

Combat Specialty

Ammunition Specialist
Combat Engineer
Infantryman
M1 Armor (tank) Crewmember
PATRIOT Missile Crewmember

Communications and Information Systems

Information Technology Specialist
NODAL Network Systems Operator
Visual Information Specialist

Construction

Carpentry and Masonry Specialist

Electronic and Electrical Equipment Repair

Radio Repairer

Engineering, Science, and Technical

Interior Electrician
Single Channel Radio Operator

Healthcare

Animal Care Specialist
Behavioral Science Specialist
Dental Laboratory Specialist
Medical Specialist
Practical Nurse
Psychological Operations Specialist
X-ray Specialist

Machine Operator and Precision Work

Crane Operator
Machinist

Media and Public Affairs

Broadcast Journalist
Multimedia Illustrator

Transportation and Material Handling

Fabric Repair Specialist
Motor Transport Operator
Watercraft Operator

Vehicle and Machinery Mechanic

Aviation Systems Repairer
Light-Wheel Vehicle Mechanic
PATRIOT System Repairer
UH-60 Helicopter Repairer

Do any of these jobs interest you? Keep in mind that to qualify for these positions, you have to receive a specified minimum score on relevant sections on the ASVAB.

Now let's review the ASVAB in greater detail so you know exactly what you will face on test day and what you will have to study to get the score you need.

The ASVAB for Non-Military Test Takers

It's important to remember that taking the ASVAB does not obligate you to join the military. If you take the ASVAB with no intention of entering the military, the test is, for you, simply an aptitude test. Your results will help you determine if you have the aptitude for certain skills or whether you should seek additional training.

There is no cost for taking the ASVAB, and they are offered in recruitment centers and at some high schools. Recruiters or guidance counselors can explain your score report and how to use it.

More Information on the ASVAB

Depending on where you take the ASVAB, you will take either the computer or paper-and-pencil version. Candidates for enlistment who take the ASVAB at a MEPS will take the computer version, while candidates for enlistment taking the ASVAB at a reserve center or Mobile Examination Team (MET) site will take the paper-and-pencil version. The content of the test is the same on both versions; only the format, the mechanics of scoring, and the number of questions asked are slightly different.

The computer version of the ASVAB is known as a *Computerized Adaptive Testing* exam, abbreviated as CAT. The main characteristic of a CAT is its design—if the correct answer is chosen, the next question will be harder. If the answer selected is incorrect, the next question will be easier. You must keep in mind, however, once an answer is selected in the CAT-ASVAB, it cannot be changed.

If you take the CAT-ASVAB test at a MEPS center, you will see that the Auto and Shop questions are broken up into their own subtests, each with 11 questions. For the purpose of this study guide, however, the Auto and Shop subtest will remain a single subtest comprised of 25 auto and shop questions.

The breakdowns for the two military recruiting tests you may take are displayed below:

MILITARY ENTRANCE PROCESSING STATION TEST (CAT-ASVAB)		
SUBTEST	NUMBER OF QUESTIONS	TIME (MINUTES)
General Science (GS)	16	8
Arithmetic Reasoning (AR)	16	39
Word Knowledge (WK)	16	8
Paragraph Comprehension (PC)	11	22
Mathematics Knowledge (MK)	16	18
Electronics Information (EI)	16	8
Auto Information (AI)	11	6
Shop Information (AS)	11	5
Mechanical Comprehension (MC)	16	20
Assembling Objects (AO)	15	25
Total	144 questions	159 minutes

MOBILE EXAMINATION TEAM TEST (PENCIL-AND-PAPER ASVAB)		
SUBTEST	NUMBER OF QUESTIONS	TIME (MINUTES)
General Science (GS)	25	11
Arithmetic Reasoning (AR)	30	36
Word Knowledge (WK)	35	11
Paragraph Comprehension (PC)	15	13
Mathematics Knowledge (MK)	25	24
Electronics Information (EI)	20	9
Auto and Shop Information (AS)	25	11
Mechanical Comprehension (MC)	25	19
Assembling Objects (AO)	25	15
Total	225 questions	149 minutes

Most sections of the ASVAB—General Science, Arithmetic Reasoning, Word Knowledge, Auto and Shop Information, Mathematics Knowledge, Mechanical Comprehension, and Electronics Information—depend on your knowlege of the subject from your high school courses or other reading. The two sections that do not depend on previous knowledge are the Paragraph Comprehension and the Assembling Objects sections. For the Paragraph Comprehension questions, you will find the answers using only the information given in the paragraph. For the Assembling Objects questions, you will find the answers by applying your skills of spatial perception and being able to determine the proper relationships of objects and shapes.

The differences between the various ASVAB tests are minor but are worth noting. The CAT-ASVAB is, of course, computerized and is taken at a dedicated computer workstation at a MEPS center. The MET-ASVAB and the Student ASVAB are both pencil-and-paper exams and can be administered in any location a Mobile Examination Team can visit or in any school testing environment. The only difference between the MET-ASVAB and the Student ASVAB is that the Student ASVAB test does not contain the Assembling Objects subtest.

The Nine ASVAB Subtests

The following is a more detailed description of each of the nine subtests in the ASVAB.

Part 1: General Science
The General Science subtest of the ASVAB consists of questions that are designed to measure your ability to recognize, apply, and analyze basic scientific principles in the areas of:

- **Life science**—botany, zoology, anatomy and physiology, ecology
- **Physical science**—force and motion, energy, fluids and gases, atomic structure, chemistry
- **Earth and space science**—astronomy, geology, meteorology, oceanography

Here's a sample General Science question, followed by its answer.

1. Substances that speed up reaction time without undergoing changes themselves are called
   a. buffers.
   b. colloids.
   c. reducers.
   d. catalysts.

The answer is **d**.

Part 2: Arithmetic Reasoning

The Arithmetic Reasoning subtest consists of word problems describing everyday life situations. The questions are designed to measure your reasoning skills and understanding of:

- Operations with whole numbers
- Operations with fractions and decimals or money
- Ratios and proportions
- Interest and percentages
- Measurements of perimeters, areas, volumes, time, and temperature

Here's a sample Arithmetic Reasoning question, followed by its answer.

1. If 12 people are needed to run four machines, how many people are needed to run 20 machines?
   a. 20
   b. 48
   c. 60
   d. 80

The answer is **c**. If four machines require 12 people to run them, that means each machine needs 3 people in order to run. 20 machines × 3 people = 60 people, choice **c**.

Part 3: Word Knowledge

The Word Knowledge subtest consists of questions that ask you to choose the correct definition of verbs, nouns, adjectives, and adverbs. These questions come in two forms:

1. Definitions presented alone, with no context
2. Words in the context of a short sentence

Here's a sample Word Knowledge question, followed by its answer.

1. *Rudimentary* most nearly means
   a. political.
   b. minute.
   c. promotional.
   d. basic.

The answer is **d**.

Part 4: Paragraph Comprehension

The Paragraph Comprehension subtest is based on several short passages written on a variety of topics. No prior knowledge of the subject is required—all the information needed to answer the questions will be found in the passage. The questions are designed to test your ability to obtain the following kinds of information from written material:

- **Literal comprehension**—your ability to identify stated facts, identify reworded facts, and determine the sequence of events
- **Implicit, inferential, or critical comprehension**—your ability to draw conclusions; identify the main idea of a paragraph; determine the author's purpose, mood, or tone; and identify style and technique

Here's a sample Paragraph Comprehension question, followed by its answer.

1. In certain areas, water is so scarce that every attempt is made to conserve it. For instance, on an oasis in the Sahara Desert, the amount of water necessary for each date palm has been carefully determined. How much water is each tree likely to be given?
   a. no water at all
   b. water on alternate days
   c. exactly the amount required
   d. water only if it is a young tree

The answer is **c**. The passage doesn't indicate how much water the tree needs, only that the exact amount is given to it.

Part 5: Auto and Shop Information

The Auto and Shop Information subtest includes questions on automotive repair and building construction. General shop practices are also included. The questions cover the following topics:

- Automotive components
- Automotive systems
- Automotive tools
- Automotive troubleshooting and repair
- Shop tools
- Building materials
- Building and construction procedures

Here's a sample Auto and Shop Information question, followed by its answer.

1. A chisel is used for
   a. drilling
   b. cutting
   c. twisting
   d. grinding

The answer is **b**.

Part 6: Mathematics Knowledge

The Mathematics Knowledge subtest is designed to measure your understanding of mathematical concepts, principles, and procedures. The emphasis is on your ability to recognize and apply basic mathematical principles. The questions cover:

- **Number theory**—factors, multiples, reciprocals, number properties, primes, integers
- **Numeration**—fractional parts, decimals, percentages, and conversions; order of operations; exponents; rounding; reducing fractions; roots and radicals; signed numbers
- **Algebraic operations and equations**—solving or determining equations, factoring, simplifying algebraic expressions, converting a sentence to an equation
- **Geometry and measurement**—coordinates and slope, angle measurement, properties of polygons and circles, perimeter, area, volume, unit conversion
- **Probability**—the likelihood of the outcomes of certain events

Here's a sample Mathematics Knowledge question, followed by its answer.

1. If 50% of $x = 66$, then x equals?
   a. 33
   b. 66
   c. 99
   d. 132

The answer is **d**. Set up an equation to help you answer this question.

$$\frac{1}{2}x = 66$$

Multiply both sides by 2

$$x = 2(66)$$

$$x = 132, \text{ choice } \mathbf{d}.$$

Part 7: Mechanical Comprehension

The Mechanical Comprehension subtest consists of questions, many of them illustrated, on general mechanics and physical principles. The questions cover simple machines, including gears, pulleys, and levers; as well as force and fluid dynamics. Problems involving basic properties of materials are also included. The questions may consist of knowledge, application, and analysis questions covering:

- **Basic compound machines**—gears, cams, pistons, cranks, linkages, belts, chains
- **Simple machines**—levers, pulleys, screws, wedges, wheels, axles
- **Mechanical motion**—friction, velocity, direction, acceleration, centrifugal force
- **Fluid dynamics**—hydraulic forces, compression
- **Properties of materials**—weight, strength, expansion/contraction, absorption, density
- **Structural support**—center of gravity, weight distribution

Here's a sample Mechanical Comprehension question, followed by its answer.

1. An elevator uses which of the following mechanical devices?
   a. a cable
   b. a pulley
   c. a motor
   d. all of the above

The answer is **d.**

Part 8: Electronics Information

The Electronics Information subtest consists of questions on electrical and electronic systems. These questions are designed to measure basic knowledge of electrical and electronic systems including:

- Electrical tools, symbols, devices, and materials
- Electrical circuits
- Electricity and electronic systems
- Electrical current: voltage, conductivity, resistance, and grounding

Here's a sample Electronics Information question, followed by its answer.

1. In electrical terms, what does the abbreviation AC stand for?
   a. additional charge
   b. alternating coil
   c. alternating current
   d. ampere current

The answer is **c.**

Part 9: Assembling Objects

The Assembling Objects subtest consists of questions that test your ability to understand and recognize the spatial relationships between different shapes. There are two types of Assembling Objects questions. The first, called Assembling Shapes, tests your ability to look at sample shapes and find the correct answer that incorporates those shapes in its design. The second, called Connectors, tests your ability to connect different shaped objects to specific, identified points on the shapes.

Here is a sampling of the two types of Assembling Objects questions, followed by its answers.

Type 1: Assembling Shapes

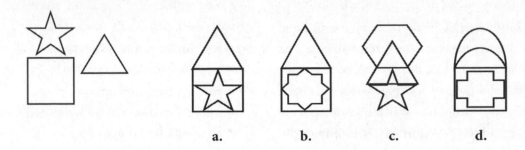

a.　　b.　　c.　　d.

The correct answer is **a**. Look for each element of the shapes to be assembled in each answer choice. Only choice **a** has a star, a triangle, and a square.

Type 2: Connectors

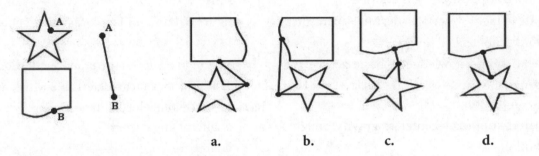

a.　　b.　　c.　　d.

The correct answer is **d**. Notice the position of points a and b on the star and trapezoidal shape. Only choice **d** attaches the line segment to the correct places—don't be confused by choice **c**; it incorrectly places point a on the point of the star, not in one of its vertices.

Now that we have reviewed the subtests of the ASVAB, it is time to address the Armed Forces Qualifying Test (AFQT).

The Armed Forces Qualifying Test (AFQT)

Although nine subtests comprise the entire ASVAB, only four of these subtests are used to determine whether you can enlist in the military. Only your scores on the Arithmetic Reasoning, Word Knowledge, Paragraph Comprehension, and Mathematics Knowledge subtests count toward your AFQT score. Simply put, if your AFQT score is not above a passing level, you will not be able to enlist. That is why it is critically important to pass each of these subtests, sometimes referred to as the ASVAB Core, to ensure that you can enlist.

The other five subtests—General Science, Auto and Shop Information, Mechanical Comprehension, Electronics Information and Assembly Objects help determine for which jobs you are suited. Even if you have a passing AFQT score, you should aim to do your best on these other subtests to improve your chances of obtaining the job you want.

How This Book Can Help You

The lessons in the rest of Section 1 offer you tips and strategies for doing your best on any test you take. The lessons found in Sections 2, 3, and 4 of this book provide you with targeted strategies for improving your basic reading, math, and vocabulary skills to get a top score on ASVAB Core subtests—Arithmatic Reasoning (AR), Word Knowledge (WK), Paragraph Comprehension (PC), and Mathematics Knowledge (MK).

While studying the math lessons, you will:

- review basic operations, such as addition, sub-traction, multiplication, and division
- get ready to tackle fractions, decimals, percents, and word problems
- gain a working knowledge of basic geometry, including lines, angles, triangles, rectangles, squares, and circles
- refresh your knowledge of math terms

In the reading comprehension lessons, you will learn to:

- find important facts while reading
- locate main ideas
- sort out fact from opinion
- understand tools used by writers, such as language choice and structure

Finally, the vocabulary lessons will help you:

- use root words to discover word meanings
- define and use common word prefixes and suffixes
- figure out unfamiliar words using context

Be sure to complete the practice questions found in each lesson, so you can determine which areas you have mastered and which still need more work.

2 ▶ The LearningExpress Test Preparation System

Taking the ASVAB demands a lot of preparation if you want to achieve a passing score. The LearningExpress Test Preparation System, developed exclusively for LearningExpress by leading test experts, gives you the discipline and attitude required to achieve winning results.

Before we cover all the ways you can succeed on this exam, here are some of the pitfalls that can keep you from your top score:

- being unfamiliar with the format and content of the exam
- having high levels of test anxiety
- leaving your preparation to the last minute
- not preparing at all
- not practicing crucial test-taking skills, such as how to pace yourself through the exam, how to use the process of elimination, and when to guess
- not being in the mental and physical shape required to complete the exam
- arriving late at the exam site, having to work on an empty stomach, or shivering through the exam because the room is cold

What is the reason for all of these test-taking pitfalls? Control. The LearningExpress Test Preparation System puts *you* in control. In nine easy-to-follow steps, you will learn everything you need to know to ensure that you are in charge of your preparation and your performance on the exam. After completing this chapter, you will have taken all the needed steps to achieve a high score on the ASVAB.

The LearningExpress Test Preparation System leads you through preparing for this or any exam. Each of the following steps includes reading about the step and one activity. It's important that you do the activities along with the reading, or you won't be getting the full benefit of the system. Each step tells you approximately how much time that step will take you to complete.

Step 1: Learn About the Exam	50 minutes
Step 2: Combat Test Anxiety	20 minutes
Step 3: Create a Study Plan	30 minutes
Step 4: Learn to Manage Your Time	10 minutes
Step 5: Practice the Process of Elimination	20 minutes
Step 6: Understand When to Guess	20 minutes
Step 7: Prepare for Peak Performance	10 minutes
Step 8: Make Final Test-Day Preparations	10 minutes
Step 9: Ace the Exam!	10 minutes
Total	**3 hours**

We estimate the entire system in this chapter will take approximately three hours. If you prefer, you can complete the whole LearningExpress Test Preparation System in one sitting. Otherwise, you can do one or two steps per day for the next several days. It's up to you—remember, *you* are in control.

Step 1: Learn about the Exam

Time to complete: 50 minutes
Activity: Read Lesson 1, "About the ASVAB"
Knowing what to expect on test day accomplishes several things. First, it lowers your test anxiety, because you can anticipate the kinds of questions asked.

Also, knowing what will be tested helps you prepare and focus your study time. For these reasons, the first step in the LearningExpress Test Preparation System is finding out everything you can about the ASVAB.

Why Do You Have to Take This Exam, Anyway?

It's important for you to remember that your score on the ASVAB does not determine the kind of person you are or even whether or not you will make a good serviceperson. An exam like this can't test whether you can follow orders; whether you can become part of a unit that works together to accomplish a task; and so on. Those kinds of things are hard to measure, while a test is easy to evaluate.

However, your chances of getting into the military *still* depend on your getting a good score on the core subtests of the ASVAB, and that's why you are here—using the LearningExpress Test Preparation System to achieve control over the exam.

Test Content and Format

If you haven't done so, stop here and read Lesson 1 of this book, which gives you an overview of the ASVAB. Once you have this information, the next steps in the LearningExpress Test Preparation System will show you what to do with it.

Step 2: Combat Test Anxiety

Time to complete: 20 minutes
Activity: Take the Test Stress Questionnaire
Knowing what is being tested and the types of questions asked is the first step toward gaining control of the exam. Next, you have to overcome one of the biggest obstacles to test success: test anxiety. Test anxiety not only impairs your performance on the exam itself; it also keeps you from preparing. In this step, you will learn stress management techniques that will help you succeed on your exam. However, don't expect to read through and master these techniques in one sitting. You will need to practice stress management the same way you practice the exams in this book, so that it will come naturally to you on test day.

The Test Anxiety Edge

It is important to understand that a little test anxiety is a good thing. Everyone gets nervous before a big exam— and if that nervousness motivates you to prepare thoroughly and stay focused on your goal, so much the better. In fact, some test anxiety gives you a little extra edge—just the kind of edge you need to do well.

On page 15 is the Test Stress Questionnaire. Stop here and answer the questions to find out whether or not your level of test anxiety is enough to provide you an edge.

Stress Management before the Test

To keep your stress level at a reasonable minimum, we suggest the following:

- **Prepare.** There's nothing like knowing what to expect and being prepared for it to put you in control of test anxiety.
- **Practice self-confidence.** A positive attitude is a great way to combat test anxiety. Don't be shy. Stand in front of the mirror and say to your reflection, "I am prepared. I am full of self-confidence. I am going to ace this test. I know I can do it." Say it once a day. If you hear it often enough, you will believe it.
- **Ignore negative messages.** Every time someone starts telling you how hard the exam is or how it's almost impossible to get a high score, repeat your self-confidence messages to yourself. Don't listen to the negative messages.
- **Visualize.** Imagine putting on your new uniform and beginning your first day of Basic Training. Visualizing success can help make it happen— and it reminds you of why you are going to this effort to prepare for the exam.
- **Exercise.** Physical activity helps relieve stress and focus your mind. Go for a run, lift weights, go swimming—and do it regularly. Being in good physical shape can actually help you do well on the exam.

Stress Management on Test Day

There are several ways you can lower your test anxiety on test day. They work best if you practice them in the weeks before the test, so you know which ones work best for you.

- **Breathe deeply.** Take a deep breath while you count to five. Hold it for a count of one, then let it out on a count of five. Repeat several times.

Test Stress Questionnaire

In general, you only need to worry about test anxiety if it is extreme enough to impair your performance. The following questions will provide an informal diagnosis of your level of test anxiety. In the blank before each statement, write the number that most accurately describes your experience.

0 = Never   1 = Once or twice   2 = Sometimes   3 = Often

_____ I have gotten so nervous before an exam that I simply put down the books and didn't study for it.

_____ I have experienced physical symptoms such as vomiting and severe headaches because I was nervous about an exam.

_____ I have simply not showed up for an exam because I was scared.

_____ I have experienced dizziness and disorientation while taking an exam.

_____ I have had trouble filling in the little circles because my hands were shaking too hard.

_____ I have failed an exam because I was too nervous to complete it.

_____ **Total: Add up the numbers in the blanks.**

Your Test Stress Score

Here are the steps you should take, depending on your score. If you scored:

- **Below 3,** your level of test anxiety is nothing to worry about; it's probably just enough to keep you driven to do your best.
- **Between 3 and 6,** your test anxiety may be enough to impair your performance, and you should practice the stress management techniques listed in this step of the LearningExpress Test Preparation System to try to lower your test anxiety to more manageable levels.
- **Above 6,** your level of test anxiety is a concern. In addition to practicing the stress management techniques listed in this step, you may want to work with a tutor, academic counselor, or mental health profession to combat your anxiety.

- **Move your body.** Try rolling your head in a circle. Rotate your shoulders. Shake your hands from the wrist. Many people find these movements very relaxing.
- **Visualize a relaxing place.** Think of the place where you are most relaxed: lying on the beach in the sun, walking through the park, or anywhere else where you feel comfortable. Now close your eyes and imagine you are actually there. If you practice in advance, you will find that you only need a few seconds of this exercise to experience a significant increase in your sense of well-being.

Stress Management during the Test

If anxiety threatens to overwhelm you during the exam, there are still things you can do to manage the stress level:

- **Visualize completing the test.** This time, visualize yourself moving smoothly and quickly through the test, answering every question correctly and finishing early. Like most visualization techniques, this one works best if you have practiced it ahead of time.
- **Find an easy question.** Find an easy question, and answer it. Finishing even one question

helps boost your sense of accomplishment and self-confidence.

- **Take a mental break.** Everyone loses concentration once in a while during a test. It's normal, so you shouldn't worry about it. Instead, accept what has happened. Say to yourself, "Hey, I lost it there for a minute. My brain is taking a break." Put down your pencil, close your eyes, and do some deep breathing for a few seconds. Then you are ready to go back to work.

Remember, do not attempt these techniques for the first time on test day. Try them while studying or taking the practice tests in this book.

Step 3: Create a Study Plan

Time to complete: 30 minutes
Activity: Construct and follow a study schedule
Maybe the most important thing you can do to get control of yourself and your exam is to make a study plan. Too many people don't plan ahead and instead spend hours the day before the exam staring at lessons and sample questions. This method only raises your level of test anxiety, and does not substitute for careful preparation and practice.

So don't wait until the last minute and cram. Take control of your preparation time by planning ahead and making a study schedule. On the following pages you will find three sample schedules, based on the amount of time you may have before you take the ASVAB. These may work for you, but don't be afraid to construct your own or to adapt them to your schedule. Be honest about how much time you have to study, and don't give up if you fall behind schedule. If something unforeseen delays your studying, make up for it when you have time.

Even more important than making a plan is making a commitment. You can't review everything you need to know for the exam in one night. You have to set time aside every day for study and practice. Shoot for at least 30 minutes a day. Thirty minutes daily is more effective than three hours on Saturday.

Schedule A: The One-Month Plan

If you have at least a month before you take the ASVAB, you have plenty of time to prepare, but don't waste it. Look at Schedule A for a suggested timeline. If you have less than a month, turn to Schedule B.

TIME	PREPARATION
Days 1–4	Use these first days to learn about the exam and work through the LearningExpress Test Preparation System. Be sure you are prepared to commit to the studying process.
Days 5–11	Review Section 2: Math for the Arithmetic Reasoning and Mathematics Knowledge Subtests. Complete all the practice questions.
Day 12	Review the answers to the practice questions. Go back and study the tips and strategies in Lessons 4, 5, 6, and 7.
Days 13–19	Review Section 3: Reading Comprehension for the Paragraph Comprehension Subtest. Complete all the practice questions.
Day 20	Review the answers to the practice questions. Go back and study the tips and strategies in Lessons 8, 9, 10, and 11.

TIME	PREPARATION
Days 21–26	Review Section 4: Vocabulary for the Word Knowledge Subtest. Complete all the practice questions.
Day 27	Once again, review the answers to the practice questions. Go back and study the tips and strategies in Lessons 12, 13, and 14.
Days 28–29	Think about which skills are your weakest. Return to those lessons and review them more thoroughly.
Day before the exam	Relax. Do something unrelated to the exam, exercise lightly, and go to bed at a reasonable hour.

Schedule B: The Two-Week Plan

If you have at least two weeks before you take the exam, use this schedule to help make the most of your time. If you have less than two weeks, turn to Schedule C.

TIME	PREPARATION
Day 1	Use the first day to learn about the exam and work through the LearningExpress Test Preparation System. Be sure you are prepared to commit to the studying process.
Days 2–4	Review Section 2: Math for the Arithmetic Reasoning and Mathematics Knowledge Subtests. Complete all the practice questions.
Day 5	Review the answers to the practice questions. Go back and study the tips and strategies in Lessons 4, 5, 6, and 7.
Days 6–8	Review Section 3: Reading Comprehension for the Paragraph Comprehension Subtest. Complete all the practice questions.
Day 9	Review the answers to the practice questions. Go back and study the tips and strategies in Lessons 8, 9, 10, and 11.
Days 10–12	Review Section 4: Vocabulary for the Word Knowledge Subtest. Complete all the practice questions.
Day 13	Once again, review the answers to the practice questions. Go back and study the tips and strategies in Lessons 12, 13, and 14.
Day before the exam	Relax. Do something unrelated to the exam, exercise lightly, and go to bed at a reasonable hour.

Schedule C: The One-Week Plan

If you have only one week before you take the exam, use this schedule to help make the most of your limited time. You will have to commit fully to preparing as best you can.

TIME	PREPARATION
Day 1	Spend some time learning about the exam and working through the Learning-Express Test Preparation System.
Day 2	Review Section 2: Math for the Arithmetic Reasoning and Mathematics Knowledge Subtests. Complete all the practice questions.
Day 3	Review Section 3: Reading Comprehension for the Paragraph Comprehension Subtest. Complete all the practice questions.
Day 4	Review Section 4: Vocabulary for the Word Knowledge Subtest. Complete all the practice questions.
Days 5–6	Think about which skills are your weakest. Return to those lessons and review them more thoroughly.
Day before the exam	Use the first part of your last study day to review areas that are still giving you trouble. By the evening, you should stop studying and relax. Do something unrelated to the exam, and go to bed at a reasonable hour.

Step 4: Learn to Manage Your Time

Time to complete: 10 minutes to read, many hours of practice!

Activity: Practice these strategies as you take the sample tests in this book

Steps 4, 5, and 6 of the LearningExpress Test Preparation System put you in charge of your exam by showing you test-taking strategies that work. Practice these strategies as you take the sample tests in this book, and you will be ready to use them on test day.

First, you will take control of your time on the exam. By doing this you will avoid a situation where there are only minutes left, and you are still far from finishing the exam.

- **Follow directions.** On test day, don't spend a lot of time reviewing the directions in detail. However, make sure you know exactly what you are required to do.

- **Pace yourself.** Whether you are taking the computer or paper-based ASVAB, use a watch or clock to keep track of time. Figure out how many minutes you can afford to spend on each question by dividing the time for each section by the number of questions in it.

- **Keep moving.** Don't waste time on one question. If you don't know the answer, skip the question and move on. You may be able to return to it later. All questions have the same point value. You should answer as many questions as you can rather than spending time answering one difficult question.

- **Don't rush.** Though you should keep moving, rushing won't help. Only careless errors and lost points come from rushing, so try to keep calm and work methodically and quickly.

Step 5: Practice the Process of Elimination

Time to complete: 20 minutes
Activity: Complete worksheet on Using the Process of Elimination

After time management, your next most important tool for taking control of your exam is using the process of elimination wisely. Standard test-taking wisdom dictates that you should always read all the answer choices before choosing your answer. This helps you find the right answer by eliminating incorrect answer choices.

Supposes you are facing an Electronics Information question that goes like this:

Which of the following has the least electrical resistence?
a. wood
b. iron
c. rubber
d. silver

Always use the process of elimination on a question like this, even if the right answer seems obvious. Sometimes the answer that jumps out isn't right after all. Let's assume, for the purpose of this exercise, that you are a little rusty on property electronics information, so you need to use some intuition to compensate for what you don't remember. Proceed through the answer choices in order.

So you start with choice **a**. This one is pretty easy to eliminate; wood doesn't conduct electricity. It absorbs it, so you can assume choice **a** is incorrect.

Choice **b** seems reasonable; make a mental note, "Good answer, I might use this one."

Choice **c** strikes you as a less likely. Rubber has a fairly high resistence. Eliminate this one since already found a choice (**b**) that is more reasonable.

Choice **d** is also a possibility. Make a mental note, "Good answer" or "Well, maybe," depending on how attractive this answer looks to you.

Now, since Electronics Information is a knowledge-based subtest, you will have to know that choice **b**, iron, is correct. However, using the process of elimination helped you narrow your choices down to only two.

If you take the ASVAB on paper, it's good to have a system for marking *good*, *bad*, and *maybe* answers. We recommend the following:

X = bad
✔ = good
? = maybe

If you don't like these marks, devise your own system. Just make sure you do it long before test day, so you won't have to worry about remembering it just before the exam.

Even when you think you are absolutely clueless about a question, you can often use process of elimination to discard at least one answer choice. If so, you are better prepared to make an educated guess, as you will see in Step 6. More often, the process of elimination allows you to get down to only two possible correct answers. Then you are in a stronger position to guess. Sometimes, even though you don't know the right answer, you find it simply by getting rid of the wrong ones, as you did in the previous example.

Try using these elimination skills on the questions in the **Using the Process of Elimination** worksheet. The questions are not sample ASVAB questions; they are just designed to show you how the process of elimination works. The answer explanations for this worksheet show one possible way you might use the process to arrive at the right answer.

The process of elimination is your tool for the next step: knowing when to guess.

Using the Process of Elimination

Use the process of elimination to answer the following questions.

1. Ilsa is as old as Meghan will be in five years. The difference between Ed's age and Meghan's age is twice the difference between Ilsa's age and Meghan's age. Ed is 29. How old is Ilsa?
   a. 4
   b. 10
   c. 19
   d. 24

2. "All drivers of commercial vehicles must carry a valid commercial driver's license whenever operating a commercial vehicle." According to this sentence, which of the following people need NOT carry a commercial driver's license?
   a. a truck driver idling the engine while waiting to be directed to a loading dock
   b. a bus operator backing a bus out of the way of another bus in the bus lot
   c. a taxi driver driving his or her personal car to the grocery store
   d. a limousine driver taking the limousine home after dropping off the last passenger of the evening

3. Smoking tobacco has been linked to
   a. increased risk of stroke and heart attack.
   b. all forms of respiratory disease.
   c. increasing mortality rates over the past ten years.
   d. juvenile delinquency.

4. Which of the following words is spelled correctly?
   a. incorrigible
   b. outragous
   c. domestickated
   d. understandible

Answers

Here are the answers, as well as some suggestions as to how you might have used the process of elimination to find them.

1. **d.** You should have eliminated choice **a** immediately. Ilsa can't be four years old if Meghan is going to be Ilsa's age in five years. The best way to eliminate other answers is to try plugging them in to the information given in the problem. For instance, for choice **b**, if Ilsa is 10, then Meghan must be 5. The difference in their ages is 5. The difference between Ed's age, 29, and Meghan's age, 5, is 24. Is 24 two times 5? No. Then choice **b** is wrong. You could eliminate choice **c** in the same way and be left with choice **d**.

2. **c.** Note the word *not* in the question, and go through the answers one by one. Is the truck driver in choice **a** "operating a commercial vehicle"? Yes, idling counts as "operating," so he needs to have a commercial driver's license. Likewise, the bus operator in choice **b** is operating a commercial vehicle; the question doesn't say the operator has to be on the street. The limo driver in choice **d** is operating a commercial vehicle, even if it doesn't have passenger in it. However, the cab driver

Using the Process of Elimination (continued)

in choice **c** is *not* operating a commercial vehicle, but his or her own private car.

3. a. You could eliminate choice **b** simply because of the presence of the word *all*. Such absolutes hardly ever appear in correct answer choices. Choice **c** looks attractive until you think a little about what you know—aren't *fewer* people smoking these days, rather than more? So how could smoking be responsible for a higher mortality rate? (If you didn't know that *mortality rate* means the rate at which people

die, you might keep this choice as a possibility, but you would still be able to eliminate two answers and have only two to choose from.) Choice **d** is not logical, so you could eliminate that one, too, leaving you with the correct choice, **a**.

4. a. How you use the process of elimination here depends on which words you recognized as spelled incorrectly. If you knew that the correct spellings were *outrageous*, *domesticated*, and *understandable*, then you were correct to choose **a**.

Step 6: Understand When to Guess

Time to complete: 20 minutes
Activity: Complete worksheet on Your Guessing Ability

Armed with the process of elimination, you are ready to take control of one of the biggest questions in test taking: "Should I guess?" The first and main answer is, yes. Some exams have a guessing penalty, in which a fraction of your incorrect answers is subtracted from your right answers—but the ASVAB doesn't work like that. The number of questions you answer correctly yields your raw score. So you have nothing to lose and everything to gain by guessing.

The more complicated answer to the question "Should I guess?" depends on you—your personality and your "guessing intuition." Ask yourself, "Am I a good guesser?"

To find out, complete the Your Guessing Ability worksheet on pages 23–24. Frankly, even if you have lousy intuition, you are still safe in guessing every time because there is no guessing penalty. The best

thing would be to overcome your anxieties and mark an answer. But you may want to have a sense of how good your intuition is before you go into the exam.

Step 7: Prepare for Peak Performance

Time to complete: 10 minutes to read, weeks to complete
Activity: Complete the Physical Preparation Checklist

To do your very best on an exam, you have to take control of your physical and mental state. Exercise, proper diet, and rest will ensure that your body works with, rather than against, your mind on exam day as well as during your preparation.

Exercise

If you don't already have an exercise routine, the time during which you are preparing for an exam is an excellent time to start one. You can incorporate your workouts into your study schedule. And if you are already keeping fit—or trying to get that way—don't let the pressure of preparing for an exam discourage your progress. Exercise helps reduce stress and increases the oxygen supply throughout your body, including your brain, so you will be at peak performance on exam day.

A half hour of vigorous activity—enough to raise a sweat—at least five times per week should be your aim. If you are pressed for time, three times per week should be the minimum. Most importantly, choose an activity you like and get out there and do it. Remember, moderation is the key. If you overdo it, you will only exhaust yourself.

Diet

The first, and perhaps the most difficult thing to do, is to cut out the junk. Chips, candy, and fast food will not improve your performance. Minimize caffeine for at least two weeks before the exam.

There is never a good time to crash diet; instead what your body needs for peak performance is balance. Be sure to eat plenty of fruits and vegetables, along with protein and carbohydrates. Foods that are high in lecithin (an amino acid), such as fish and beans, are especially good brain foods.

The night before the exam, you might eat plenty

Your Guessing Ability

The following are five difficult questions. You are not supposed to know the answers. This is an assessment of your ability to guess when you don't have much information. Read each question carefully, just as if you did expect to answer it. If you have any knowledge at all of the subject of the question, use that knowledge to help you eliminate incorrrect answers.

1. September 7 is Independence Day in
- **a.** India.
- **b.** Costa Rica.
- **c.** Brazil.
- **d.** Australia.

2. American author Gertrude Stein was born in
- **a.** 1713.
- **b.** 1830.
- **c.** 1874.
- **d.** 1901.

3. The third Chief Justice of the U.S. Supreme Court was
- **a.** John Blair.
- **b.** William Cushing.
- **c.** James Wilson.
- **d.** John Jay.

4. Which of the following is the poisonous portion of a daffodil?
- **a.** the bulb
- **b.** the leaves
- **c.** the stem
- **d.** the flowers

5. The state with the highest per capita personal income in 1980 was
- **a.** Alaska.
- **b.** Connecticut.
- **c.** New York.
- **d.** Texas.

Your Guessing Ability (continued)

Answers

Check your answers against the following correct answers.

1. c.   4. a.
2. c.   5. a.
3. b.

The Results

How did you do? If you are lucky, you may have actually known the answer to one question. In addition, your guessing may have been more successful if you were able to use the process of elimination on any of the questions. Maybe you didn't know who the third Chief Justice was (question 3), but you knew that John Jay was the first. In that case, you would have eliminated choice **d** and therefore improved your odds of guessing right from one in four to one in three.

According to probability, you should get at least one question correct. If you answered two or three correctly, you may be a really terrific guesser. If you got none right, you may be a really bad guesser.

Keep in mind, though, that this is only a small sample. You should continue to keep track of your guessing ability as you work through the sample questions in this book. Circle the numbers of questions you guess on as you make your guess; or, if you don't have time during the practice tests, go back afterward, and try to remember at which questions you guessed the answers. Remember, on a test with four answer choices, your chance of getting a correct answer is one in four. So keep a separate guessing score for each exam. For example, how many questions did you guess? How many did you get right? If the number you got right is at least one-fourth of the number of questions you guessed on, you are at least an average guesser, maybe better—and you should always go ahead and guess on the real exam. If the number you got right is significantly lower than one-fourth of the number you guessed on, you would, frankly, be safe guessing anyway, but you might feel more comfortable if you guessed selectively, when you can eliminate a wrong answer or at least have a good feeling about one of the answer choices.

---

of carbohydrates, the way athletes do before a contest. Enjoy a big plate of spaghetti, rice and beans, or your own favorite carbohydrate.

Rest

You probably know how much sleep you need every night to be at your best, even if you don't always get it. Make sure you do get that much sleep for at least a week before the exam. Moderation is important here, too. Extra sleep will just make you feel groggy.

If you are not a morning person and your exam will be given in the morning, you should adjust your internal clock so that your body doesn't think you are taking an exam at 3 A.M. You have to start this process well before the exam: Get up half an hour earlier each morning, and then go to bed half an hour earlier that night. Don't try it the other way around; you will just toss and turn if you go to bed early without waking up early that same day. The next morning, get up another half an hour earlier, and so on. How long you will have to do this depends on how late you are used to waking up. Use the Physical Preparation Checklist below to help track your progress.

Physical Preparation Checklist

For the week before the exam, write down (1) what physical exercise you engaged in and for how long and (2) what you ate for each meal. Remember, you are trying for at least half an hour of exercise three days per week (preferably five days per week) and a balanced diet, which minimizes junk food intake.

7 days before the exam

Exercise:_____ for _____ minutes

Breakfast:_____

Lunch:_____

Dinner: _____

Snacks: _____

6 days before the exam

Exercise:_____ for _____ minutes

Breakfast:_____

Lunch:_____

Dinner: _____

Snacks: _____

5 days before the exam

Exercise:_____ for _____ minutes

Breakfast:_____

Lunch:_____

Dinner: _____

Snacks: _____

4 days before the exam

Exercise:_____ for _____ minutes

Breakfast:_____

Lunch:_____

Dinner: _____

Snacks: _____

3 days before the exam

Exercise:_____ for _____ minutes

Breakfast:_____

Lunch:_____

Dinner: _____

Snacks: _____

2 days before the exam

Exercise:_____ for _____ minutes

Breakfast:_____

Lunch:_____

Dinner: _____

Snacks: _____

1 day before the exam

Exercise:_____ for _____ minutes

Breakfast:_____

Lunch:_____

Dinner: _____

Snacks: _____

Step 8: Make Final Test-Day Preparations

Time to complete: 10 minutes to read; time to complete will vary
Activity: Complete Final Preparations Checklist
If you remember some of the test-taking pitfalls from the beginning of this chapter, they included arriving late to the exam site and being cold as you complete the test. In this part of the LearningExpress Test Preparation System, you will learn how to take control over these external factors. Remember, you have already prepared your mind and body to take the exam, so now it's time to focus on these equally important details.

Find Out Where the Exam Is and Make a Trial Run

Do you know how to get to the exam site? Do you know how long it will take to get there? If not, make a trial run, preferably on the same day of the week at the same time of day. On the Final Preparations Checklist on page 26 make a note of the amount of time it will take you to get to the exam site. Plan on arriving at least 30–45 minutes early so you can orient yourself, use the bathroom, and calm down. Then calculate how early you need to wake up that morning, and make sure you wake up that early every day for a week before the exam. Remember, whether you are driving yourself or taking public transportation, you should leave ample time for any possible travel delays, including weather and traffic.

Gather Your Materials

The night before the exam, lay out your clothes and the materials you have to bring with you. Plan on dressing in layers; you won't have any control over the temperature of the examination room. Have a sweater or jacket you can take off if it's warm. Use the Final Preparations Checklist to help you gather everything you will need.

Don't Skip Breakfast

Even if you don't usually eat breakfast, do so on exam morning. A cup of coffee doesn't count. Don't have doughnuts or other sweet foods, either. A sugar high will leave you with a sugar low in the middle of the exam. A mix of protein and carbohydrates is best: Cereal (low sugar) with milk, or eggs with toast, will give your body what it needs on test day.

Step 9: Ace the Exam!

Time to complete: 10 minutes, plus test-taking time
Activity: Take the ASVAB and do your best!
Now that you have almost completed the LearningExpress Test Preparation System, you only have one more task. Imagine it is test day. You are ready. You made a study plan and followed through. You practiced your test-taking strategies while working through this book. You are in control of your physical, mental, and emotional state. You know when and where to show up and what to bring with you. In other words, you are better prepared than many of the other people taking the ASVAB with you.

When you are done with the exam, you will have earned a reward, so plan a celebration. Call up your friends and plan a party, or have a nice dinner for two—give yourself something to look forward to.

Go into the exam full of confidence, armed with the test-taking strategies you practiced until they became automatic. You are in control of yourself, your environment, and your performance on the exam. You are ready to succeed. So do it. Go in there and ace the exam. And look forward to your future in the military!

Final Preparations Checklist

Getting to the Exam Site

Location of exam site: _____

Date: _____

Departure time: _____

Do I know how to get to the exam site?   Yes   No

If no, make a trial run.

Time it will take to get to the exam site: _____

Things to lay out the night before

Clothes I will wear _____

Sweater/jacket/scarf _____

Watch_____

Photo ID_____

No. 2 pencils_____

LESSON

3 ▶ Multiple-Choice Test Strategies

In this lesson, you will learn how to deal with the multiple-choice format and with questions requiring recall or recognition of material.

All multiple-choice test questions are geared to test your knowledge of a subject or to measure your skills at performing some task. Some test questions require you to recall specific items of information, while others ask you only to recognize information by separating it from similar choices. Others have you deduce answers based on ideas presented in the test itself.

Generally speaking, multiple-choice questions are considered to be objective because they are fact-based; they do not allow for the opinion or interpretation of the test taker. In addition, multiple-choice tests are easier and quicker to grade, and they do not penalize test takers who know the information but have poorly developed writing skills or problems with expressive language.

Parts of a Multiple-Choice Question

You may remember taking tests that contained questions like this one:

1. The largest of the Great Lakes is
   a. Huron.
   b. Superior.
   c. Erie.
   d. Mississippi.

The question contains the three elements of most multiple-choice questions—stems, options, and distracters.

> **Stem:** "The largest of the Great Lakes is"
> **Options:** All answer choices
> **Distracters:** Incorrect answer choices

The answer is **b**.

Stems

Stems contain the core information on which the question is based. In some tests, the stems of the questions may be as long as a paragraph and could contain a lot of information that you must sift through before you can choose an answer. Sometimes question stems are phrased as situations, which set a scene or provide facts. You base your answers to the following series of questions on these scenarios.

Stems can also be simply a word, a math example, or a fragment of a sentence that serves to frame the question.

Options

Options are the answer choices offered to you. Many options require that you simply recognize a correct choice among several others.

2. As president, Ronald Reagan came to be known as
   a. Old Hickory.
   b. The Great Communicator.
   c. Speaker of the House.
   d. Old Ironsides.

The answer is **b**.

In the next sample, the question is trying to test the accuracy of your knowledge by offering two or more options that are similar.

3. The word in the following sentence that means the same or almost the same as *flammable* is
   a. fireproof.
   b. fire resistant.
   c. easily burned.
   d. burning.

To answer this question, it wouldn't be enough to know that flammable has something to do with fire. All of the options offer that choice. You have to know that the meaning of flammable is *easily burned*, answer **c**.

Distracters

Distracters are the incorrect answers, which often present a challenge to detect. In question 2, the distracters are **a**, **c**, and **d**; and in question 3, they are **a**, **b**, and **d**.

Distracters are often written to force you to be very careful in your selections. In question 2, for instance, if you didn't know that Reagan was known as The Great Communicator, you could be distracted by the two choices that refer to age. Since Reagan was one of our oldest presidents while in office, you might be tempted to choose one of them.

The wise test taker will eliminate the clearly impossible options first. In question 2, both Old Ironsides, which is the name of a ship, and Speaker of the House, which is an office that cannot be held by a sitting president, should be eliminated. Then, between Old Hickory and The Great Communicator, you would have to make a choice. If you remembered that Old Hickory was the term used to describe President Andrew Jackson, you would eliminate it, and then the correct choice would be obvious.

Recognition and Recall Questions

As noted before, multiple-choice questions require you to recall or recognize specific information that is surrounded by other similar, but incorrect, options. These other options are written to confuse many test takers.

4. Choose the word or phrase that most nearly means *secession*.
   a. a meeting
   b. an act of breaking away from a political body
   c. a surgical birth
   d. a parade

5. From the following group, circle the word that is correctly spelled.
   a. chenal
   b. chanle
   c. channel
   d. chanell

6. Choose the correct word for the following sentence: I went to _____ house for lunch.
   a. they're
   b. their
   c. there
   d. the're

In questions 4–6, you would have to rely on your memory for the definition of secession, the spelling of the word *channel*, and the correct word *their*, or you would have to be able to recognize the correct answer in comparison to the other choices. The correct answers are: 4 is **b**, 5 is **c**, and 6 is **b**.

Note distracters **c** and **d** in question 4. Many multiple-choice questions are designed to confuse you by offering options that sound like the stem word or have associations with the stem word. In this instance, the similarity between *procession* and *secession*, and the distant but confusing sound similarities between *secession* and the medical shorthand *C-section* (for cesarean section) could trap the unwary test taker.

Reading Questions

Some multiple-choice questions are geared toward measuring your ability to take information directly from the text and answer questions based on that text. These kinds of multiple-choice questions typically measure reading comprehension—you will see them mostly in the Paragraph Comprehension subtest.

Generally, reading comprehension tests start with a passage on a particular subject, followed by as few as two or as many as ten questions based on the content of that passage.

These questions usually are aimed at four skills:

- **Vocabulary**—recognizing the definition of a vocabulary word in the passage
- **Main Idea**—identifying the main idea of the passage
- **Specific Fact or Detail**—noting a specific fact or detail in the passage
- **Conclusion**—making an inference or conclusion based on information in the passage that is not directly stated

Read the following passage and the four questions that follow. Identify each type of question from the previous list.

The "broken window" theory was originally developed to explain how minor acts of vandalism or disrespect can quickly escalate to crimes and attitudes that break down the entire social fabric of an area or unit. It is an idea that can easily be applied to any situation in society. The theory contends that if a broken window in an abandoned building is not replaced quickly, soon all the windows in that building will be broken.

In other words, a small violation, if condoned, leads others to commit similar or greater violations. Thus, after all the windows have been broken, the building is likely to be further vandalized. According to this theory, violations increase exponentially. Thus, if disrespect to a superior is tolerated, others will be tempted to be disrespectful as well. A management crisis could erupt literally overnight.

For example, if one firefighter begins to disregard proper housewatch procedure by neglecting to maintain the housewatch administrative journal, and this firefighter is not reprimanded, others will follow suit by committing similar violations of procedure, thinking, "If he can get away with it, why can't I?" So what starts out as a small violation that may not seem to warrant disciplinary action, may actually ruin the efficiency of the entire firehouse, risking the lives of the people the firehouse serves.

7. In this passage, the word *reprimanded* means
   a. scolded.
   b. praised.
   c. rewarded.
   d. fired.

Question type _____

8. The best title for this passage would be
   a. Broken Windows: Only the First Step.
   b. The Importance of Housewatch.
   c. How to Write an Administrative Journal.
   d. A Guide to Window Repair.

Question type _____

9. The passage suggests that
   a. firefighters are sloppy administrators.
   b. firefighters will blame others for mistakes.
   c. discipline starts with small infractions.
   d. discipline is important for the efficiency of the firehouse.

Question type _____

10. According to the passage, which of the following could be the result of broken windows?
    a. The building would soon be vandalized.
    b. Firefighters would lose morale.
    c. There could be a management crisis.
    d. The efficiency of the firehouse could be destroyed.

Question type _____

Answers

7. **a.** Reprimanded means scolded. (Vocabulary)
8. **a.** The passage is about the "broken window" theory, showing that a minor violation or breach of discipline can lead to major violations. (Main idea)
9. **d.** The passage applies the broken window theory to firehouse discipline, showing that even small infractions have to be dealt with to avoid worse problems later. (Inference)
10. **a.** As stated in the third sentence of the passage. (Detail)

Strategies for Answer Reading Questions

A successful test taker will approach multiple-choice questions with several good strategies. They include:

1. **Always circle or underline the key words in the question.** Key words in the stem often direct you to the correct answer.
2. **Immediately eliminate all clearly incorrect distracters.** This will usually mean that you have to choose between two similar choices.
3. **Carefully read each question.** Beware of look-alike options, easily confused options, and silly options. Watch for tricky wording such as, *All of the following are true EXCEPT . . .*
4. **Understand exactly what is being asked.** You will find distracters that are accurate and may sound right but do not apply to the question.
5. **Beware of the absolute.** Read carefully for words like *always*, *never*, *none*, or *all*. An answer may sound perfectly correct and the general principal may be correct, however, it may not be true in all circumstances. For example, think about the statement "All roses are red." *All* roses?
6. **Do the easiest questions first.** Many tests are arranged so that the questions move from easy to more difficult. Don't lose points by skipping those early questions and risk running out of time.

Math Questions

Math questions on the ASVAB assess how you apply basic math skills to workplace situations.

Most questions are numerical in format:

1. What is the reciprocal of $3\frac{7}{8}$?
   a. $\frac{31}{28}$
   b. $\frac{8}{31}$
   c. $\frac{8}{21}$
   d. $\frac{31}{8}$

Other questions are introduced by stems in which the numerical information is embedded. In other words, they are word problems.

2. A city worker is paid time-and-a-half per hour in overtime pay. He earns $20 per hour. If he works four hours more than his contracted work week, how much does he make in overtime pay?
   a. $80.00
   b. $120.00
   c. $400.00
   d. $60.00

Answers
1. b. $3\frac{7}{8} = \frac{31}{8}$, whose reciprocal is $\frac{8}{31}$.
2. b. The worker makes $20 \times 1\frac{1}{2} = \$30$ per hour in overtime. Now multiply the hourly overtime wage by the number of overtime hours: $30 \times 4 = \$120$.

Strategies for Answering Math Questions

Even though you are dealing with numbers and not words in math questions, the way you analyze the questions and consider the possible answers is very similar.

- **Don't panic because it's math.** They're only numbers—they conform to rules and logic.
- **Read the stem carefully.** Underline or circle the most important information in the stem.
- **Read all the options carefully.** Don't be confused by distracting answer choices.
- **Work through the problem.** If you immediately see an answer that matches, you can move on. Do all calculations on paper, not in your head.
- **Skip unfamiliar or difficult questions on the first pass through the test.** Put a dot in the margin of the test or keep a list on scrap paper so that you can locate the question quickly and easily if you are in a hurry.
- **Be careful when you write your calculations.** The number 1 can look like 7, 3 like 8, and 6 like 0 when you are in a hurry. If you don't take your time and write carefully, you risk choosing a wrong answer or wasting time recalculating an answer to find something that fits from your choice of answers.
- **Translate between math and English.** *Reciprocal* in question 1 means the inverse of the fractional number. Time and a half in question 2 means $1\frac{1}{2}$ or $\frac{3}{2}$. Take some time to translate words from English into math.

Managing Your Time

It's important to manage your time so that you don't get stuck on any one question. The following section will help you pace yourself so that you increase your chances for getting all the points possible in the time allowed.

Read or Listen to Directions Carefully

If you are allowed to write in the test booklet, always underline or circle key words in the instructions that cue you to what the question requires. Follow the directions to the letter.

Preview the Test

There should be no surprises on any section of the test. It's always helpful to know what you will encounter.

There are two reasons that you should preview a test carefully before you start working:

- To locate your weak spots, so that you can prepare to spend more time on those sections.
- To be familiar with the content and format of the whole test so that you have a good overall picture of what topics are stressed and how questions are presented.

Don't Linger Too Long on Any One Question

Answer the questions that you know the answers to for certain right away. Remember, if you are unsure about a question, put a dot in the margin next to that question so that you can find it easily when you want to come back to it later. Don't linger too long over questions you can't answer immediately.

When You Have Time Left Over

If you have followed the strategies and conscientiously maintained control over your timing, you may find that you have time left over after finishing the test. Do not throw down your pen and sigh with relief that the test is over. Remember, this is not a race. You don't win by being first over the finish line. Here are some suggestions for making the best possible use of any left over time:

- **Don't leave anything out.** Make sure that you did not skip any questions and that you have answers for any questions you may have left blank the first time through the test. Use the tips you learned about guessing to help you answer questions about which you are still uncertain.

- **Double-check your answers.** Make sure each answer you have chosen is entered on the correct spot on the answer sheet. If you change an answer, make sure you change it completely. Review any difficult questions you flagged and ensure you answered them correctly.

The strategies in this lesson should help you prepare for, take, and excel on the ASVAB. The rest of the lessons in this book will help improve your skills for the Arithmetic Reasoning, Mathematics Knowledge, Paragraph Comprehension, and Word Knowledge portions of the ASVAB.

2

Math for the Arithmetic Reasoning and Mathematics Knowledge Subtests

The Arithmetic Reasoning and Mathematics Knowledge subtests of the ASVAB cover math skills. Arithmetic Reasoning is mostly composed of math word problems. Mathematics Knowledge focuses on knowledge of math concepts, principles, and procedures. You don't have to do a lot of calculation in the Mathematics Knowledge subtest; but you do need to know basic terminology (like *sum* and *perimeter*), formulas (such as the area of a square), and computation rules. Both subtests cover the subjects you might have studied in school. This section of the book reviews concepts you will need for both Arithmetic Reasoning and Mathematics Knowledge.

Math Strategies

- **Don't work in your head!** Use your test book or scratch paper to take notes, draw pictures, and calculate. Although you might think that you can solve math questions more quickly in your head, that's a good way to make mistakes. Write out each step; if nothing else, it will help you check your answers later.
- **Read a math question in chunks rather than straight through from beginning to end.** As you read each chunk, stop to think about what it means and make notes or draw a picture to represent that chunk.
- **When you get to the actual question, circle it.** This will keep you more focused as you solve the problem.
- **Glance at the answer choices for clues.** If they are fractions, you probably should do your work in fractions; if they are decimals, work in decimals; etc.

- **Make a plan of attack to help you solve the problem.**
- **If a question stumps you, try one of the *backdoor* approaches explained in the next section.** These are particularly useful for solving word problems.
- **When you get your answer, reread the circled question to make sure you have answered it.** This helps avoid the careless mistake of answering the wrong question.
- **Check your work after you get an answer.** Test takers get a false sense of security when they get an answer that matches one of the multiple-choice answers. Here are some good ways to check your work *if you have time:*
  - Ask yourself if your answer is reasonable, if it makes sense.
  - Plug your answer back into the problem to make sure the problem holds together.
  - Do the question a second time, but use a different method.
- **Approximate when appropriate.** For example:
  - $5.98 + $8.97 is a little less than $15. (Add: $6 + $9)
  - .9876 × 5.0342 is close to 5. (Multiply: 1×5)
- **Skip hard questions and return to them later.** Mark them in your test book, or keep a list on a piece of scrap paper, so you can find them quickly.

Backdoor Approaches for Answering Tough Questions

Many word problems are actually easier to solve by backdoor approaches. The two techniques that follow are time-saving ways to solve perplexing multiple-choice word problems with a straightforward approach. The first technique, *nice numbers*, is useful when there are unknowns (like *x*) in the text of the word problem, making the problem too abstract for you. The second technique, *working backward*, presents a quick way to substitute numeric answer choices back into the problem to see which one works.

Nice Numbers

1. When a question contains unknowns, like *x*, plug in nice numbers for the unknowns. A nice number is easy to calculate with and makes sense in the problem.
2. Read the question with the nice numbers in place. Then solve it.
3. If the answer choices are all numbers, the choice that matches your answer is the right one.
4. If the answer choices contain unknowns, substitute the same nice numbers into all the answer choices. The choice that matches your answer is the right one. If more than one answer matches, do the problem again with different nice numbers. You will only have to check the answer choices that have already matched.

Example:

1. Judi went shopping with *p* dollars in her pocket. If the price of shirts was *s* shirts for *d* dollars, what is the maximum number of shirts Judi could buy with the money in her pocket?
   a. *psd*
   b. $\frac{ps}{d}$
   c. $\frac{pd}{s}$
   d. $\frac{ds}{p}$

To solve this problem, let's try these nice numbers: *p* = $100, *s* = 2; *d* = $25. Now reread it with the numbers in place:

Judi went shopping with $100 in her pocket. If the price of shirts was 2 shirts for $25, what is the maximum number of shirts Judi could buy with the money in her pocket?

Since 2 shirts cost $25, that means that 4 shirts cost $50, and 8 shirts cost $100. So our answer is 8. Let's substitute the nice numbers into all 4 answers:

   a. $\$100 \times 2 \times \$25 = 5{,}000$

   b. $\dfrac{\$100 \times 2}{\$25} = 8$

   c. $\dfrac{\$100 \times \$25}{2} = 1{,}250$

   d. $\dfrac{\$25 \times 2}{\$100} = \dfrac{1}{2}$

The answer is **b** because it is the only one that matches our answer of 8.

Working Backward

You can frequently solve a word problem by plugging the answer choices back into the text of the problem to see which one fits all the stated facts. The process is faster than you think because you will probably only have to substitute one or two answers to find the right one.

   This approach works *only* when:

- all of the answer choices are numbers;
- you are asked to find a simple number, not a sum, product, difference, or ratio.

Here's What to Do

1. Look at all the answer choices and begin with the one in the middle of the range. For example, if the answers are 14, 8, 2, 20, and 25, begin by plugging 14 into the problem.
2. If your choice doesn't work, eliminate it. Determine if you need a bigger or smaller answer.
3. Plug in one of the remaining choices.
4. If none of the answers work, you may have made a careless error. Begin again or look for your mistake.

Example:

1. Juan ate $\frac{1}{3}$ of the jellybeans. Maria then ate $\frac{3}{4}$ of the remaining jellybeans, which left 10 jellybeans. How many jellybeans were there to begin with?
   a. 60
   b. 80
   c. 90
   d. 120

Starting with the middle answer, let's assume there were 90 jellybeans to begin with:

Since Juan ate $\frac{1}{3}$ of them, that means he ate 30 ($\frac{1}{3} \times 90 = 30$), leaving 60 of them ($90 - 30 = 60$). Maria then ate $\frac{3}{4}$ of the 60 jellybeans, or 45 of them ($\frac{3}{4} \times 60 = 45$). That leaves 15 jellybeans ($60 - 45 = 15$).

The problem states that there were 10 jellybeans left, and we wound up with 15 of them. That indicates that we started with too big a number. Thus, 90 and 120 are incorrect! With only two choices left, let's use common sense to decide which one to try. The next lower answer is only a little smaller than 90 and may not be small enough. So, let's try 60:

Since Juan ate $\frac{1}{3}$ of them, that means he ate 20 ($\frac{1}{3} \times 60 = 20$), leaving 40 of them ($60 - 20 = 40$). Maria then ate $\frac{3}{4}$ of the 40 jellybeans, or 30 of them ($\frac{3}{4} \times 40 = 30$). That leaves 10 jellybeans ($40 - 30 = 10$).

Because this result of 10 jellybeans remaining agrees with the problem, the correct answer is **a.**

Glossary of Terms

Denominator   the bottom number in a fraction. *Example:* 2 is the denominator in $\frac{1}{2}$.

Difference   Finding the difference between two numbers means subtracting one number from the other.

Divisible by   a number is divisible by a second number if that second number divides *evenly* into the original number. *Example:* 10 is divisible by 5 (10 ÷ 5 = 2, with no remainder). However, 10 is not divisible by 3. (See *multiple of*)

Even Integer   integers that are divisible by 2, like . . . –4, –2, 0, 2, 4. . . (See *integer*)

Integer   numbers along the number line, like . . . –3, –2, –1, 0, 1, 2, 3. . . Integers include the whole numbers and their opposites. (See *whole number*)

Multiple of   a number is a multiple of a second number if that second number can be multiplied by an integer to get the original number. *Example:* 10 is a multiple of 5 (10 = 5 × 2); however, 10 is not a multiple of 3. (See *divisible by*)

Negative Number   a number that is less than zero, like . . . –1, –18.6, $-\frac{3}{4}$. . .

Numerator   the top part of a fraction. *Example:* 1 is the numerator of $\frac{1}{2}$.

Odd Integer   integers that are not divisible by 2, like . . . –5, –3, –1, 1, 3. . .

Positive Number   a number that is greater than zero, like . . . 2, 42, $\frac{1}{2}$, 4.63. . .

Prime Number   integers that are divisible only by 1 and themselves, like . . . 2, 3, 5, 7, 11. . . All prime numbers are odd, except for the number 2. The number 1 is not considered prime.

Product   The product of two numbers is the result of multiplying them together.

Quotient   the answer you get when you divide. *Example:* 10 divided by 5 is 2; the quotient is 2.

Real Number   all the numbers you can think of, like . . . 17, –5, $\frac{1}{2}$, –23.6, 3.4329, 0. . . Real numbers include the integers, fractions, and decimals. (See *integer*)

Remainder   the number left over after division. *Example:* 11 divided by 2 is 5, with a remainder of 1.

Sum   The sum of two numbers is the result of adding them together.

Whole Number   numbers you can count on your fingers, like . . . 1, 2, 3. . . All whole numbers are positive.

Basic Arithmetic Functions

Adding Whole Numbers

When we add numbers, we are combining two or more groups to find the total. The total is often called the **sum**.

For example, suppose you have 5 cans of soup in your kitchen cupboard, and you buy 4 more. Now you have a total of 9 cans of soup. The number 9 is the sum (total), of the two groups.

Now, suppose you want to add two or more larger groups. To add larger numbers correctly, follow these simple rules:

1. Line up the numbers in a straight column. Arrange the numbers according to place value.
2. Add each column. Start the addition at the right with the ones column.
3. Make sure your answers are in the correct columns.

Example: At the store where you buy your soup, there are 132 cans on the shelves. The stocker adds 56 more cans. You want to know how many cans there are in all. The problem, written out, would look like this: 132 + 56.

To find the answer, follow the three steps:

1. Line up the numbers in a straight column.

   132 = 1 hundred 3 tens 2 ones

   +56 =   5 tens 6 ones

2. Add each column. Start the addition at the right with the ones column:

   ```
   1 hundred  3 tens  2 ones
   +          5 tens  6 ones
   ───────────────────────────
   1          8       8
   ```

3. Make sure your answers are in the correct columns:

   132 = 1 hundred 3 tens 2 ones

   +56 =   5 tens 6 ones

   188 = 1 hundred 8 tens 8 ones

Copy the numbers into columns and add.

_____ **1.** 567 + 12

_____ **2.** 3,004 + 1,790

_____ **3.** 24 + 831

_____ **4.** 22 + 513 + 104

_____ **5.** 1,526 + 40

_____ **6.** 10,412 + 30 + 1,547

Carrying

When you add a column of numbers, the sum may be 10 or more. For example, if your ones column adds up to 14, you have a total of 1 ten and 4 ones. Now you must carry the 1 to the tens column.

To carry, follow these simple rules:

1. Line up the numbers to be added in a straight column.
2. Add the numbers in the ones place.
3. If the sum is 10 or more, write the number in the tens place at the top of the next column.
4. Add the tens column, starting with the number you carried.
5. Add the other columns in the same way.

Example: 238 + 76

1. Line up the numbers to be added in a straight column:

   ```
    238
   +76
   ───
   ```

2. Add the numbers in the ones place:

   ```
    6
   +8
   ──
   14
   ```

3. If the sum is 10 or more, carry the number in the tens place to the top of the next column:

   ```
    1
    238
   +76
   ───
      4
   ```

4. Add the tens column, starting with the number you carried:

   ```
    1
    3
   +7
   ──
   11
   ```

5. Add the other columns in the same way:

   ```
    1 1
    238
   +76
   ───
    314
   ```

Copy the numbers into columns and add.

_____ **7.** 499 + 78

_____ **8.** 16 + 9 + 27

_____ **9.** 1,465 + 2,808

_____ **10.** 367 + 20,553

_____ **11.** 351 + 42 + 86 + 5

_____ **12.** 19 + 1,600 + 782 + 62

Subtracting

When you subtract two numbers, you are finding the difference between them.

Here are some questions answered by subtraction:

- When we take 4 away from 9, how many are left?
- What is the difference between 4 and 9?
- What is 9 minus 4?
- How much more is 9 than 4?
- To get 9, how much must be added to 4?

To subtract, follow these simple rules:

1. Line up the numbers in a column. Arrange the numbers according to place value.
2. Start the subtraction at the right with the ones column.
3. Make sure your answers are in the correct columns.

Example: 98 − 75

1. Line up the numbers in a column. Arrange the numbers according to place value:

$$98 = \quad 9 \text{ tens and } 8 \text{ ones}$$
$$-75 = -7 \text{ tens and } 5 \text{ ones}$$

2. Start the subtraction at the right with the ones column:

$$9 \text{ tens and } 8 \text{ ones}$$
$$-7 \text{ tens and } 5 \text{ ones}$$
$$\quad 2 \qquad\qquad 3$$

3. Make sure your answers are in the correct columns:

$$98 = \quad 9 \text{ tens and } 8 \text{ ones}$$
$$-75 = -7 \text{ tens and } 5 \text{ ones}$$
$$23 \qquad 2 \text{ tens and } 3 \text{ ones}$$

Copy the numbers into columns and subtract.

_____ **13.** 48 − 17

_____ **14.** 79 − 39

_____ **15.** 156 − 44

_____ **16.** 992 − 61

_____ **17.** 3,667 − 2,005

_____ **18.** 235 − 112

Borrowing

Sometimes the top number in a column is larger than the bottom number. Then you must borrow from the next column. Borrowing is also known as **regrouping**.

To borrow, follow these simple rules:

1. Line up the columns by place value, as usual.

2. Start with the right column, the ones place. If you cannot subtract the bottom number from the top number, borrow from the tens place. Write the new numbers at the top of each column.

3. Continue subtracting from right to left.

4. Optional: Check the result by adding.

Example: 52 − 36

1. Line up the columns by place value, as usual:

    52 = 5 tens and 8 ones

    −36 = − 3 tens and 6 ones
    _____

2. Start with the right column, the ones place. If you cannot subtract the bottom number from the top number, borrow from the tens place. (Since you cannot subtract 6 from 2, you must borrow from the 5 in the tens place.) Write the new numbers at the top of each column:

    4 12 =   4 tens   and 12 ones
    ~~52~~ =   ~~5 tens and 8 ones~~

    −36 = − 3 tens and 6 ones
    _____

    Notice that you are taking 1 ten (10 ones) and adding it to the ones place. Now you have 12 ones: 2 + 10 = 12. You have also taken one ten away from the tens place: 5 − 1 = 4.

3. Continue subtracting from right to left:

    4 12
    ~~52~~
    −36
    ____
    16

4. Optional: Check the result by adding:

    16 + 36 = 52.

Practice.

_____ **19.** 37 − 28

_____ **20.** 61 − 14

_____ **21.** 193 − 88

_____ **22.** 465 − 277

_____ **23.** 1,381 − 497

_____ **24.** 22,623 − 13,884

Multiplying Whole Numbers

Multiplication is the short method of adding a number to itself several times. (The sign for multiplication is ×.) For example, 4 × 2, (read 4 times 2) means 2 + 2 + 2 + 2. If you add 4 twos together, you will get a total of 8. So 4 × 2 = 8. In multiplication, the two numbers multiplied are called **factors**. The result of multiplying one number by another is called the **product**. This means that 8 is the product of 4 times 2.

We use multiplication to put together equal groups. Suppose you had 3 packs of gum. Each pack has 5 sticks. You have 3 groups of 5. You want to find out how many sticks of gum you have total. You could add 5 + 5 + 5. But a shorter way is to multiply 3 times 5.

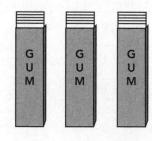

3 × 5 = 15

Sometimes it is helpful to view equal groups in rows or columns. If you add all the blocks in the figure below, you will get a total of 24. A shorter way is to multiply. There are 6 blocks in the rows across. There are 4 blocks in the up-and-down rows.

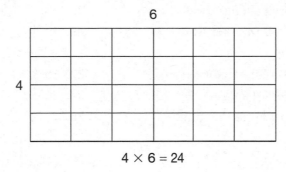

$4 \times 6 = 24$

Multiplication Table

It is important that you commit to memory all the multiplication facts up to 12. Use the multiplication table to help you. The second row will give you the result of all the numbers multiplied by 1 ($1 \times 1 = 1$; $1 \times 2 = 2$; $1 \times 3 = 3$; and so forth). The third row will give you the result of all the numbers multiplied by 2 ($2 \times 1 = 2$; $2 \times 2 = 4$). Memorize the multiplication table before you read the preceding math chapters. Making flashcards or downloading a quiz app for your mobile device may also be useful.

	1	2	3	4	5	6	7	8	9	10	11	12
1	1	2	3	4	5	6	7	8	9	10	11	12
2	2	4	6	8	10	12	14	16	18	20	22	24
3	3	6	9	12	15	18	21	24	27	30	33	36
4	4	8	12	16	20	24	28	32	36	40	44	48
5	5	10	15	20	25	30	35	40	45	50	55	60
6	6	12	18	24	30	36	42	48	54	60	66	72
7	7	14	21	28	35	42	49	56	63	70	77	84
8	8	16	24	32	40	48	56	64	72	80	88	96
9	9	18	27	36	45	54	63	72	81	90	99	108
10	10	20	30	40	50	60	70	80	90	100	110	120
11	11	22	33	44	55	66	77	88	99	110	121	132
12	12	24	36	48	60	72	84	96	108	120	132	144

Here are a few more tips to help you learn multiplication.

- You may have already noticed that the order of the numbers (factors) doesn't change the result: $7 \times 2 = 14$ and $2 \times 7 = 14$. In other words, 7 groups of 2 equals 2 groups of 7.
- In multiplication, when one of the factors is zero, the product is zero: $7 \times 0 = 0$ and $0 \times 7 = 0$. This is true no matter how large the number: $1 \times 0 = 0$ and $1,000,000 \times 0 = 0$.

Multiplying by One-Digit Numbers

To multiply whole numbers:

1. Line up the numbers by place value.
2. Begin multiplying in the ones place. If necessary, carry to the next column.
3. Continue multiplying from right to left. Add any numbers that were carried.

Example: 6×27

1. Line up the numbers by place value:

   $$\begin{array}{r} 27 \\ \times\ 6 \\ \hline \end{array}$$

2. Begin multiplying in the ones place. If necessary carry to the next column. ($6 \times 7 = 42$. Carry 4 tens to the tens place.)

   $$\begin{array}{r} ^4 \\ 27 \\ \times\ 6 \\ \hline 2 \end{array}$$

3. Continue multiplying from right to left. Add any numbers that were carried.
   ($6 \times 2 = 12$ and $12 + 4 = 16$):

   $$\begin{array}{r} ^4 \\ 27 \\ \times\ 6 \\ \hline 162 \end{array}$$

Multiply.

_____ **25.** 63×2

_____ **26.** 79×7

_____ **27.** 48×3

_____ **28.** 109×8

_____ **29.** 530×6

_____ **30.** 800×9

_____ **31.** $14,000 \times 8$

Multiplying by Numbers with Two or More Digits

The following will help you learn to multiply with two (or more) digit numbers. There are three steps:

1. Multiply as usual by the number in the ones place.
2. Multiply by the number in the tens place. (For larger numbers continue to line up the numbers according to place value.) Write this product (result) in the tens place under the first product.
3. Add the columns.

Example: 34×26

1. Multiply as usual by the number in the ones place: ($6 \times 34 = 204$)

   $$\begin{array}{r} ^2 \\ 34 \\ \times\ 26 \\ \hline 204 \end{array}$$

2. Multiply by the number in the tens place. Write this product (result) in the tens place under the first product. If you want, you can put a zero in the ones place as a place holder. (2 × 34 = 68):

$$
\begin{array}{r}
34 \\
\times\,26 \\
\hline
204 \\
680 \\
\end{array}
$$

Note that the 8 is aligned with the 2 in the multiplier and that the zero serves as a place holder so that you align the numbers correctly. To multiply with three or more digit numbers, multiply the third product in the hundreds place.

3. Add the columns:

$$
\begin{array}{r}
34 \\
\times\,26 \\
\hline
204 \\
+\,680 \\
\hline
884 \\
\end{array}
$$

Multiply.

_____ **32.** 77 × 11

_____ **33.** 98 × 32

_____ **34.** 85 × 45

_____ **35.** 456 × 53

_____ **36.** 612 × 22

_____ **37.** 128 × 141

Dividing Whole Numbers

Division means dividing an amount into equal groups. Suppose you have 12 cookies. You want to divide them equally among 3 people. You want 3 groups out of a total of 12. To do this, you need to use division.

$$12 \div 3 = 4$$

When you divide 12 equally into 3 groups, you have 4 in each group. The sign ÷ means *divided by*.

Division Is the Opposite of Multiplication

You learned earlier that subtraction is the opposite of addition. Division is the opposite of multiplication:

$$12 \div 3 = 4 \text{ and } 4 \times 3 = 12$$

You need practice to learn basic division facts. Memorize them as you did multiplication. You can use the multiplication table as a guide. Read it in reverse.

The Language of Division

The quantity to be divided is called the **dividend**. The number of equal parts is called the **divisor**. The result is called the **quotient**.

$$40 \text{ (dividend)} \div 5 \text{ (divisor)} = 8 \text{ (quotient)}$$

Another way to write out this problem would be:

$$5\overline{)40}\,^{8}$$

One more way to write this problem would be:

$$\frac{40}{5} = 8$$

More to Remember about Division

When you divide any number by itself, the result is 1: $8 \div 8 = 1$

When you divide any number by 1, the result is the number itself: $8 \div 1 = 8$

When zero is divided by another number, the result is zero: $0 \div 8 = 0$

Dividing by One-Digit Numbers

There are several steps to division. In these steps, you will use addition, subtraction, and multiplication.

Here are the steps to division:

1. Write the problem correctly.
2. Estimate and divide.
3. Write your answer on top.
4. Multiply and write your answer below.
5. Subtract.
6. Bring down.
7. Repeat the steps if necessary.

Example: $216 \div 9$

1. Write the problem correctly:

$$9\overline{)216}$$

2. Estimate and divide: You cannot divide 9 into 2. So you must divide 9 into 21. Think about how many times 9 will go into 21. Nine times $3 = 27$ is too large, so try 2.

3. Write your answer on top:

$$\begin{array}{r} 2 \\ 9\overline{)216} \end{array}$$

Notice that your answer is written above the tens place. (If you are able to divide evenly into the hundreds place, the answer is written above the hundreds place.)

4. Multiply ($9 \times 2 = 18$) and write your answer below:

$$\begin{array}{r} 2 \\ 9\overline{)216} \\ 18 \end{array}$$

5. Subtract ($21 - 18 = 3$):

$$\begin{array}{r} 2 \\ 9\overline{)216} \\ -18 \\ \hline 3 \end{array}$$

6. Bring down (6):

$$\begin{array}{r} 2 \\ 9\overline{)216} \\ -18 \\ \hline 36 \end{array}$$

7. Repeat the steps if necessary ($36 \div 9 = 4$):

$$\begin{array}{r} 24 \\ 9\overline{)216} \\ -18 \\ \hline 36 \\ -36 \\ \hline 0 \end{array}$$

$$216 \div 9 = 24$$

Remainders

Sometimes the quotient (answer) will not be exact. You will have a number left over. This number is called a **remainder**. This means that you have a certain number of equal groups with one or more left over. Let's say you have 13 cookies instead of 12. You want to divide them into 3 groups. You will still have 3 groups of 4. But now you will have one cookie remaining. You can show that there is a remainder by writing an *r* and the number left over beside the answer. $13 \div 3 = 4\ r1$

Checking Your Work

To check your work in division:

1. multiply your answer (the quotient) by the divisor;
2. add any remainder. Is your answer the dividend (the number you divided into)? Then your work is correct.

Divide.

_____ **38.** 65 ÷ 5

_____ **39.** 256 ÷ 4

_____ **40.** 37 ÷ 6

_____ **41.** 188 ÷ 3

_____ **42.** 5,511 ÷ 4

_____ **43.** 2,929 ÷ 9

Dividing by Two- or Three-Digit Numbers

The steps for dividing by two- or three-digit numbers are the same. However, you are dividing by a larger number in the first step.

Divide.

_____ **44.** 325 ÷ 25

_____ **45.** 381 ÷ 127

_____ **46.** 1,941 ÷ 96

_____ **47.** 4,207 ÷ 18

_____ **48.** 40,000 ÷ 20

_____ **49.** 11,000 ÷ 550

_____ **50.** 15,600 ÷ 130

Answers

1. 579		**26.** 553	
2. 4,794		**27.** 144	
3. 855		**28.** 872	
4. 639		**29.** 3,180	
5. 1,566		**30.** 7,200	
6. 11,989		**31.** 112,000	
7. 577		**32.** 847	
8. 52		**33.** 3,136	
9. 4,273		**34.** 3,825	
10. 20,920		**35.** 24,168	
11. 484		**36.** 13,464	
12. 2,463		**37.** 18,048	
13. 31		**38.** 13	
14. 40		**39.** 64	
15. 112		**40.** 6 r1	
16. 931		**41.** 62 r2	
17. 1,662		**42.** 1,377 r3	
18. 123		**43.** 325 r4	
19. 9		**44.** 13	
20. 47		**45.** 3	
21. 105		**46.** 20 r21	
22. 188		**47.** 233 r13	
23. 884		**48.** 2,000	
24. 8,739		**49.** 20	
25. 126		**50.** 120	

5 ▶ Fractions, Decimals, Percents, and Averages

Fractions

Problems involving fractions may be straightforward calculation questions, or they may be word problems. Typically, they ask you to add, subtract, multiply, divide, or compare fractions.

Working with Fractions

A fraction is a part of something.

> *Example:* Let's say that a pizza was cut into eight equal slices and you ate three of them. The fraction $\frac{3}{8}$ tells you what part of the pizza you ate. The pizza below shows this: the three pieces you ate are shaded.

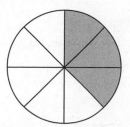

Three Kinds of Fractions

Proper fraction	The top number is less than the bottom number: $\frac{1}{2}$, $\frac{2}{3}$, $\frac{4}{9}$, $\frac{8}{13}$ The value of a proper fraction is less than 1.
Improper fraction	The top number is greater than or equal to the bottom number: $\frac{3}{2}$, $\frac{5}{3}$, $\frac{14}{9}$, $\frac{12}{12}$ The value of an improper fraction is 1 or more.
Mixed number	A fraction written to the right of a whole number: $3\frac{1}{2}$, $4\frac{2}{3}$, $12\frac{3}{4}$, $24\frac{3}{4}$ The value of a mixed number is more than 1: It is the sum of the whole number plus the fraction.

Changing Improper Fractions into Mixed or Whole Numbers

It's easier to add and subtract fractions that are mixed numbers rather than improper fractions. To change an improper fraction, say $\frac{13}{2}$, into a mixed number, follow these steps:

1. Divide the bottom number (2) into the top number (13) to get the whole number portion (6) of the mixed number:

$$
\begin{array}{r}
6 \\
2{\overline{\smash{)}13}} \\
\underline{12} \\
1
\end{array}
$$

2. Write the remainder of the division (1) over the old bottom number (2): $6\frac{1}{2}$
3. Check: Change the mixed number back into an improper fraction (see steps below).

Changing Mixed Numbers into Improper Fractions

It's easier to multiply and divide fractions when you're working with improper fractions rather than mixed numbers. To change a mixed number, say $2\frac{3}{4}$, into an improper fraction, follow these steps:

1. Multiply the whole number (2) by the bottom number (4): $2 \times 4 = 8$
2. Add the result (8) to the top number (3): $8 + 3 = 11$
3. Put the total (11) over the bottom number (4): $\frac{11}{4}$
4. Check: Reverse the process by changing the improper fraction into a mixed number. If you get the same number you started with, your answer is correct.

Reducing Fractions

Reducing a fraction means writing it in *lowest terms,* that is, with smaller numbers. For instance, 50¢ is $\frac{50}{100}$ of a dollar, or $\frac{1}{2}$ of a dollar. In fact, if you have 50¢ in your pocket, you could say that you have half a dollar. Reducing a fraction does not change its value.

Follow these steps to reduce a fraction:

1. Find a whole number that divides *evenly* into both numbers that make up the fraction.
2. Divide that number into the top of the fraction, and replace the top of the fraction with the quotient (the answer you got when you divided).
3. Do the same thing to the bottom number.
4. Repeat the first three steps until you can't find a number that divides evenly into both numbers of the fraction.

For example, let's reduce $\frac{8}{24}$. We could do it in two steps: $\frac{8 \div 4}{24 \div 4} = \frac{2}{6}$; then $\frac{2 \div 2}{6 \div 2} = \frac{1}{3}$. Or we could do it in a single step: $\frac{8 \div 8}{24 \div 8} = \frac{1}{3}$.

Shortcut: When the top and bottom numbers both end in zeroes, cross out the same number of zeroes in both numbers to begin the reducing process. For example $\frac{300}{4,000}$ reduces to $\frac{3}{40}$ when you cross out two zeroes in both numbers.

Whenever you do arithmetic with fractions, reduce your answer. On a multiple-choice test, don't panic if your answer isn't listed. Make sure it's reduced as far as possible and then compare it to the choices.

Reduce these fractions to lowest terms.

1. $\frac{3}{12} =$

2. $\frac{14}{35} =$

3. $\frac{27}{72} =$

Raising Fractions to Higher Terms

Before you can add and subtract fractions, you have to know how to raise a fraction to higher terms. This is actually the opposite of reducing a fraction.

Follow these steps to raise $\frac{2}{3}$ to 24ths:

1. Divide the old bottom number (3) into the new one (24): $\frac{3}{24} = 8$

2. Multiply the answer (8) by the old top number (2): $2 \times 8 = 16$

3. Put the answer (16) over the new bottom number (24): $\frac{16}{24}$

4. Check: Reduce the new fraction to see if you get back the original one: $\frac{16 \div 8}{24 \div 8} = \frac{2}{3}$

Raise these fractions to higher terms.

1. $\dfrac{5}{12} = \dfrac{}{24}$

2. $\dfrac{2}{9} = \dfrac{}{27}$

3. $\dfrac{2}{5} = \dfrac{}{500}$

Adding Fractions

If the fractions have the same bottom numbers, just add the top numbers together and write the total over the bottom number.

Examples: $\dfrac{2}{9} + \dfrac{4}{9} = \dfrac{6}{9}$ Reduce the sum: $\dfrac{2}{3}$.

$\dfrac{5}{8} + \dfrac{7}{8} = \dfrac{12}{8}$ Change the sum to a mixed number: $1\dfrac{4}{8}$; then reduce: $1\dfrac{1}{2}$.

There are a few extra steps to add mixed numbers with the same bottom numbers, say $2\dfrac{3}{5} + 1\dfrac{4}{5}$:

1. Add the fractions: $\dfrac{3}{5} + \dfrac{4}{5} = \dfrac{7}{5}$

2. Change the improper fraction into a mixed number: $\dfrac{7}{5} = 1\dfrac{2}{5}$

3. Add the whole numbers: $2 + 1 = 3$

4. Add the results of steps 2 and 3: $1\dfrac{2}{5} + 3 = 4\dfrac{2}{5}$

Finding the Least Common Denominator

If the fractions you want to add don't have the same bottom number, you will have to raise some or all of the fractions to higher terms so that they all have the same bottom number, called the **common denominator**. All of the original bottom numbers divide evenly into the common denominator. If it is the smallest number that they all divide evenly into, it is called the **least common denominator (LCD).**

Here are a few tips for finding the LCD:

- See if all the bottom numbers divide evenly into the biggest bottom number.
- Look at a multiplication table of the largest bottom number until you find a number that all the other bottom numbers evenly divide into.
- When all else fails, multiply all the bottom numbers together.

Example: $\frac{2}{3} + \frac{4}{5}$

1. Find the LCD. Multiply the bottom numbers: $\quad 3 \times 5 = 15$

2. Raise each fraction to 15ths:
$$\frac{2}{3} = \frac{10}{15}$$
$$+\frac{4}{5} = \frac{12}{15}$$
$$\overline{\phantom{+\frac{4}{5}=}\ \frac{22}{15}}$$

3. Add as usual:

Try these addition problems.

4. $\frac{3}{4} + \frac{1}{6} =$

5. $\frac{7}{8} + \frac{2}{3} + \frac{3}{4} =$

6. $4\frac{1}{3} + 2\frac{3}{4} + \frac{1}{6} =$

Subtracting Fractions

If the fractions have the same bottom numbers, just subtract the top numbers and write the difference over the bottom number.

Example: $\frac{4}{9} - \frac{3}{9} = \frac{4-3}{9} = \frac{1}{9}$

If the fractions you want to subtract don't have the same bottom number, you will have to raise some or all of the fractions to higher terms, so that they all have the same bottom number, or LCD. If you forgot how to find the LCD, just read the previous section on adding fractions with different bottom numbers.

Example: $\frac{5}{6} - \frac{3}{4}$

1. Raise each fraction to 12ths because 12 is the LCD, the smallest number that 6 and 4 both divide into evenly:

2. Subtracting mixed numbers with the same bottom number is similar to adding mixed numbers.

Example: $4\frac{3}{5} - 1\frac{2}{5}$

1. Subtract the fractions: $\qquad \frac{3}{5} - \frac{2}{5} = \frac{1}{5}$
2. Subtract the whole numbers: $\qquad 4 - 1 = 3$
3. Add the results of steps 1 and 2: $\qquad \frac{1}{5} + 3 = 3\frac{1}{5}$

Sometimes there is an extra step where you borrow when subtracting mixed numbers with the same bottom numbers, for example, $7\frac{3}{5} - 2\frac{4}{5}$:

1. You can't subtract the fractions the way they are because $\frac{4}{5}$ is larger than $\frac{3}{5}$. So you borrow 1 from the 7, making it 6, and change that 1 to $\frac{5}{5}$ because 5 is the bottom number: $7\frac{3}{5} = 6\frac{5}{5} + \frac{3}{5}$

2. Add the numbers from Step 1: $\qquad 6\frac{5}{5} + \frac{3}{5} = 6\frac{8}{5}$

3. Now you have a different version of the original problem: $\qquad 6\frac{8}{5} - 2\frac{4}{5}$

4. Subtract the fractional parts of the two mixed numbers: $\qquad \frac{8}{5} - \frac{4}{5} = \frac{4}{5}$

5. Subtract the whole number parts of the two mixed numbers: $\qquad 6 - 2 = 4$

6. Add the results of the last two steps together: $\qquad 4 + \frac{4}{5} = 4\frac{4}{5}$

Try these subtraction problems.

7. $\frac{4}{5} - \frac{2}{3} =$

8. $\frac{7}{8} - \frac{1}{4} - \frac{1}{2} =$

9. $4\frac{1}{3} - 2\frac{3}{4} =$

Now let's put what you have learned about adding and subtracting fractions to work in some real-life problems.

10. Manuel drove $3\frac{1}{2}$ miles to work. Then he drove $4\frac{3}{4}$ miles to the store. When he left there, he drove 2 miles to the dry cleaners. Then he drove $3\frac{2}{3}$ miles back to work for a meeting. Finally, he drove $3\frac{1}{2}$ miles home. How many miles did he travel in total?

   a. $17\frac{5}{12}$

   b. $16\frac{5}{12}$

   c. $15\frac{7}{12}$

   d. $15\frac{5}{12}$

11. Before leaving the warehouse, a truck driver noted that the mileage gauge registered $4{,}357\frac{4}{10}$ miles. When he arrived at the delivery location, the mileage gauge then registered $4{,}400\frac{1}{10}$ miles. How many miles did he drive from the warehouse to the delivery location?

   a. $42\frac{3}{10}$

   b. $42\frac{7}{10}$

   c. $43\frac{7}{10}$

   d. $47\frac{2}{10}$

Multiplying Fractions

Multiplying fractions is actually easier than adding them. All you do is multiply the top numbers and then multiply the bottom numbers.

Examples: $\frac{2}{3} \times \frac{5}{7} = \frac{2 \times 5}{3 \times 7} = \frac{10}{21}$

                $\frac{1}{2} \times \frac{3}{5} \times \frac{7}{4} = \frac{1 \times 3 \times 7}{2 \times 5 \times 4} = \frac{21}{40}$

Sometimes you can *cancel* before multiplying. Canceling is a shortcut that makes the multiplication go faster because you're multiplying with smaller numbers. It's very similar to reducing: If there is a number that divides evenly into a top number and bottom number, do that division before multiplying. If you forget to cancel, you will still get the right answer, but you will have to reduce it.

Example: $\frac{5}{6} \times \frac{9}{20}$

  1. Cancel the 6 and the 9 by dividing 3 into both of them: $6 \div 3 = 2$ and $9 \div 3 = 3$. Cross out the 6 and the 9.
  2. Cancel the 5 and the 20 by dividing 5 into both of them: $5 \div 5 = 1$ and $20 \div 5 = 4$. Cross out the 5 and the 20.
  3. Multiply across the new top numbers and the new bottom numbers: $\frac{1 \times 3}{2 \times 4} = \frac{3}{8}$.

  Try these multiplication problems.

12. $\frac{1}{5} \times \frac{2}{3} =$

13. $\frac{2}{3} \times \frac{4}{7} \times \frac{3}{5} =$

14. $\frac{3}{4} \times \frac{8}{9} =$

To multiply a fraction by a whole number, first rewrite the whole number as a fraction with a bottom number of 1.

Example: $5 \times \frac{2}{3} = \frac{5}{1} \times \frac{2}{3} = \frac{10}{3}$

(Optional: Convert $\frac{10}{3}$ to a mixed number: $3\frac{1}{3}$)

To multiply with mixed numbers, it's easier to change them to improper fractions before multiplying.

Example: $4\frac{2}{3} \times 5\frac{1}{2}$

1. Convert $4\frac{2}{3}$ to an improper fraction: $4\frac{2}{3} = \frac{(4 \times 3) + 2}{3} = \frac{14}{3}$

2. Convert $5\frac{1}{2}$ to an improper fraction: $5\frac{1}{2} = \frac{(5 \times 2) + 1}{2} = \frac{11}{2}$

3. Cancel and multiply the fractions: $\frac{\overset{7}{\cancel{14}}}{3} \times \frac{11}{\underset{1}{\cancel{2}}} = \frac{77}{3}$

4. Optional: Convert the improper fraction to a mixed number: $\frac{77}{3} = 25\frac{2}{3}$

Now try these multiplication problems with mixed numbers and whole numbers.

15. $4\frac{1}{3} \times \frac{2}{5} =$

16. $2\frac{1}{2} \times 6 =$

17. $3\frac{3}{4} \times 4\frac{2}{5} =$

Here are a few more real-life problems to test your skills.

18. After driving $\frac{2}{3}$ of the 15 miles to work, Mr. Stone stopped to make a phone call. How many miles had he driven when he made his call?
   a. 5
   b. $7\frac{1}{2}$
   c. 10
   d. 12

19. If Henry worked $\frac{3}{4}$ of a 40-hour week, how many hours did he work?
   a. $7\frac{1}{2}$
   b. 10
   c. 25
   d. 30

20. Technician Chin makes $14.00 an hour. When she works more than 8 hours a day, she gets overtime pay of $1\frac{1}{2}$ times her regular hourly wage for the extra hours. How much did she earn for working 11 hours in one day?

a. $77

b. $154

c. $175

d. $210

21. Of the incoming 640 freshmen in a certain high school, $\frac{3}{8}$ attended the nearest middle school. How many came from schools other than the nearest middle school?

a. 240

b. 320

c. 400

d. 560

Dividing Fractions

To divide one fraction by a second fraction, invert the second fraction (that is, flip the top and bottom numbers) and then multiply.

Example: $\frac{1}{2} \div \frac{3}{5}$

1. Invert the second fraction ($\frac{3}{5}$): $\frac{5}{3}$

2. Change the division sign ($\div$) to a multiplication sign ($\times$).

3. Multiply the first fraction by the new second fraction: $\frac{1}{2} \times \frac{5}{3} = \frac{1 \times 5}{2 \times 3} = \frac{5}{6}$

To divide a fraction by a whole number, first change the whole number to a fraction by putting it over 1. Then follow the division steps above.

Example: $\frac{3}{5} \div 2 = \frac{3}{5} \div \frac{2}{1} = \frac{3}{5} \times \frac{1}{2} = \frac{3 \times 1}{5 \times 2} = \frac{3}{10}$

When the division problem has a mixed number, convert it to an improper fraction, and then divide as usual.

Example: $2\frac{3}{4} \div \frac{1}{6}$

1. Convert $2\frac{3}{4}$ to an improper fraction: $\qquad 2\frac{3}{4} = \frac{(2 \times 4) + 3}{4} = \frac{11}{4}$

2. Divide $\frac{11}{4}$ by $\frac{1}{6}$, flip $\frac{1}{6}$ to $\frac{6}{1}$ change $\div$ to $\times$: $\qquad \frac{11}{4} \div \frac{1}{6} = \frac{11}{4} \times \frac{6}{1}$

3. Cancel and multiply: $\qquad \frac{11}{\overset{}{\underset{2}{4}}} \times \overset{3}{\cancel{6}} \; \frac{}{1} = \frac{11 \times 3}{2 \times 1} = \frac{33}{2}$

Here are a few division problems to try.

22. $\frac{1}{3} \div \frac{2}{3} =$

23. $2\frac{3}{4} \div \frac{1}{2} =$

24. $\frac{3}{5} \div 3 =$

25. $3\frac{3}{4} \div 2\frac{1}{3} =$

Let's wrap this up with some real-life problems.

26. If four friends evenly split $6\frac{1}{2}$ pounds of candy, how many pounds of candy does each friend get?

    a. $\frac{8}{13}$

    b. $1\frac{5}{8}$

    c. $1\frac{1}{2}$

    d. $1\frac{5}{13}$

27. How many $2\frac{1}{2}$-pound chunks of cheese can be cut from a single 20-pound piece of cheese?

    a. 2

    b. 4

    c. 6

    d. 8

28. Ms. Goldbaum earned $36.75 for working $3\frac{1}{2}$ hours. What was her hourly wage?

    a. $10.00

    b. $10.50

    c. $10.75

    d. $12.00

Decimals

A decimal is a special kind of fraction. You use decimals every day when you deal with money—$10.35 is a decimal that represents 10 dollars and 35 cents. The decimal point separates the dollars from the cents. Because there are 100 cents in one dollar, 1¢ is $\frac{10}{10}$ of a dollar, or $.01.

Each decimal digit to the right of the decimal point has a name:

Examples: .1 = 1 tenth = $\frac{1}{10}$

$$.02 = 2 \text{ hundredths} = \frac{2}{100}$$
$$.003 = 3 \text{ thousandths} = \frac{3}{1,000}$$
$$.0004 = 4 \text{ ten-thousandths} = \frac{4}{10,000}$$

When you add zeros after the rightmost decimal place, you don't change the value of the decimal. For example, 6.17 is the same as all of these:

6.170

6.1700

6.17000000000000000

If there are digits on both sides of the decimal point (like 10.35), the number is called a **mixed decimal**. If there are digits only to the right of the decimal point (like .53), the number is called a **decimal**. A whole number (like 15) is understood to have a decimal point at its right (15.). Thus, 15 is the same as 15.0, 15.00, 15.000, and so on.

Changing Fractions to Decimals

To change a fraction to a decimal, divide the bottom number into the top number after you put a decimal point and a few zeros on the right of the top number. When you divide, bring the decimal point up into your answer.

Example: Change $\frac{3}{4}$ to a decimal.

1. Add a decimal point and two zeros to the top number (3):   3.00
2. Divide the bottom number (4) into 3.00:
   Bring the decimal point up into the answer:

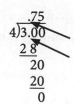

$$\begin{array}{r} .75 \\ 4\overline{)3.00} \\ \underline{2\ 8} \\ 20 \\ \underline{20} \\ 0 \end{array}$$

3. The quotient (result of the division) is the answer: .75

Some fractions may require you to add many decimal zeros in order for the division to come out evenly. In fact, when you convert a fraction like $\frac{2}{3}$ to a decimal, you can keep adding decimal zeros to the top number forever because the division will never come out evenly. As you divide 3 into 2, the number 6 will keep repeating:

$$2 \div 3 = .6666666666 \text{ etc.}$$

This is called a **repeating decimal** and it can be written as $.66\overline{6}$ or as $.66\frac{2}{3}$. You can approximate it as .67, .667, .6667, and so on.

Changing Decimals to Fractions

To change a decimal to a fraction, write the digits of the decimal as the top number of a fraction and write the decimal's name as the bottom number of the fraction. Then reduce the fraction, if possible.

Example: .018

1. Write 18 as the top of the fraction: $\underline{18}$
2. Three places to the right of the decimal means *thousandths*, so write 1,000 as the bottom number: $\frac{18}{1,000}$
3. Reduce by dividing 2 into the top and bottom numbers: $\frac{18 \div 2}{1,000 \div 2} = \frac{9}{500}$

Change these decimals or mixed decimals to fractions.

29. .005 =

30. 3.48 =

31. 123.456 =

Comparing Decimals

Because decimals are easier to compare when they have the same number of digits after the decimal point, tack zeros onto the end of the shorter decimals. Then all you have to do is compare the numbers as if the decimal points weren't there.

Example: Compare .08 and .1.

1. Tack one zero at the end of .1: .10
2. To compare .10 to .08, just compare 10 to 8.
3. Since 10 is larger than 8, .1 is larger than .08.

Adding and Subtracting Decimals

To add or subtract decimals, line them up so their decimal points are aligned. You may want to tack on zeros at the end of shorter decimals so you can keep all your digits lined up evenly. Remember, if a number doesn't have a decimal point, then put one at the right end of the number.

Example: 1.23 + 57 + .038 =

   1. Line up the numbers like this: 1.230
   2. Add.   57.000
                                        + .038
                                      58.268

Example: 1.23 − .038 =

   1. Line up the numbers like this: 1.230
   2. Subtract.   − .038
                                      1.192

Try these addition and subtraction problems.

32. .905 + .02 + 3.075 =

33. .005 + 8 + .3 =

34. 3.48 − 2.573 =

35. 123.456 − 122 =

36. A park ranger drove 3.7 miles to the state park. He then walked 1.6 miles around the park to make sure everything was all right. He got back into the car, drove 2.75 miles to check on a broken light and then drove 2 miles back to the ranger station. How many miles did he drive in total?
   a. 8.05
   b. 8.45
   c. 10
   d. 10.05

37. The average number of customers at a diner fell from 486.4 per week to 402.5 per week. By how many customers per week did the average fall?
   a. 73.9
   b. 83
   c. 83.1
   d. 83.9

Multiplying Decimals

To multiply decimals, ignore the decimal points and just multiply the numbers. Then count the total number of decimal digits (the digits to the *right* of the decimal point) in the numbers you are multiplying. Count off that number of digits in your answer beginning at the right side and put the decimal point to the *left* of those digits.

Example: 215.7×2.4

1. Multiply 2157 times 24:

$$\begin{array}{r} 2157 \\ \times\ 24 \\ \hline 8628 \\ 4314\ \\ \hline 51768 \end{array}$$

2. Because there is a total of two decimal digits in 215.7 and 2.4, count off two places from the right in 51768, placing the decimal point to the *left* of the last two digits: 517.68

   If your answer doesn't have enough digits, tack zeros on to the left of the answer.

Example: $.03 \times .006$

1. Multiply 3 times 6: $3 \times 6 = 18$
2. You need five decimal digits in your answer, so tack on three zeros: 00018
3. Put the decimal point at the front of the number (which is five digits in from the right):   .00018

You can practice multiplying decimals with these.

38. $.05 \times .6 =$

39. $.053 \times 6.4 =$

40. $38.1 \times .0184 =$

41. Joe earns \$14.50 per hour. Last week, he worked 37.5 hours. How much money did he earn that week?
   a. \$518.00
   b. \$518.50
   c. \$536.50
   d. \$543.75

42. Nuts cost $3.50 per pound. Approximately how much will 4.25 pounds of nuts cost?

   a. $12.25

   b. $12.88

   c. $14.50

   d. $14.88

Dividing Decimals

To divide a decimal by a whole number, set up the division, $8\overline{).256}$, and immediately bring the decimal point straight up into the answer, $8\overline{).256}$. Then divide as you would normally divide whole numbers.

Example:

$$\begin{array}{r} .032 \\ 8\overline{).256} \\ \underline{0} \\ 25 \\ \underline{24} \\ 16 \\ \underline{16} \\ 0 \end{array}$$

There is an extra step to perform before you can divide any number by a decimal. Move the decimal point to the very right of the number you are dividing by, counting the number of places you are moving it. Then move the decimal point the same number of places to the right in the number you are dividing into. In other words, first change the problem to one in which you are dividing by a whole number.

Example: $.06\overline{)1.218}$

1. Because there are two decimal digits in .06, move the decimal point two places to the right in both numbers and move the decimal point straight up into the answer:

   $.06_\smile\overline{)1.21_\smile8}$

2. Divide using the new numbers:

$$\begin{array}{r} 20.3 \\ 6\overline{)121.8} \\ \underline{12} \\ 01 \\ \underline{00} \\ 18 \\ \underline{18} \\ 0 \end{array}$$

   $6\overline{)121.8} = 20.3$

Under certain conditions, you have to tack on zeros to the right of the last decimal digit in the number you are dividing into:

- if there are not enough digits for you to move the decimal point to the right;
- if the answer doesn't come out evenly when you do the division;
- if you are dividing a whole number by a decimal. Then you will have to tack on the decimal point as well as some zeros.

Try your skills on these division problems.

43. $7\overline{)9.8}=$

44. $.0004\overline{).0512}=$

45. $.5\overline{)28.6}=$

46. $.14\overline{)196}=$

47. If James Worthington drove his truck 92.4 miles in 2.1 hours, what was his average speed in miles per hour?
  a. 41 MPH
  b. 44 MPH
  c. 90.3 MPH
  d. 94.5 MPH

48. Mary Sanders walked a total of 18.6 miles in 4 days. On average, how many miles did she walk each day?
  a. 4.15
  b. 4.60
  c. 4.65
  d. 22.60

Percents

A percent is a special kind of fraction or part of something. The bottom number (the **denominator**) is always 100. For example, 17% is the same as $\frac{17}{100}$. Literally, the word *percent* means *per 100 parts*. The root *cent* means 100: A *century* is 100 years; there are 100 *cents* in a dollar, etc. Thus, 17% means 17 parts out of 100. Because fractions can also be expressed as decimals, 17% is also equivalent to .17, which is 17 hundredths.

You come into contact with percents every day. Sales tax, interest, and discounts are just a few common examples.

If your fraction skills need work, you may want to review that section again before reading further.

Changing a Decimal to a Percent and Vice Versa

To change a decimal to a percent, move the decimal point two places to the right and tack on a percent sign (%) at the end. If the decimal point moves to the very right of the number, you don't have to write the decimal point. If there aren't enough places to move the decimal point, add zeros on the right before moving the decimal point.

To change a percent to a decimal, drop the percent sign and move the decimal point two places to the left. If there aren't enough places to move the decimal point, add zeros on the left before moving the decimal point.

Try changing these decimals to percents.

49. $.45 =$

50. $.008 =$

51. $.16\frac{2}{3} =$

Now, change these percents to decimals.

52. $12\% =$

53. $87\frac{1}{2}\% =$

54. $250\% =$

Changing a Fraction to a Percent and Vice Versa

To change a fraction to a percent, there are two techniques. Each is illustrated by changing the fraction $\frac{1}{4}$ to a percent:

Technique 1:   Multiply the fraction by 100%.

Multiply $\frac{1}{4}$ by 100%: $\frac{1}{\cancel{4}_{1}} \times \frac{\cancel{100}^{25}\%}{1} = 25\%$.

Technique 2:   Divide the fraction's bottom number into the top number; then move the decimal point two places to the right and add on a percent sign (%).

Divide 4 into 1 and move the decimal point two places to the right:

$$4\overline{)1.00}^{\,.25} \qquad\qquad .25 = 25\%$$

To change a percent to a fraction, remove the percent sign and write the number over 100. Then reduce if possible.

Example: Change 4% to a fraction.

1. Remove the % and write the fraction 4 over 100: $\frac{4}{100}$

2. Reduce: $\frac{4 \div 4}{100 \div 4} = \frac{1}{25}$

Here's a more complicated example: Change $16\frac{2}{3}$% to a fraction.

1. Remove the % and write the fraction $16\frac{2}{3}$ over 100: $\frac{16\frac{2}{3}}{100}$

2. Since a fraction means "top number divided by bottom number," rewrite the fraction as a division problem: $16\frac{2}{3} \div 100$

3. Change the mixed number ($16\frac{2}{3}$) to an improper fraction ($\frac{50}{3}$): $\frac{50}{3} \div \frac{100}{1}$

4. Flip the second fraction ($\frac{100}{1}$) and multiply: $\frac{\overset{1}{\cancel{50}}}{3} \times \frac{1}{\underset{2}{\cancel{100}}} = \frac{1}{6}$

Try changing these fractions to percents.

55. $\frac{1}{8} =$

56. $\frac{13}{25} =$

57. $\frac{7}{12} =$

Now change these percents to fractions.

58. 95% =

59. $37\frac{1}{2}$% =

60. 125% =

Sometimes it is more convenient to work with a percentage as a fraction or a decimal. Rather than always *calculating* the equivalent fraction or decimal, consider memorizing the equivalence table on the next page. Not only will this increase your efficiency on the math test, but it will also be practical for real-life situations.

CONVERSION TABLE		
DECIMAL	**%**	**FRACTION**
.25	25%	$\frac{1}{4}$
.50	50%	$\frac{1}{2}$
.75	75%	$\frac{3}{4}$
.10	10%	$\frac{1}{10}$
.20	20%	$\frac{1}{5}$
.40	40%	$\frac{2}{5}$
.60	60%	$\frac{3}{5}$
.80	80%	$\frac{4}{5}$
.33$\overline{3}$	$33\frac{1}{3}$%	$\frac{1}{3}$
.66$\overline{6}$	$66\frac{2}{3}$%	$\frac{2}{3}$

Percent Word Problems

Word problems involving percents come in three main varieties:

- Find a percent of a whole.
  Example: What is 30% of 40?

- Find what percent one number is of another number.
  Example: 12 is what percent of 40?

- Find the whole when the percent of it is given.
  Example: 12 is 30% of what number?

While each variety has its own approach, there is a single shortcut formula you can use to solve each of these:

$$\frac{is}{of} = \frac{\%}{100}$$

The **is** number usually follows or comes just before the word *is* in the question.
The **of** number usually follows the word *of* in the question.
The **%** is the number that is in front of the % or *percent* in the question.

Or you may think of the shortcut formula as:

$$\frac{part}{whole} = \frac{\%}{100}$$

$$part \times 100 = whole \times \%$$

To solve each of the three varieties, let's use the fact that the **cross-products** are equal. The cross-products are the products of the numbers diagonally across from each other. Remembering that *product* means *multiply,* here's how to create the cross-products for the percent shortcut:

$$\frac{part}{whole} = \frac{\%}{100}$$

$$part \times 100 = whole \times \%$$

Here's how to use the shortcut with cross-products:

■ Find a percent of a whole.

What is 30% of 40?

30 is the % and 40 is the *of* number: $\quad \frac{is}{40} = \frac{30}{100}$

Cross-multiply and solve for *is*: $\quad is \times 100 = 40 \times 30$

$$is \times 100 = 1,200$$

$$is = \frac{1,200}{100}$$

$$is = 12$$

Thus, **12 is** 30% of 40.

■ Find what percent one number is of another number.

12 is what percent of 40?

12 is the *is* number and 40 is the *of* number: $\frac{12}{40} = \frac{\%}{100}$

Cross-multiply and solve for %: $\quad 12 \times 100 = 40 \times \%$

$$1,200 = 40 \times \%$$

$$\% = \frac{1,200}{40}$$

$$\% = \mathbf{30}$$

Thus, 12 is **30% of** 40.

■ Find the whole when the percent of it is given.

12 is 30% of what number?

12 is the *is* number and 30 is the %: $\quad \frac{12}{of} = \frac{30}{100}$

Cross-multiply and solve for the *of* number: $\quad 12 \times 100 = of \times 30$

$$1,200 = of \times 30$$

$$of = \frac{1,200}{30}$$

$$of = \mathbf{40}$$

Thus 12 is 30% **of 40**.

You can use the same technique to find the percent increase or decrease. The *is* number is the actual increase or decrease, and the *of* number is the original amount.

Example: If a merchant puts his $20 hats on sale for $15, by what percent does he decrease the selling price?

1. Calculate the decrease, the *is* number: $20 - $15 = $5
2. The *of* number is the original amount, $20.
3. Set up the equation and solve for *of* by cross-multiplying: $\frac{5}{20} = \frac{\%}{100}$

$$5 \times 100 = 20 \times \%$$

$$500 = 20 \times \%$$

$$\frac{500}{20} = \%$$

$$25 = \%$$

4. Thus, the selling price is decreased by **25%**.

If the merchant later raises the price of the hats from $15 back to $20, don't be fooled into thinking that the percent increase is also 25%! It's actually more, because the increase amount of $5 is now based on a lower original price of only $15:

$$\frac{5}{15} = \frac{\%}{100}$$

$$5 \times 100 = 15 \times \%$$

$$500 = 15 \times \%$$

$$\frac{500}{15} = \%$$

$$33\frac{1}{3} = \%$$

Thus, the selling price is increased by **33%**.

Find a percent of a whole.

61. 1% of 25 =

62. 18.2% of 50 =

63. $37\frac{1}{2}$% of 100 =

64. 125% of 60 =

Find what percent one number is of another number.

65. 10 is what % of 20?

66. 4 is what % of 12?

67. 12 is what % of 4?

Find the whole when the percent of it is given.

68. 15% of what number is 15?

69. $37\frac{1}{2}$% of what number is 3?

70. 200% of what number is 20?

Now try your percent skills on some real-life problems.

71. Last Monday, 20% of 140 staff members were absent. How many employees were absent that day?
   a. 14
   b. 28
   c. 112
   d. 126

72. Forty percent of Vero's postal service employees are women. If there are 80 women in Vero's postal service, how many men are employed there?
   a. 32
   b. 112
   c. 120
   d. 160

73. Of the 840 shirts sold at a retail store last month, 42 had short sleeves. What percent of the shirts were short sleeved?
   a. .5%
   b. 2%
   c. 5%
   d. 20%

74. Sam's Shoe Store put all of its merchandise on sale for 20% off. If Jason saved $10 by purchasing one pair of shoes during the sale, what was the original price of the shoes before the sale?
   a. $12
   b. $20
   c. $40
   d. $50

Averages

An average, also called an **arithmetic mean**, is a number that *typifies* a group of numbers, a measure of central tendency. You come into contact with averages on a regular basis: your bowling average, the average grade on a test, the average number of hours you work per week.

To calculate an average, add up the number of items being averaged and divide by the number of items.

Example: What is the average of 6, 10, and 20?

Solution: Add the three numbers together and divide by 3: $\frac{6 + 10 + 20}{3} = 12$

Shortcut

Here's a neat shortcut for some average problems.

- Look at the numbers being averaged. If they are equally spaced, like 5, 10, 15, 20, and 25, then the average is the number in the middle, or 15 in this case.
- If there is an even number of such numbers, say 10, 20, 30, and 40, then there is no middle number. In this case, the average is halfway between the two middle numbers. In this case, the average is halfway between 20 and 30, or 25.

Try these average questions.

75. Bob's bowling scores for the last five games were 180, 182, 184, 186, and 188. What was his average bowling score?

   a. 182

   b. 183

   c. 184

   d. 185

76. Conroy averaged 30 miles per hour for the two hours he drove in town and 60 miles per hour for the two hours he drove on the highway. What was his average speed in miles per hour?

   a. 18

   b. $22\frac{1}{2}$

   c. 45

   d. 60

77. There are 10 men and 20 women in a history class. If the men achieved an average score of 85 and the women achieved an average score of 95, what was the class average? (Hint: Don't fall for the trap of taking the average of 85 and 95; there are more scores of 95 being averaged than 85.)

a. $90\frac{2}{3}$

b. $91\frac{2}{3}$

c. 92

d. $92\frac{2}{3}$

Answers

Fractions

1. Divide 3 and 12 by 3:

$$\frac{3 \div 3}{12 \div 3} = \frac{1}{4}$$

2. Divide 14 and 35 by 7:

$$\frac{14 \div 7}{35 \div 7} = \frac{2}{5}$$

3. Divide 27 and 72 by 9:

$$\frac{27 \div 9}{72 \div 9} = \frac{3}{8}$$

4. Divide 12 into 24:

$$24 \div 12 = 2$$

Multiply 5 by 2:

$$\frac{5 \times 2}{12 \times 2} = \frac{10}{24}$$

$$\frac{5}{12} = \frac{10}{24}$$

5. Divide 9 into 27:

$$27 \div 9 = 3$$

Multiply 2 by 3:

$$\frac{2 \times 3}{9 \times 3} = \frac{6}{27}$$

$$\frac{2}{9} = \frac{6}{27}$$

6. Divide 5 into 500:

$$500 \div 5 = 100$$

Multiply 2 by 100:

$$\frac{2 \times 100}{5 \times 100} = \frac{200}{500}$$

$$\frac{2}{5} = \frac{200}{500}$$

7. The LCD of 4 and 6 is 12. Raise each fraction to 12ths:

$$\frac{3}{4} = \frac{9}{12}$$

$$+ \ \frac{1}{6} = \frac{2}{12}$$

$$\overline{\qquad \frac{11}{12} \qquad}$$

8. The LCD of 8, 3, and 4 is 24. Raise each fraction to 24ths:

$$\frac{7}{8} = \frac{21}{24}$$

$$\frac{2}{3} = \frac{16}{24}$$

$$+\frac{3}{4} = \frac{18}{24}$$

$$\frac{55}{24}$$

To convert $\frac{55}{24}$ into a mixed number, divide 24 into 55:

$$\begin{array}{r} 2\frac{7}{24} \\ 24\overline{)\,55} \\ -48 \\ \hline 7 \end{array}$$

9. The LCD of 3, 4, and 6 is 12. Raise each fraction to 12ths:

$$4\frac{1}{3} = 4\frac{4}{12}$$

$$2\frac{3}{4} = 2\frac{9}{12}$$

$$+0\frac{1}{6} = 0\frac{2}{12}$$

$$6\frac{15}{12}$$

Convert $\frac{15}{12}$ into a mixed number and add to 6:

$$\frac{15}{12} = 1\frac{3}{12} = 1\frac{1}{4}$$

$$6 + 1\frac{1}{4} = 7\frac{1}{4}$$

10. The LCD of 5 and 3 is 15. Raise each fraction to 15ths and subtract:

$$\frac{4}{5} = \frac{12}{15}$$

$$-\frac{2}{3} = \frac{10}{15}$$

$$\frac{2}{15}$$

11. The LCD of 8, 4, and 2 is 8. Raise each fraction to 8ths:

$$\frac{7}{8} = \frac{7}{8}$$

$$\frac{1}{4} = \frac{2}{8}$$

$$\frac{1}{2} = \frac{4}{8}$$

You can finish this problem in two steps.

Subtract $\frac{2}{8}$ from $\frac{7}{8}$:

$$\frac{7}{8} - \frac{2}{8} = \frac{5}{8}$$

Subtract $\frac{4}{8}$ from $\frac{5}{8}$:

$$\frac{5}{8} - \frac{4}{8} = \frac{1}{8}$$

12. The LCD of 3 and 4 is 12. Raise each fraction to 12ths.

$$4\frac{1}{3} = 4\frac{4}{12}$$

$$2\frac{3}{4} = 2\frac{9}{12}$$

The bottom fraction, $\frac{9}{12}$, is larger than the top fraction $\frac{4}{12}$. Borrow 1 from 4 and add it, as $\frac{12}{12}$, to $\frac{4}{12}$:

$$4\frac{1}{3} = 3\frac{12}{12} + \frac{4}{12} = 3\frac{16}{12}$$

Subtract $2\frac{9}{12}$ from $3\frac{16}{12}$:

$$3\frac{16}{12} - 2\frac{9}{12} = 1\frac{7}{12}$$

13. a. The total distance driven can be found by adding the lengths of the separate trips.

The LCD of 2,3, and 4 is 12, so raise all fractions to 12ths:

$$3\frac{1}{2} = 3\frac{6}{12}$$

$$4\frac{3}{4} = 4\frac{9}{12}$$

$$3\frac{2}{3} = 3\frac{8}{12}$$

$$3\frac{1}{2} = 3\frac{6}{12}$$

Next, add all the whole numbers:

$$3 + 4 + 2 + 3 + 3 = 15$$

Now, add all the fractions:

$$\frac{6}{12} + \frac{9}{12} + \frac{8}{12} + \frac{6}{12} = \frac{29}{12}$$

Convert $\frac{29}{12}$ to a mixed number and add it to 15:

$$\frac{29}{12} = 2\frac{5}{12}$$

$$15 + 2\frac{5}{12} = 17\frac{5}{12}$$

14. b. Subtract the starting mileage from the ending mileage to find the distance traveled.

$$4400\frac{1}{10} - 4357\frac{4}{10}$$

Since $\frac{4}{10}$ is greater than $\frac{1}{10}$, borrow 1 from 4400 and add it, as $\frac{10}{10}$, to $\frac{1}{10}$.

$$4400\frac{1}{10} = 4399\frac{10}{10} + \frac{1}{10} = 4399\frac{11}{10}$$

Subtract $4357\frac{4}{10}$ from $4399\frac{11}{10}$.

$$4399\frac{11}{10} - 4357\frac{4}{10} = 42\frac{7}{10}$$

15. $\frac{1}{5} \times \frac{2}{3} = 1 \times \frac{2}{5} \times 3 = \frac{2}{15}$

16. Cancel the 3's by dividing each by 3: $3 \div 3 = 1$

Multiply across the new top and bottom numbers:

$$\frac{2}{3} \times \frac{4}{7} \times \frac{\overset{1}{3}}{\underset{1}{5}} = \frac{8}{35}$$

17. Cancel the 3 and 9 by dividing each by 3. Cancel the 4 and 8 by dividing each 4:

$$\frac{3}{4} \times \frac{8}{9} = \frac{\overset{1}{3}}{\underset{1}{4}} \times \frac{\overset{2}{8}}{\underset{3}{9}} = \frac{2}{3}$$

18. Convert $4\frac{1}{3}$ to an improper fraction:

$$4\frac{1}{3} = \frac{13}{3}$$

Multiply the fractions:

$$\frac{13}{3} \times \frac{2}{5} = \frac{26}{15}$$

If necessary, convert $\frac{26}{15}$ to a mixed number.

$$\frac{26}{15} = 1\frac{11}{15}$$

19. Convert $2\frac{1}{2}$ to an improper fraction:

$$2\frac{1}{2} = \frac{5}{2}$$

Multiply the fractions and cancel as required:

$$\frac{5}{2} \times \frac{\overset{3}{6}}{\underset{1}{1}} = \frac{5 \times 3}{1 \times 1} = 15$$

20. Convert both mixed numbers to improper fractions:

$$3\frac{3}{4} = \frac{15}{4} \qquad 4\frac{2}{5} = \frac{22}{5}$$

Multiply the fractions and cancel:

$$\overset{3}{\underset{2}{\cancel{\frac{15}{4}}}} \times \overset{11}{\underset{1}{\cancel{\frac{22}{5}}}} = \frac{3 \times 11}{2 \times 1} = \frac{33}{2}$$

Convert $\frac{33}{2}$ to a mixed number if necessary:

$$\frac{33}{2} = 16\frac{1}{2}$$

21. c. "Of" means multiply, so multiply $\frac{2}{3}$ by 15:

$$\underset{1}{\frac{2}{3}} \times \overset{5}{\cancel{\frac{15}{1}}} = \frac{2 \times 5}{1 \times 1} = 10$$

22. d. Multiply $\frac{3}{4}$ by 40:

$$\underset{1}{\frac{3}{4}} \times \overset{10}{\cancel{\frac{40}{1}}} = \frac{3 \times 10}{1 \times 1} = 30$$

23. c. Multiply 8×14 to find Chin's regular pay:

$$8 \times 14 = 112$$

Next, find Chin's overtime pay and multiply by 3, the number of overtime hours:

$$1\frac{1}{2} \times 14 \times 3 = \underset{1}{\frac{3}{2}} \times \overset{7}{\cancel{\frac{14}{1}}} \times \frac{3}{1} = 63$$

Add the regular and overtime pay:

$$112 + 63 = \$175$$

24. c. Find the number of students from the nearby middle school and subtract that number from 640:

$$\frac{640}{1} \times \frac{3}{8} = 240$$

$$640 - 240 = 400$$

25.

$$\frac{1}{3} \div \left(\frac{2}{3}\right) = \underset{1}{\frac{1}{3}} \times \overset{1}{\frac{3}{2}} = \frac{1}{2}$$

26.

$$2\frac{3}{4} \div \frac{1}{2} = \underset{2}{\frac{11}{4}} \times \overset{1}{\frac{2}{1}} = 1\frac{1}{2} = 5\frac{1}{2}$$

27.

$$\frac{3}{5} \div \frac{3}{1} = \frac{3}{5} \times \overset{1}{\underset{1}{\frac{1}{3}}} = \frac{1}{5}$$

28. $3\frac{3}{4} \div 2\frac{1}{3} = \frac{15}{4} \times \frac{3}{7} = \frac{45}{28}$ or $1\frac{17}{28}$

29. b. Convert $6\frac{1}{2}$ to an improper fraction and divide by 4:

$$6\frac{1}{2} = \frac{13}{2}$$

$$\frac{13}{2} \div \frac{4}{1} = \frac{13}{2} \times \frac{1}{4} = \frac{13}{8} = 1\frac{5}{8}$$

30. d. Divide 20 by $2\frac{1}{2}$:

$$20 \div 2\frac{1}{2} = 20 \div \frac{5}{2} = \overset{4}{\cancel{\frac{20}{1}}} \times \underset{1}{\frac{2}{5}} = 8$$

31. b. Convert \$36.75 into $36\frac{3}{4}$ dollars. Next, convert $36\frac{3}{4}$ and $3\frac{1}{2}$ into improper fractions:

$$36\frac{3}{4} = \frac{147}{4}$$

$$3\frac{1}{2} = \frac{7}{2}$$

Divide $\frac{147}{4}$ by $\frac{7}{2}$:

$$\frac{147}{4} \div \frac{7}{2} = \frac{147}{4} \times \frac{2}{7} = \frac{\overset{21}{\cancel{147}}}{\underset{2}{\cancel{4}}} \times \frac{\overset{1}{\cancel{2}}}{\underset{1}{\cancel{7}}} = 10\frac{1}{2}$$

Ms. Goldbaum earned $10\frac{1}{2}$ dollars, or 10.50, per hour.

Decimals

32. $005 = \frac{5}{1000}$

Divide the top and bottom by 5:

$$\frac{5 \div 5}{1000 \div 5} = \frac{1}{200}$$

33. Convert the decimal to a fraction:

$$.48 = \frac{48}{100} = \frac{48 \div 4}{100 \div 4} = \frac{12}{25}$$

Add 3 to the number to get $3\frac{12}{25}$.

34. $.123.456 = 123\frac{456}{1000}$

Divide 456 and 1000 by 8:

$$\frac{456 \div 8}{1000 \div 8} = \frac{57}{125}$$

Add $\frac{57}{125}$ to 123:

$$123 + \frac{57}{125} = 123\frac{57}{125}$$

35. Align the decimals, tacking on zeroes as needed, and add:

$$
\begin{array}{r}
.905 \\
.020 \\
+3.075 \\
\hline
4.000 \text{ or } 4.
\end{array}
$$

36.
$$
\begin{array}{r}
.005 \\
8.000 \\
+.300 \\
\hline
8.305
\end{array}
$$

37.
$$
\begin{array}{r}
3.480 \\
-2.573 \\
\hline
.907
\end{array}
$$

38.
$$
\begin{array}{r}
123.456 \\
-122.000 \\
\hline
1.456
\end{array}
$$

39. b. Add all the distances driven to get the total distance:

$$
\begin{array}{r}
3.70 \\
2.75 \\
+2.00 \\
\hline
8.45
\end{array}
$$

40. d. Subtract 402.5 from 486.4 to find the decrease:

$$
\begin{array}{r}
486.4 \\
-402.5 \\
\hline
83.9
\end{array}
$$

41. First, multiply 5 by 6:

$5 \times 6 = 30$

You need 3 decimal digits, so tack on a zero:

030

Put the decimal point in front of the number:

.030

Since the 0 after the 3 does not affect the value, it should be dropped:

$.030 = .03$

42. $53 \times 64 = 3,392$

Move the decimal point four places to the left: 0.3392

43. $381 \times 184 = 70,104$

Move the decimal point five places to the left: 0.70104

44. d. Multiply $14.50 by 37.5 to get Joe's pay that week. First, multiply 1,450 by 375:

$1,450 \times 375 = 543,750$

Move the decimal point three places to the left: 543.750

The last digit, 0, can be ignored to arrive at $543.75

45. d. Multiply $3.50 by 4.25 to find the total cost. First, Multiply 350 by 425: $350 \times 425 = 148,750$

Move the decimal point four places to the left: 14.8750

Round to the nearest cent: 14.88

46. $\dfrac{1.4}{7 \overline{)9.8}}$

47. Move the decimal point four places to the right in both numbers:

$0512 \div .0004 = 512 \div 4 = 128$

48. Move the decimal point one place to the right in both numbers:

$28.6 \div .5 = 286.0 \div 5 = 57.2$

49. Move the decimal point two places to the right. You will have to add two zeroes to 196.

$196 \div .14 = 19,600 \div 14 = 1,400$

50. b. Divide 92.4 by 2.1 to find the average speed:

$92.4 \div 2.1 = 924 \div 21 = 44$

51. c. Divide 18.6 by 4 to find the average miles walked per day.

$18.6 \div 4 = 4.65$

Percents

52. Move the decimal point two places to the right and add %:

$.45 = 45\%$

53. $.008 = .8\%$

54. Change $\frac{2}{3}$ into a decimal:

$\frac{2}{3} = .666...$

Thus, $.16\frac{2}{3} = .1666...$

Change .1666 to a percent: $.1666... = 16.67\%$

55. To change a percent to a decimal, drop the % and move the decimal point two places to the left: $12\% = .12$

56. $87\frac{1}{2}\% = 87.5\% = .875$

57. $250\% = 2.5$

58. Multiply $\frac{1}{8}$ by 100%:

$\overset{}{\underset{2}{\frac{1}{8}}} \times \frac{\overset{25}{\cancel{100\%}}}{1} = \frac{25}{2}\% = 12.5\%$ or $12\frac{1}{2}\%$

59. Let's try technique #2.

$\frac{13}{25} = 13 \div 25 = .52 = 52\%$

60.

$\overset{}{\underset{3}{\frac{7}{\cancel{12}}}} \times \frac{\overset{25}{\cancel{100\%}}}{1} = \frac{175\%}{3} = 58.33\%$ or $58\frac{1}{3}\%$

61. $95\% = \frac{95}{100} = \frac{95 \div 5}{100 \div 5} = \frac{19}{20}$

62. $37\frac{1}{2}\% = 37.5\% = \frac{375}{1000} = \frac{375 \div 125}{1000 \div 125} = \frac{3}{8}$

63. $125\% = \frac{125}{100} = \frac{125 \div 25}{100 \div 25} = \frac{5}{4}$ or $1\frac{1}{4}$

64. Think of the problem as: "What is 1% of 25?"

$\frac{is}{of} = \frac{\%}{100}$

$\frac{is}{25} = \frac{1}{100}$

Cross-multiply and solve for *is*:

$100 \times is = 25 \times 1$

$100 \times .25 = 25$

1% of 25 is .25 or $\frac{1}{4}$.

65. Let's try $\frac{part}{whole} = \frac{\%}{100}$:

$\frac{part}{50} = \frac{18.2}{100}$

Cross-multiply and solve for *part*:

$50 \times 18.2 = part \times 100$

$910 = part \times 100$

$910 = 9.1 \times 100$

18.2% of 50 is 9.1

66. Let's try changing the percent into a decimal first:

$37\frac{1}{2}\%$ of $100 = 37.5\%$ of $100 = .375 \times 100 =$

37.5 or $37\frac{1}{2}$

67. 125% of $60 = 125\% \times 60 = 1.25 \times 60 = 75$

68. $\frac{is}{of} = \frac{\%}{100}$

$\frac{10}{20} = \frac{\%}{100}$

Cross-multiply and solve for %:

$10 \times 100 = 20 \times \%$

$1000 = 20 \times \%$

$1000 = 20 \times 50$

10 is 50% of 20

69. $\frac{4}{12} = \frac{\%}{100}$

$4 \times 100 = 12 \times \%$

$400 = 12 \times \%$

$400 = 12 \times 33\frac{1}{3}$

4 is $33\frac{1}{3}\%$ of 12

70. $\frac{12}{4} = \frac{\%}{100}$

$12 \times 100 = 4 \times \%$

$1,200 = 4 \times \%$

$1,200 = 4 \times 300$

12 is 300% of 4

71. $\frac{15}{of} = \frac{15}{100}$

$15 \times 100 = 15 \times of$

$1,500 = 15 \times of$

$1,500 = 15 \times 100$

15 is 15% of 100

72. $\frac{3}{of} = \frac{37.5}{100}$

Cross-multiply and solve for *of*:

$3 \times 100 = 37.5 \times of$

$300 = 37.5 \times of$

Divide 300 by 37.5 to find the value of *of*

$300 \div 37.5 = 8$

3 is 37.5% of 8

73. $\frac{20}{of} = \frac{200}{100}$

Cross-multiply and solve for *of*:

$20 \times 100 = 200 \times of$

$2,000 = 200 \times of$

$2,000 = 200 \times 10$

20 is 200% of 10

74. b. Convert 20% to a decimal and multiply by 140:

$20\% = .20$

$.20 \times 140 = 28$

75. c. This is a multi-step problem.

1. Find the total number of employees by using $\frac{part}{whole} = \frac{\%}{100}$.

$\frac{80}{whole} = \frac{40}{100}$

2. Cross-multiply and solve for *whole*.

$80 \times 100 = 40 \times whole$

$8,000 = 40 \times whole$

$8,000 = 40 \times 200$

3. Find the number of men by subtracting the number of women from 200:

$200 - 80 = 120$

76. c. Use $\frac{part}{whole} = \frac{\%}{100}$.

$$\frac{42}{840} = \frac{\%}{100}$$

Cross-multiply and solve for %:

$$42 \times 100 = 840 \times \%$$

$$4{,}200 = 840 \times \%$$

$$4{,}200 = 84 \times 5$$

The short sleeve shirts represent 5% of the 840 shirts that were sold.

77. d. Use $\frac{part}{whole} = \frac{\%}{100}$ to find the original cost of the shoes.

$$\frac{10}{whole} = \frac{20}{100}$$

Cross-multiply and solve for *whole*:

$$10 \times 100 = 20 \times whole$$

$$1{,}000 = 20 \times whole$$

$$1{,}000 = 20 \times 50$$

The shoes were originally priced at 50.

Averages

78. c. Add the scores and divide by 5:

$$\frac{180 + 182 + 184 + 186 + 188}{5} = \frac{920}{5} = 184$$

79. c. If Conroy averaged 30 miles per hour for two hours, then he drove 60 miles. Similarly, if he drove 60 miles per hour for two hours, he drove 120 miles. Add all the miles driven and divide by the number of hours spent driving.

$$\frac{60 + 120}{4} = \frac{180}{4} = 45$$

80. b. Multiply the number of men, 10, by their average score, 85:

$$10 \times 85 = 850$$

Next, multiply the number of women, 20, by their average score, 95;

$$20 \times 95 = 1{,}900$$

Add all the points scored and divide by the number of students.

$$\frac{850 + 1{,}900}{30} = 91\frac{2}{3}$$

Geometry and Algebra

Geometry

Typically, there are very few geometry problems on the math sections of the ASVAB. The problems that are included tend to cover the basics: lines, angles, triangles, rectangles, squares, and circles. You may be asked to find the area, perimeter, or volume of a figure or the size of an angle. The arithmetic involved is pretty simple, so all you really need are a few definitions and formulas.

Glossary of Geometry Terms

Angle two rays with a common endpoint. The endpoint is called a vertex.
There are four types of angles:

> **Acute:** less than 90°
>
> **Obtuse:** more than 90°
>
> **Right:** 90°
>
> **Straight:** 180°

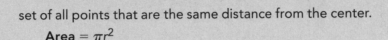

Circle set of all points that are the same distance from the center.

> **Area** $= \pi r^2$
>
> **Circumference** $= 2\pi r$
>
> ($\pi = 3.14$; $r =$ radius)

radius

Circumference distance around a circle. (See *circle*)

Cube a solid with six congruent square faces.

> **Volume** $= (side)^3$

Diameter a line through the center of a circle. The diameter is twice the length of the radius. (See *circle*, *radius*)

Line extends endlessly in both directions. It is referred to by a letter at the end of it or

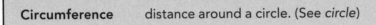

by two points on it. Thus, the line below may be referred to as line *l* or as $\overleftrightarrow{AB}$.

Parallel lines two lines in the same plane that do not intersect.

$l \,\|\, m$

l _____

m _____

Perimeter distance around a figure, such as a triangle or a rectangle. The perimeter of a circle is called its *circumference*.

> **Perimeter** = sum of length of all sides

Perpendicular lines two lines in the same plane that intersect to form four right angles. (See *right angle*)

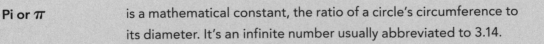

Pi or π is a mathematical constant, the ratio of a circle's circumference to its diameter. It's an infinite number usually abbreviated to 3.14.

Glossary of Geometry Terms

Point
has a location but no size or dimension. It is referred to by a letter close to it, like this: • *A*

Radius
line segment from the center to any point on a circle. The radius is half the diameter. (See *circle, diameter*)

Rectangle
four-sided figure with a right angle and both pairs of opposite sides parallel (which implies that all four sides are right angles and that opposite sides are equal in length).

> **Area** = *length × width*
>
> **Perimeter** = 2 × *length* + 2 × *width*

Rectangular Solid
a solid with six rectangular faces.

Volume = length × width × height

Square
rectangle with four equal sides (See *rectangle*).

> **Area** = (*side*)^2
>
> **Perimeter** = 4 × *side*

Triangle
three-sided figure.

> **Area** = $\frac{1}{2}$(*base × height*)
>
> **Perimeter** = sum of the lengths of all three sides
>
> **Angles:** The sum of the three angles of a triangle is always° 180

height

base

Volume
the measure of the amount of space in a solid figure.

Practice Problems in Geometry

1. What is the area in inches of a triangle with base 10" and height 8"?

    a. 80

    b. 40

    c. 20

    d. 10

2. Find the perimeter of a triangle with sides 3, 4, and 5 units in length.

    a. 60 units

    b. 20 units

    c. 12 units

    d. 9 units

3. If the area of a square field measures 256 square feet, how many feet of fencing are needed to completely surround the field?

    a. 256

    b. 128

    c. 64

    d. It cannot be determined.

4. The length of a rectangle is twice its width. If the perimeter of the rectangle is 30 units, what is the width of the rectangle?

    a. 30

    b. 20

    c. 15

    d. 5

5. A circular opening has a diameter of $8\frac{1}{2}$ inches. What is the radius in inches of a circular disk that will exactly fit into the opening?

    a. 17

    b. 8.5

    c. 8

    d. 4.25

6. The radius of a hoop is 10". If you roll the hoop along a straight path through 6 complete revolutions, approximately how far will it roll, in inches? (Use a value of 3.14 for π.)

   a. 31.4

   b. 62.8

   c. 188.4

   d. d. 376.8

7. What is the perimeter of a square with an area measuring 64 square inches?

   a. 96

   b. 64

   c. 32

   d. 8

8. The sum of three equal angles is the same as the measure of a straight angle. What is the measure of one of the equal angles?

   a. 180

   b. 90

   c. 75

   d. 60

9. A rectangle has a perimeter of 48 and a width of 8. What is the measure of the length?

   a. 24

   b. 16

   c. 8

   d. 4

10. A triangle has two equal angles and a smaller angle which measures 26°. What is the measure of one of the larger angles?

   a. 77

   b. 66

   c. 55

   d. 44

11. Each of the square faces of a cube has an area of 25 square inches. What is the volume of the cube?

   a. 250

   b. 125

   c. 50

   d. 25

12. The volume of a rectangular solid is 120 cubic inches. If the height is 4 inches and the width is 5 inches, what is the measure of the height?

a. 30

b. 10

c. 6

d. 3

13. What is the length of the diameter of a circle with an area of 144π?

a. 24

b. 16

c. 12

d. 6

14. The difference between an obtuse angle and an acute angle is 14°. If the acute angle measures 84°, what is the measure of the obtuse angle?

a. 166

b. 116

c. 98

d. 91

15. What is the area of a circle with circumference 12π?

a. 144π

b. 72π

c. 48π

d. 36π

16. What is the circumference of a circle with an area of 121π?

a. 60.5π

b. 22π

c. 11π

d. 5.5π

17. A triangle has three equal sides, each side measuring 6 inches. If a square has the same perimeter as the triangle, what is the length of one of its sides?

a. 4.5

b. 9

c. 13.5

d. 18

18. What is the perimeter of a rectangle with an area measuring 96 square inches and a width of 6 inches?

    a. 48

    b. 44

    c. 24

    d. 16

19. What is the height of a triangle with an area of 36 square inches and a base of 6 inches?

    a. 24

    b. 18

    c. 12

    d. 6

20. How many cubes, 2 inches on an edge, can fit into a rectangular solid with dimensions 6" by 4" by 8"?

    a. 84

    b. 64

    c. 48

    d. 24

Algebra

Algebra questions do not appear on every test. However, when they do, they typically cover the material you learned in pre-algebra or in the first few months of your high school algebra course. Popular topics for algebra questions include:

- solving equations
- positive and negative numbers
- algebraic expressions

What Is Algebra?

Algebra is a way to express and solve problems using numbers and symbols. These symbols, called **unknowns** or **variables**, are letters of the alphabet that are used to represent numbers.

For example, say you are asked to find out what number, when added to 3, gives you a total of 5. Using algebra, you could express the problem as $x + 3 = 5$. The variable x represents the number you are trying to find. Subtracting 3 from 5 tells you $x = 2$.

Here's another example, but this one uses only variables. To find the distance traveled, multiply the rate of travel (speed) by the amount of time traveled: $d = r \times t$. The variable d stands for *distance,* r stands for *rate,* and t stands for *time.*

In algebra, the variables may take on different values. In other words, they *vary,* and that's why they're called *variables.*

Operations

Algebra uses the same operations as arithmetic: addition, subtraction, multiplication, and division. In arithmetic, we might say $3 + 4 = 7$, while in algebra, we would talk about two numbers whose values we don't know that add up to 7, or $x + y = 7$. Here's how each operation translates to algebra:

ALGEBRAIC OPERATIONS	
The sum of two numbers	$x + y$
The difference of two numbers	$x - y$
The product of two numbers*	$x \times y$ or $x \bullet y$ or xy
The quotient of two numbers	$\frac{x}{y}$

*In algebra, the familiar multiplication symbol, "x" is often replaced with a dot, or eliminated altogether (two variables can be placed right next to one another for clarity).

Equations

An equation is a mathematical sentence stating that two quantities are equal. For example:

$$2x = 10$$
$$x + 5 = 8$$

The idea is to find a replacement for the unknown that will make the sentence true. That's called *solving* the equation. Thus, in the first example, $x = 5$ because $2 \times 5 = 10$ (or $10 \div 2 = 5$). In the second example, $x = 3$ because $3 + 5 = 8$.

Sometimes you can solve an equation by inspection, as with the above examples. Other equations may be more complicated and require a step-by-step solution:

$$\frac{n+4}{2} + 1 = 3$$

The general approach is to consider an equation like a balanced scale. Essentially, whatever you do to one side, you must also do to the other side to maintain the balance. Thus, if you were to add 2 to the left side, you would also have to add 2 to the right side.

Let's apply this balance concept to our complicated equation above. Remembering that we want to solve it for n, we must somehow rearrange it so the n is isolated on one side of the equation. What it is equal to will then be on the other side. Looking at the equation, you can see that n has been increased by 2 and then divided by 4 and ultimately added to 1. Therefore, we will undo these operations to isolate n.

Begin by subtracting 1 from both sides of the equation:

$$\frac{n+2}{4} + 1 = 3$$
$$\underline{\quad -1 \quad -1 \quad}$$
$$\frac{n+2}{4} = 2$$

Next, multiply both sides by 4:

$$4 \times \frac{n+2}{4} = 2 \times 4$$
$$n + 2 = 8$$

Finally, subtract 2 from both sides:

$$\underline{\quad -2 \quad -2 \quad}$$

This isolates n and solves the equation:

$$n = 6$$

Notice that each operation in the original equation was undone by using the inverse operation. That is, addition was undone by subtraction, and division was undone by multiplication. In general, each operation can be undone by its **inverse**:

ALGEBRAIC INVERSES	
OPERATION	**INVERSE**
Addition	Subtraction
Subtraction	Addition
Multiplication	Division
Division	Multiplication

After you solve an equation, check your work by plugging the answer back into the original equation to make sure it balances.

When more than one arithmetic operation appears, you must know the correct sequence in which to perform the operations. For example, do you know what to do first to calculate $2 + 3 \times 4$? You are right if you said, multiply first. The correct answer is 14. If you add first, you will get the wrong answer of 20. The correct sequence of operations is:

1. parentheses
2. exponents
3. multiplication
4. division
5. addition
6. subtraction

If you remember this saying, you will know the order of operations: **Please Excuse My Dear Aunt Sally** or **PEMDAS**.

Observe what happens when we plug 6 in for n:

$$\frac{6+2}{4} + 1 = 3$$
$$\frac{8}{4} + 1 = 3$$
$$2 + 1 = 3$$
$$3 = 3$$

Solve each equation for x:

21. $x + 5 = 12$

22. $3x + 6 = 18$

23. $\frac{1}{4}x = 7$

Positive and Negative Numbers

Positive and negative numbers, also known as **signed** numbers, are best shown as points along the number line:

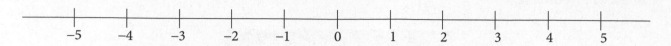

Numbers to the left of 0 are **negative** and those to the right are **positive**. Zero is neither negative nor positive. If a number is written without a sign, it is assumed to be **positive**. Notice that when you are on the negative side of the number line, numbers with bigger values are actually smaller. For example, –5 is *less than* –2. You come into contact with negative numbers more often than you might think; for example, very cold temperatures are recorded as negative numbers, or decreases in attendence might be measured with negatives.

As you move to the right along the number line, the numbers get larger. Mathematically, to indicate that one number, say 4, is *greater than* another number, like –2, the *greater than* sign (>) is used:

$$4 > -2$$

On the other hand, to say that –2 is *less than* 4, we use the *less than* sign, (<):

$$-2 < 4$$

Arithmetic with Positive and Negative Numbers

The following table illustrates the rules for doing arithmetic with signed numbers. Notice that when a negative number follows an operation (as it does in the second example below), it is enclosed in parentheses to avoid confusion.

RULE	EXAMPLES
ADDITION	
• If both numbers have the same sign, just add them. The answer has the same sign as the numbers being added.	$3 + 5 = 8$ $-3 + (-5) = -8$
• If both numbers have different signs, subtract the smaller number from the larger. The answer has the same sign as the larger number.	$-3 + 5 = 2$ $3 + (-5) = -2$
• If both numbers are the same but have opposite signs, the sum is zero.	$3 + (-3) = 0$
SUBTRACTION	
• Change the sign of the number to be subtracted and then add as above.	$3 - 5 = 3 + (-5) = -2$ $-3 - 5 = -3 + (-5) = -8$ $-3 - (-5) = -3 + 5 = 2$

RULE	EXAMPLES
MULTIPLICATION	
• Multiply the numbers together. If two numbers have the same sign, the answer is positive.	$3 \times 5 = 15$ $-3 \times (-5) = 15$
• If two numbers have different signs, the answer is negative.	$-3 \times 5 = -15$ $3 \times (-5) = -15$
• If one number is zero, the answer is zero.	$3 \times 0 = 0$
DIVISION	
• Divide the numbers. If two numbers have the same sign, the answer is positive.	$15 \div 3 = 5$ $-15 \div (-3) = 5$
• If two numbers have different signs, the answer is negative.	$15 \div (-3) = -5$ $-15 \div 3 = -5$
• If the top number is zero, the answer is zero.	$0 \div 3 = 0$

Even when signed numbers appear in an equation, the PEMDAS step-by-step solution works exactly as it does for positive numbers. You just have to remember the arithmetic rules for negative numbers. For example, let's solve $14x + 2 = 5$.

1. Subtract 2 from both sides:
$$-14x + 2 = -5$$
$$\underline{ -2 \quad -2}$$
$$-14x = -7$$

2. Divide both sides by –14:
$$-14x \div -14 = -7 \div -14$$
$$x = \tfrac{1}{2}$$

Now try these problems with signed numbers. Solve for x.

24. $1 - 3 \times (-4) = x$

25. $-3x + 6 = -18$

26. $\frac{x}{-4} + 3 = -7$

Algebraic Expressions

An algebraic expression is a group of numbers, unknowns, and arithmetic operations, like: $3x - 2y$. This one may be translated as, "3 times some number minus 2 times another number." To *evaluate* an algebraic expression, replace each variable with its value. For example, if $x = 5$ and $y = 4$, we would evaluate $3x - 2y$ as follows:

$$3(5) - 2(4) = 15 - 8 = 7$$

Evaluate these expressions.

27. $4a + 3b$; $a = 2$ and $b = -1$

28. $3mn - 4m + 2n$; $m = 3$ and $n = -3$

29. $-2x - \frac{1}{2}y + 4z$; $x = 5$, $y = -4$, and $z = 6$

30. The volume of a cylinder is given by the formula $V = \pi r^2 h$, where r is the radius of the base and h is the height of the cylinder. What is the volume of a cylinder with a base radius of 3 and height of 4? (Leave π in your answer.)

31. If $x = 3$, what is the value of $3x - x$?

Exponents and Factoring

Solving a problem such as $4 \times 4 \times 4 = 64$ can be written using an exponent. An exponent is a number that indicates how many times a factor multiplies by itself.

Example: Write the expression $4 \times 4 \times 4$ using an exponent.

Answer: $4 \times 4 \times 4 = 4^3$

The smaller number 3 is the *exponent* and the 4 is the *base*. Another name for an exponent is power, as in 4 to the third power (4^3)

Variables can also have exponents. For example, $m \times m = m^2$ and $m \times m \times m = m^3$. When you multiply similar variables with exponents, add the exponents.

Example: What is the product of m^2 and m^3?

Answer: Since the variables are same, add the exponents:

$$m^2 \times m^3 = m^{2+3} = m^5$$

The properties of exponents are useful when multiplying algebraic expressions. A useful acronym, **FOIL**, guides us in this process.

F: Multiply the *first* terms
O: Multiply the *outer* terms
I: Multiply the *inner* terms
L: Multiply the *last* terms

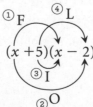

Example: Multiply $(m + 5)(m + 2)$ using the FOIL method.

Multiply the first terms: $m \times m = m^2$
Multiply the outer terms: $m \times 2 = 2m$
Multiply the inner terms: $5 \times m = 5m$
Multiply the last terms: $5 \times 2 = 10$

Arrange the terms in descending order, combining like terms:

$$m^2 + (2m + 5m) + 10 = m^2 + 7m + 10$$

There will only be a few FOIL problems on the ASVAB, so it will be useful to memorize these patterns:

1. $(m + n)^2 = (m + n)(m + n) = m^2 + 2mn + n^2$
2. $(m - n)^2 = (m - n)(m - n) = m^2 - 2mn + n^2$
3. $m^2 - n^2 = (m + n)(m - n)$

Example: Simplify the following expression:

$$\frac{m^2 - 2mn + n^2}{m^2 - n^2}$$

1. Simplify the numerator and the denominator by reversing the FOIL process.

$$\frac{m^2 - 2mn + n^2}{m^2 - n^2} = \frac{(m - n)(m - n)}{(m + n)(m - n)}$$

2. Cancel equivalent expressions that appear on the top and bottom:

$$\frac{(m - n)(m - n)}{(m + n)(m - n)} = \frac{(m - n)\cancel{(m - n)}}{(m + n)\cancel{(m - n)}} = \frac{(m - n)}{(m + n)}$$

Try these sample problems.

32. $\sqrt{\frac{216}{6}} =$
   a. 6
   b. 12
   c. 18
   d. 24

33. $\sqrt{8} + \sqrt{18} =$

   a. $\sqrt{26}$

   b. 12

   c. $2\sqrt{5}$

   d. $5\sqrt{2}$

34. $(3x^2y^2)(-2x^3y) =$

35. Multiply: $(x + 3)^2 =$

36. Simplify: $\frac{m^2 - n^2}{(m + n)^2} =$

Squares and Square Roots

A number multiplied by itself is called a square. For example, 25 is a square because $5 \times 5 = 25$. The square root of a number is that number that has been multiplied by itself. The symbol $\sqrt{\ }$ means *the square root*.

Example: $6^2 =$

   Calculate the product by multiplying 6 by 6: $6 \times 6 = 36$

Example: $\sqrt{36} =$

   Since $6 \times 6 = 36$, the square root of 36 is 6 ($\sqrt{36} = 6$)

It will be helpful to memorize a few squares and square roots.

$1^2 = 1$	$7^2 = 49$	$\sqrt{1} = 1$	$\sqrt{49} = 7$
$2^2 = 4$	$8^2 = 64$	$\sqrt{4} = 2$	$\sqrt{64} = 8$
$3^2 = 9$	$9^2 = 81$	$\sqrt{9} = 3$	$\sqrt{81} = 9$
$4^2 = 16$	$10^2 = 100$	$\sqrt{16} = 4$	$\sqrt{100} = 10$
$5^2 = 25$	$11^2 = 121$	$\sqrt{25} = 5$	$\sqrt{121} = 11$
$6^2 = 36$	$12^2 = 144$	$\sqrt{36} = 6$	$\sqrt{144} = 12$

Try these problems.

37. If $2x^2 = 162$, what is the positive value of x?

   a. 81

   b. 40.5

   c. 9

   d. 3

38. $\sqrt{169} - \sqrt{25} =$

   a. 12

   b. 11

   c. 8

   d. 6

39. Solve for x: $\frac{x^2}{2} - 3 = 29$

   a. 4

   b. 8

   c. 32

   d. 64

40. Solve for x: $3(x - 4) = -12$

   a. 0

   b. 4

   c. 8

   d. 12

Answers

Geometry

1. b. Use the formula $Area = \frac{1}{2}(base \times height)$

$$Area = \frac{1}{2}(10 \times 8) = \frac{1}{2} \times 80 = 40$$

2. c. To find the perimeter, find the sum of the sides:

$$3 + 4 + 5 = 12$$

3. c. The area of a square is found by using the formula $Area = (side)^2$. Substitute 256 for Area to find the length of one side:

$$256 = (side)^2$$

$$16 = side$$

The length of one side is 16 because $16 \times 16 = 256$. Next, multiply 16 by 4, the number of equal sides in a square:

$$4 \times 16 = 64$$

4. d. The perimeter of a rectangle is found by using the formula:

$$P = (2 \times width) + (2 \times length)$$

Since the length is twice the width, we can rewrite the formula for perimeter as:

$$P = (2 \times width) + [2 \times (2 \times width)]$$

Solve for width:

$$(2 \times width) + (4 \times width) = 30$$

$$6 \times width = 30$$

$$6 \times 5 = 30$$

The width of the rectangle is 5.

5. d. The radius of a circle is one-half the diameter.

$$\frac{1}{2} \times 8\frac{1}{2} = \frac{1}{2} \times \frac{17}{2} = \frac{17}{4} = 4\frac{1}{4} \text{ or } 4.25.$$

6. d. A hoop rolled six times is equivalent to multiplying the circle's circumference by 6. To find one circumference, use the formula $2\pi r$ and multiply that product by 6:

$$2 \times 3.14 \times 10 \times 6 = 376.8$$

7. c. The area of a square is found by using the formula $Area = (side)^2$. Substitute 64 for *Area* to find the length of a side:

$$64 = (side)^2$$

$$8 = side$$

Since the lengths of all four sides are equal, multiply 4 by 8 to find the perimeter.

$$4 \times 8 = 32$$

8. d. A straight angle measures 180°. Divide 180 by 3 to find the measure of one of the angles:

$$180 \div 3 = 60$$

9. b. The perimeter of a rectangle is found by using the formula $Perimeter = 2 \times length + 2 \times width$. Substitute 8 for the width and subtract from 48:

$$48 = 2 \times length + 2 \times 8$$

$$48 = 2 \times length + 16$$

$$32 = 2 \times length$$

Divide 32 by 2 to find the measure of one of the lengths:

$$32 \div 2 = 16$$

10. a. The sum of the measures of the three angles in a triangle is 180°. Subtract 26 from 180 to find the measure of the remaining angles:

$$180 - 26 = 144$$

Since the two remaining angles are equal, divide 144 by 2 to find the measure of one of the angles:

$$144 \div 2 = 77$$

11. b. The formula for the area of a square is *Area* = (*side*)². Substitute 25 for *Area* to find the length of one side:

$$25 = (side)^2$$

$$5 = side$$

Use the formula *Volume* = (*side*)³ to find the cube's volume:

$$Volume = (5)^3 = 125$$

12. c. Use the formula *Volume* = *length* × *width* × *height* and input the known values.

$$120 = length \times 4 \times 5$$

$$120 = length \times 20$$

$$120 = 6 \times 20$$

The length of the rectangular solid is 6.

13. a. Use the formula *Area* = πr^2 and substitute 144π for Area:

$$144\pi = \pi r^2$$

Divide both sides by π and solve for *r*:

$$144 = r^2$$

$$12 = r$$

Double the radius to find the diameter:

$$2 \times 12 = 24$$

14. c. An obtuse angle must be greater than 90° :

$$Obtuse\ angle -14 = 84$$

$$98 - 14 = 84$$

The obtuse angle measures 98°.

15. d. Use the formula *Circumference* = 2π*r* to find the radius:

$$12\pi = 2\pi r$$

$$\frac{12\pi}{2\pi} = \frac{2\pi r}{2\pi}$$

$$6 = r$$

Use the formula *Area* = πr^2 substituting 6 for *r*:

$$Area = \pi(6)^2$$

$$Area = 36\pi$$

16. b. Use the formula $Area = \pi r^2$ to find the radius:

$$121\pi = \pi r^2$$

$$121 = r^2$$

$$11 = r$$

Use the formula $Circumference = 2\pi r$, substituting 11 for r:

$$Circumference = 2 \times \pi \times 11$$

$$Circumference = 22\pi$$

17. a. The perimeter of the triangle and the square is 18 inches. Divide 18 by 4, to find a side of the square:

$$18 \div 4 = 4.5$$

18. b. Use the formula $Area = length \times width$ to find the length:

$$96 = 6 \times length$$

$$96 = 6 \times 16$$

The length is 16. Use the formula $Perimeter = 2 \times length + 2 \times width$ to finish the problem:

$$Perimeter = 2 \times 16 + 2 \times 6$$

$$Perimeter = 44$$

19. c. Use the formula $Area = \frac{1}{2}(base \times height)$ to find the height:

$$36 = \frac{1}{2}(6 \times height)$$

$$36 = 3 \times height$$

$$36 = 3 \times 12$$

The height is 12 inches.

20. d. Divide the volume of the rectangular solid by the volume of the cube:

Volume of the rectangular solid: $6 \times 4 \times 8 = 192 \; inches^3$

Volume of the cube: $2 \times 2 \times 2 = 8 \; inches^3$

$$192 \div 8 = 24$$

21. Subtract 5 from both sides:

$$x + 5 - 5 = 12 - 5$$

$$x = 7$$

Check your answer: $7 + 5 = 12$

22. Subtract 6 from both sides:

$$3x + 6 - 6 = 18 - 6$$

$$3x = 12$$

Divide both sides by 3:

$$\frac{3x}{3} = \frac{12}{3}$$

$$x = 4$$

Check your answer:

$$3 \times 4 + 6 = 18$$

$$12 + 6 = 18$$

23. Although you can divide both sides by $\frac{1}{4}$, it is easier to multiply both sides by 4:

$$4\left(\frac{1}{4}x\right) = 7 \times 4$$

$$x = 28$$

Check your answer: $\frac{1}{4} \times 28 = 7$

24. Multiply 3 and –4:

$1 - 3(-4) = x$

$1 - (-12) = x$

Subtract –12 from 1:

$1 - (-12) = 1 + 12 = 13 = x$

$x = 13$

25. Subtract 6 from both sides:

$-3x + 6 - 6 = -18 - 6$

$-3x = -24$

Divide both sides by –3:

$\frac{-3x}{-3} = \frac{-24}{-3}$

$x = 8$

26. Subtract 3 from both sides:

$\frac{x}{-4} + 3 - 3 = -7 - 3$

$\frac{x}{-4} = -10$

Multiply both sides by –4:

$\frac{x}{-4} \times -4 = -10 \times -4$

$x = 40$

27. $4(2) + 3(-1) = 8 + -3 = 5$

28. $3(3)(-3) - 4(3) + 2(-3) = -27 - 12 - 6 = -45$

29. $-2(5) - \frac{1}{2}(-4) + 4(6) =$

$-10 - (-2) + 24 =$

$-10 + 2 + 24 = 16$

30. $V = \pi r^2 h$

$V = \pi(3^2)(4)$

$V = \pi(9)(4)$

$V = 36\pi$

31. $3(3) - 3 = 9 - 3 = 6$

32. a. $\sqrt{\frac{216}{6}} = \sqrt{36} = 6$

33. d. Simplify each radical:

$\sqrt{8} = \sqrt{4} \times \sqrt{2} = 2\sqrt{2}$

$\sqrt{18} = \sqrt{9} \times \sqrt{2} = 3\sqrt{2}$

Add the simplified radicals:

$2\sqrt{2} + 3\sqrt{2} = 5\sqrt{2}$

34. Multiply 3 and -2, x^2 and x^3, and y^2 and y (remember, $y = y^1$):

$-6x^5y^3$

35. Rewrite the problem:

$(x + 3)^2 = (x + 3)(x + 3)$

Use the FOIL method to multiply:

First: $x \bullet x = x^2$

Outer: $x \bullet 3 = 3x$

Inner: $3 \bullet x = 3x$

Last: $3 \bullet 3 = 9$

Arrange the terms in descending order, combining like terms:

$x^2 + 3x + 3x + 9 = x^2 + 6x + 9$

36. Factor the numerator and the denominator separately:

$$m^2 - n^2 = (m + n)(m - n)$$

$$(m + n)^2 = (m + n)(m + n)$$

Next, divide and simplify:

$$\frac{(m + n)(m - n)}{(m + n)(m + n)} = \frac{\cancel{(m + n)}(m - n)}{\cancel{(m + n)}(m + n)} = \frac{m - n}{m + n}$$

37. c. Divide both sides by 2 to isolate x^2

$$\frac{2x^2}{2} = \frac{162}{2}:$$

$$x^2 = 81$$

Take the square root of both sides:

$$\sqrt{x^2} = \sqrt{81}$$

$$x = 9$$

38. c. Simplify each square root first:

$$\sqrt{169} = 13$$

$$\sqrt{25} = 5$$

$$13 - 5 = 8$$

39. b. $\frac{x^2}{2} - 3 = 29$

$$\frac{x^2}{2} - 3 + 3 = 29 + 3$$

$$\frac{x^2}{2} = 32$$

$$(2)\left(\frac{x^2}{2}\right) = (32)(2)$$

$$x^2 = 64$$

$$x = 8$$

40. a. Multiply each term in the parentheses by 3:

$$3(x - 4) = -12$$

$$3x - 12 = -12$$

Solve for x:

$$3x - 12 + 12 = -12 + 12$$

$$3x = 0$$

$$\frac{3x}{3} = \frac{0}{3}$$

$$x = 0$$

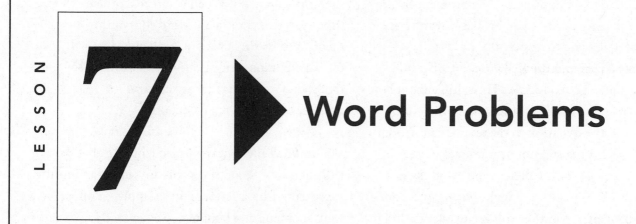

Word Problems

A word problem tells a story. It may present a situation with numbers and/or unknown information (also called a **variable**). Your job is to translate that word problem into a solvable math problem. Many of the math problems on the ASVAB are word problems. A word problem can include any kind of math, including simple arithmetic, fractions, decimals, percentages—even algebra and geometry. This chapter will give you some helpful hints to use when solving word problems.

Steps to Solving Word Problems

Some simple word problems can be solved by common sense. Most word problems, however, require several steps. Here are some steps to help you solve word problems:

1. **Read a word problem in chunks, rather than straight through.** As you read each chunk, stop to think about what it means. To represent that chunk, take notes, draw a diagram, or a picture, or write an

equation. You may even want to underline important information in each chunk. Repeat this process with each chunk. Reading a word problem in sections makes the problem easier to understand. Also, you probably won't have to read it again to answer it.

2. **Make a plan of attack.** Figure out what information you already have. Then think about how you're going to use it to solve the problem.

3. **Reread the question** to make sure you've been solving for the right information after you get your answer. This will help you avoid the careless mistake of answering the wrong question.

4. **Check your work after you get an answer.** In a multiple-choice test, don't assume your answer is correct just because it matches one of the answers given. Answers arrived at by making the most common mistakes are often included in the answer choices. You should always check your work if you have time. Here are a few suggestions:

- Ask yourself if the answer is reasonable: Does it make sense?
- Plug your answer back into the problem: Does it hold together?
- Work the problem a second time, using a different method if you can.

Translating Word Problems

The hardest part of any word problem is translating the story into math. When you read a problem, sometimes you can translate it word for word from statements into math. For many problems, you will write out an equation. An equation is a number sentence that shows two parts that are equal: $45 + 12 = 57$ is a number sentence *and* an equation.

An equation may involve an unknown amount. The unknown is a way of placeholding that part of the equation. Sometimes this unknown amount is represented by a letter. For example, suppose you went shopping and bought a sweater for $45. You also bought a pair of gloves, but you can't remember how much they cost. You do remember that you spent $57 in all. The amount of the gloves is the unknown. Use the letter x to represent the price of the gloves. The equation looks like this: $45 + x = 57$. When you solve the problem by subtracting $45 from $57 you learn that $x = 12$. The gloves cost $12.

Often, key words in the problem hint at the mathematical operation to be performed and how to translate that story into math. Think of the key word as a word to look for that will signal what operations you need to set up the equation and solve the problem. The following are some translation tips:

EQUALS   Key words: *is, are, has*

STATEMENT	MATH
Judi **has** 5 books.	$J = 5$
Bob **is** 18 years old.	$B = 18$
There **are** 7 hats.	$H = 7$

ADDITION   Key words: *sum; more, greater, older than; total; altogether*

STATEMENT	MATH
The **sum** of two numbers is 10.	$X + Y = 10$
Karen has $5 **more** than Sam.	$K = 5 + S$
Judi is 2 years **older** than Tony.	$J = 2 + T$
The **total** of three numbers is 25.	$A + B + C = 25$
The base is 3" **greater than** the height.	$B = 3 + H$
How much do Joan and Tom have **altogether**?	$J + T = ?$

SUBTRACTION   Key words: *difference, less or younger than, remain, left over*

STATEMENT	MATH
Jay is 2 years **younger** than Brett.	$J = B - 2$
After Carol ate 3 apples, R apples **remained**.	$R = A - 3$
The **difference** between two numbers is 17.	$X + Y = 17$
Mike has 5 **less** cats than twice the number Jan has.	$M = 2J - 5$

MULTIPLICATION   Key words: *of, product, times*

STATEMENT	MATH
Half **of** the boys	$\frac{1}{2} \times B$
The **product** of two numbers is 12.	$A \times B = 12$
20% **of** Matthew's baseball caps	$.20 \times M$

DIVISION   Key word: *per*

STATEMENT	MATH
22 miles **per** gallon	22 miles/gallon
15 drops **per** teaspoon	15 drops/teaspoon

DISTANCE Formula: distance = rate × time
Key words are: movement words like *walk, run, climb, swim*; time and distance words like *far, long*; or vehicle words like *plane, train, car.*

STATEMENT	MATH
How **far** did the plane travel in 4 hours if it averaged 300 miles per hour?	$D = 300 \times 4$ $D = 1{,}200$ miles
Ben **walked** 20 miles in 4 hours. What was his average **speed**?	$20 = r \times 4$ 5 miles per hour $= r$

Solving Word Problems Using the Translation Table

Let's try to solve the following problem using our translation rules.

Example

Carla is reading a novel that has a total of 336 pages. On Friday, she read 35 pages. On Saturday, she read twice the number of pages she read on Friday. How many more pages does she have left to read?

- **a.** 105
- **b.** 231
- **c.** 266
- **d.** 301

Here's how we marked up the question. Notice how we underlined key phrases and we used letters to represent words: *t* for total, *F* for Friday, and *S* for Saturday.

Carla is reading a novel that has a total of 336 pages. On Friday, she read 35 pages. On Saturday, she read twice the number of pages she read on Friday. How many more pages does she have left to read?

$t = 336$
$F = 35$
$S = 2 \times 35$
$? = \text{left}$

The words *more* and *left* hint at both addition and subtraction. The word *twice* (meaning *two times more*) hints at multiplication.

What we know:

- Carla read 35 pages one day.
- Carla read 2 times 35 pages the next day.
- The book has a total of 336 pages.

The question itself: How many more pages does she have left to read?

Plan of attack:

- Find the number of pages she has already read.
- Find out how many pages are left.

Solution

You know how many pages Carla read on Friday: 35. If you want to find out how many pages she read on Saturday, you will use multiplication: $2 \times 35 = 70$. Next, you will use addition to find out how many pages she has already read: $35 + 70 = 105$. But the question asks, "How many pages does she have left to read?" The word *left* indicates that you will subtract the total number of pages minus the number of pages already read: $366 - 105 = 231$. So, to answer this question, you must take three steps—addition, subtraction, and multiplication.

Step 1: $2 \times 35 = 70$
Step 2: $35 + 70 = 105$
Step 3: $366 - 105 = 231$

Answer: Carla has 231 pages left to read.

Check Your Work

Check your work by plugging your answer back into the original problem. See if the whole thing makes sense:

Carla is reading a novel that has a total of 336 pages. On Friday, she read 35 pages. On Saturday, she read 70 pages. She has 231 pages left to read.

Carla has already read 105 pages (25 + 70). If she reads 231 more (105 + 231 = 336), she will have read all 336 pages.

Practice Word Problems

Practice using the translation table to help you solve problems that require you to work with basic arithmetic. Answers are at the end of the chapter.

1. Mark went shopping with $100 and returned home with only $18.42. How much money did he spend?
   a. $81.58
   b. $72.68
   c. $72.58
   d. $71.68

2. Joan invited ten friends to a party. Each friend brought three guests. How many people came to the party, excluding Joan?
   a. 3
   b. 10
   c. 30
   d. 40

3. The office secretary can type 80 words per minute on his word processor. How many minutes will it take him to type a report containing 760 words?
   a. 8
   b. 8.5
   c. 9
   d. 9.5

4. Mr. Wallace is writing a budget request to upgrade his personal computer system. He wants to purchase 4 MB of RAM, which will cost $100, two new software programs at $350 each, external hard drive for $249, and an additional mouse for $25. What is the total amount Mr. Wallace should write on his budget request?
   a. $724
   b. $974
   c. $1,049
   d. $1,074

5. A roast needs to be cooked 20 minutes per pound. If an 8 pound roast needs to be served at 5:30 P.M., when should it be placed in the oven?
   a. 2:50 P.M.
   b. 3:00 P.M.
   c. 3:20 P.M.
   d. 3:30 P.M.

6. On a certain day, the low temperature in City A was −6° while the high temperature was 22°. How much had the temperature risen that day?
   a. 34°
   b. 28°
   c. 16°
   d. 6°

7. A number increased by 12 is 135. What is the number?
   a. 133
   b. 123
   c. 33
   d. 23

8. The sum of two integers is 40 and their difference is 8. What are the two integers?

   a. 30 and 10

   b. 28 and 12

   c. 24 and 16

   d. 20 and 20

9. A shuttle can transport 9 people per trip. How many trips must it make to transport 40 people?

   a. $6\frac{5}{9}$

   b. 5

   c. $4\frac{4}{9}$

   d. 4

10. Sam bought two turkeys. The heavier turkey weighed 16 pounds, 2 ounces while the lighter turkey weighed 14 pounds, 10 ounces. What is the difference between the weights of the two turkeys?

   a. 30 pounds, 12 ounces

   b. 10 pounds, 2 ounces

   c. 1 pound, 8 ounces

   d. 12 ounces

11. On a class trip, the seventh and eighth graders ate 84 hot dogs. If the eighth graders ate 16 more hot dogs than the seventh graders, how many hot dogs did the eighth graders eat?

   a. 68

   b. 50

   c. 42

   d. 34

12. Wilma planned to spend 120 to feed the 15 guests at her party. Later, she realized she would be entertaining 20 guests. How much *more* will she need to spend on the party?

   a. $40

   b. $80

   c. $160

   d. $240

Fractions

13. The length of a table plus $\frac{1}{5}$ of its length is 36 inches. How long is the table, in inches?

   a. 30

   b. 40

   c. 42

   d. 45

14. An outside wall is $5\frac{7}{8}$ inches thick. The wall consists of $\frac{1}{2}$ inch of drywall and $3\frac{3}{4}$ inches of insulation, and $\frac{5}{8}$ inch of wall sheathing. The remaining thickness is siding. How thick is the siding?

   a. $\frac{1}{8}$ inch

   b. $\frac{1}{4}$ inch

   c. $\frac{1}{2}$ inch

   d. 1 inch

15. A certain test is scored by adding 1 point for each correct answer and subtracting $\frac{1}{4}$ of a point for each incorrect answer. If Jan answered 31 questions correctly and 9 questions incorrectly, what was her score?

   a. $28\frac{3}{4}$

   b. $28\frac{1}{4}$

   c. 26

   d. $22\frac{1}{4}$

16. Bart took a taxi $\frac{1}{4}$ of the distance to Mandy's house. He took a bus for $\frac{1}{3}$ of the distance to her house. Finally, he walked the remaining 5 miles to her house. How many miles did Bart travel in all?

a. 9

b. 10

c. $11\frac{3}{4}$

d. 12

17. Ursula can walk $3\frac{1}{2}$ miles per hour. If she walks for $2\frac{1}{4}$ hours, how far will she walk, in miles?

a. $5\frac{3}{4}$

b. $6\frac{1}{4}$

c. $7\frac{7}{8}$

d. 18

18. What is $\frac{1}{2}$ of $\frac{1}{3}$ of 60?

a. 30

b. 20

c. 15

d. 10

19. A tree that was $7\frac{1}{4}$ feet tall grew 10 inches one year and $\frac{1}{6}$ of a foot the following year. How tall was the tree after two years?

a. 8 feet, 3 inches

b. 8 feet

c. 7 feet, 6 inches

d. 7 feet

20. Cashews sell for .65 per ounce. What is the cost of $\frac{3}{4}$ of a pound? (1 pound = 16 ounces)

a. $7.80

b. $6.50

c. $5.20

d. $2.60

21. Sam can type 2 pages in 13 minutes. At this rate, how many minutes will it take him to type 15 pages?

a. 97.5

b. 80

c. 64

d. 26

22. A tennis racket that normally sells for $80 now sells for $64. In lowest terms, what fraction represents the former price compared to the current price?

a. $\frac{3}{4}$

b. $\frac{4}{5}$

c. $\frac{6}{5}$

d. $\frac{5}{4}$

23. If 11-inch pieces are cut from a rope that measures $7\frac{1}{2}$ feet, how much rope will remain?

a. 1 inch

b. 2 inches

c. 1 foot 2 inches

d. 2 feet 2 inches

24. At the beginning of the semester, 36 students were in a chemistry class. After the first exam, $\frac{1}{3}$ of the students dropped the class. After the second exam, $\frac{1}{4}$ of the remaining students dropped the class. How many students were in the class after the second exam?

a. 18

b. 24

c. 28

d. 36

Decimals

25. At a certain discount store, if you purchase five pairs of socks, you get another pair of socks free. If one pair of socks costs $1.25, and Jeff left the store with 18 pairs of socks, how much did he spend?
a. $18.75
b. $20.00
c. $21.25
d. $22.50

26. Selma has a stack of small boxes, all the same size. If the stack measures 55.5 centimeters high and each box is 9.25 centimeters high, how many boxes does she have?
a. 5
b. 6
c. 7
d. 8

27. Roland bought four items at the grocery store that cost $1.98, $2.65, $4.29, and $6.78. He gave the clerk a $20 bill. How much change did he receive?
a. $3.30
b. $4.30
c. $4.40
d. $15.70

28. At a price of $.82 per pound, which of the following comes closest to the cost of a turkey weighing $9\frac{1}{4}$ pounds?
a. $6.80
b. $7.00
c. $7.60
d. $8.20

29. Roxy must drive a 160 mile distance in 2.5 hours. What must her average driving speed be during the trip?
a. 72 MPH
b. 64 MPH
c. 56 MPH
d. 48 MPH

30. Beth rented a car for 3 days. The cost was $27 per day and $.12 per mile. If Beth drove the car for 111 miles during the 3-day trip, what was her rental fee?
a. $13.32
b. $47.53
c. $81.00
d. $94.32

31. Tim has 11 quarters, 6 dimes, 15 nickels, and 5 pennies. What is the total value of Tim's change?
a. $3.15
b. $3.75
c. $4.00
d. $4.15

Percents

32. If the price of a bottle of maple syrup is reduced from $4 to $3, by what percent is the price reduced?
a. $\frac{1}{4}$%
b. $\frac{1}{3}$%
c. 1%
d. 25%

33. A credit card company charges $12\frac{1}{4}$% interest on the unpaid balance. If Mona has an unpaid balance of $220, how much interest will she be charged for one month?
a. $2.75
b. $14.40
c. $24.00
d. $26.95

34. Fifteen percent of the 3,820 employees at TechnoCorps were hired this year. How many of TechnoCorps employees were NOT hired this year?
a. 573
b. 1,910
c. 3,247
d. 3,805

35. Gilbert won 12 out of the 19 tennis matches he played in. What percent of his matches did he lose, rounded to the nearest percent?
a. 37%
b. 39%
c. 59%
d. 63%

36. A coat, originally priced at $120, was offered at a 20% discount. When the coat did not sell, the vendor offered an additional 20% discount off the sale price. What was the final price of the coat?
a. $80.00
b. $76.80
c. $76.00
d. $72.00

37. Jean received grades of 75% and 65% on her first two tests. What does she need to score on the next exam to have an 80% average on all three tests?
a. 85
b. 90
c. 95
d. 100

38. There are 5 blue marbles, 11 green marbles and 4 red marbles in a box. What percent of the marbles are green?
a. 100
b. 80
c. 55
d. 20

39. What number is 40% of 2?
a. 800
b. 80
c. 8
d. .8

40. What percent of 25 is 19?
a. 84
b. 76
c. 72
d. 48

Answers

1. a. To find the amount Mark spent, subtract $18.42 from $100.00:

$100.00 – $18.42 = $81.58

2. d. This is a two-step problem. First, multiply 10 by 3 to find the number of guests that were invited by Joan's friends:

$10 \times 3 = 30$

Now add the 10 guests Joan originally invited to find the total number of people at the party:

$30 + 10 = 40$

Remember, Joan is not to be included in the final tally of guests.

3. d. Divide the number of words, 760, by the number of words the secretary can type per minute, 80:

$760 \div 80 = 9.5$

4. d. To calculate the budget request, add all the costs:

4 mb of RAM: $100

2 software programs: $2 \times $350 = $700

External harddrive: $249

Additional mouse: $25

$100 + $700 + $249 + $25 = $1,074

5. a. An 8 pound roast needs 160 minutes to cook because $8 \times 20 = 160$. Convert 160 minutes to hours and minutes and subtract that time from 5:30 P.M.:

160 minutes ÷ 60 minutes = 2 hours 40 minutes

5:30 P.M. – 2 hours, 40 minutes = 2:50 P.M.

6. b. Subtract the low temperature from the high temperature to find out how much the temperature had risen:

$22 - (-6) = 22 + 6 = 28$

7. b. Let x = the original number

$x + 12 = 135$

$x + 12 - 12 = 135 - 12$

$x = 123$

8. c. Quickly add and subtract the numbers to find the correct answer:

$24 + 16 = 40$

$24 - 16 = 8$

9. b. Divide 40 by 9 to see how many trips the shuttle must make:

$40 \div 9 = 4\frac{4}{9}$

10. c. Subtract the lighter turkey from the heavier turkey:

16 pounds, 2 ounces

− 14 pounds, 10 ounces

Borrow 1 pound from 16 pounds and add it as 16 ounces to 2 ounces:

15 pounds, 18 ounces

− 14 pounds, 10 ounces

1 pound, 8 ounces

11. b. Let n = hot dogs eaten by the seventh grade

$n + 16$ = hot dogs eaten by the eighth grade

$n + (n + 16) = 84$

$2n + 16 = 84$

$2n + 16 - 16 = 84 - 16$

$2n = 68$

$\frac{2n}{2} = \frac{68}{2}$

$n = 34$

$n + 16 = 50$

The eighth grade ate 50 hot dogs.

12. a. Use the proportion $\frac{dollars}{guests} = \frac{dollars}{guests}$ and input the known values:

$$\frac{120}{15} = \frac{dollars}{20}$$

Cross-multiply and solve for *dollars*:

$120 \times 20 = 15 \times dollars$

$2{,}400 = 15 \times dollars$

$2{,}400 = 15 \times 160$

Wilma needs to spend $160. Subtract 120 from 160 to find her additional expense:

$160 - 120 = 40$

13. a. Let x represent the length of the table. Therefore, $\frac{1}{5}x$ equals $\frac{1}{5}$ of the table's length:

$x + \frac{1}{5}x = 36$

$1\frac{1}{5}x = 36$

$\frac{6}{5}x = 36$

$\left(\frac{5}{6}\right)\left(\frac{6}{5}x\right) = (36)\left(\frac{5}{6}\right)$

$x = 30$

14. d. To find the thickness of the siding, add the wall's other components and subtract that sum from $5\frac{7}{8}$. Remember to convert all the fractions to eighths, the LCD.

$5\frac{7}{8} - \left(\frac{1}{2} + 3\frac{3}{4} + \frac{5}{8}\right) =$

$5\frac{7}{8} - \left(\frac{4}{8} + 3\frac{6}{8} + \frac{5}{8}\right) =$

$5\frac{7}{8} - 4\frac{7}{8} = 1$

15. a. Subtract the points deducted from the points earned:

Correct: $31 \times 1 = 31$

Incorrect: $9 \times \frac{1}{4} = \frac{9}{4} = 2\frac{1}{4}$

$31 - 2\frac{1}{4} = 28\frac{3}{4}$

16. d. Let x equal the total distance Bart traveled. Therefore $\frac{1}{4}x$ is the distance traveled by taxi and $\frac{1}{3}x$ is the distance traveled by bus.

$\frac{1}{4}x + \frac{1}{3}x + 5 = x$

Rewrite the problem using twelfths, the LCD:

$\frac{3}{12}x + \frac{4}{12}x + 5 = \frac{12}{12}x$

Combine like terms and solve for x:

$\frac{3}{12}x + \frac{4}{12}x + 5 = \frac{12}{12}x$

$\frac{7}{12}x + 5 = \frac{12}{12}x$

$\frac{7}{12}x - \frac{7}{12}x + 5 = \frac{12}{12}x - \frac{7}{12}x$

$5 = \frac{5}{12}x$

$(\frac{12}{5})(5) = (\frac{5}{12}x)(\frac{12}{5})$

$12 = x$

Bart traveled 12 miles.

17. c. Use the formula $rate \times time = distance$ to find the distance walked:

$3\frac{1}{2} \times 2\frac{1}{4} = distance$

$\frac{7}{2} \times \frac{9}{4} = \frac{63}{8} = 7\frac{7}{8} = distance$

18. d. *Of* means multiply:

$\frac{1}{2} \times \frac{1}{3} \times \frac{60}{1} = \frac{60}{6} = 10$

19. a. Convert all fractions to inches (1 foot =12 inches)

$\frac{1}{4} foot = \frac{1}{4} \times \frac{12}{1} = 3$

$\frac{1}{6} foot = \frac{1}{6} \times \frac{12}{1} = 2 :$

Add all the inches:

$10 + 3 + 2 = 15 = 1$ foot, 3 inches

Add 1 foot 3 inches to 7 feet:

7 feet + 1 foot + 3 inches = 8 feet, 3 inches

20. a. Find the number of ounces in $\frac{3}{4}$ of a pound:

$\frac{3}{4} \times \frac{16}{1} = 12$

Multiply 12 by $.65, the cost of 12 ounces of cashews:

$12 \times \$.65 = \$7.80$

21. a. Use the proportion $\frac{pages}{minutes} = \frac{pages}{minutes}$ and input the known values:

$\frac{2}{13} = \frac{15}{minutes}$

Cross-multiply and solve for *minutes*:

$2 \times minutes = 13 \times 15$

$2 \times minutes = 195$

$2 \times 97.5 = 195$

Sam will need 97.5 minutes to type 15 pages.

22. d. Use the fraction $\frac{former\ price}{current\ price}$ and simplify:

$\frac{80}{64} \div \frac{16}{16} = \frac{5}{4}$

A bus cannot make $\frac{4}{9}$ of a trip. Thus, the bus must make 5 trips to transport 40 people.

23. b. Find the number of inches in $7\frac{1}{2}$ feet:

$$7\frac{1}{2} \times 12 = 90$$

Divide 90 by 11:

$$90 \div 11 = 8 \ \textit{remainder} \ 2$$

There are eight 11-inch pieces of rope with 2 inches remaining.

24. a. Find $\frac{1}{3}$ of 36 and subtract that amount from 36:

$$\frac{1}{3} \times \frac{36}{1} = 12$$
$$36 - 12 = 24$$

Find $\frac{1}{4}$ of 24 and subtract that amount from 24:

$$\frac{1}{4} \times \frac{24}{1} = 6$$
$$24 - 6 = 18$$

25. a. Another way to view this problem is to say that you are paying for $\frac{5}{6}$ of your socks. Multiply $\frac{5}{6}$ by 18 to find the pairs of socks that are purchased:

$$\frac{5}{6} \times \frac{\overset{3}{\cancel{18}}}{\underset{1}{1}} = 15$$

Multiply 15 by $1.25 to find the cost of the purchase:

$$15 \times \$1.25 = \$18.75$$

26. b. Divide 55.5 by 9.25 to find the number of stacked boxes:

$$55.5 \div 9.25 = 6$$

27. b. Add all the purchases and subtract from $20.00:

$$\$20.00 - (1.98 + 2.65 + 4.29 + 6.78) =$$
$$\$20.00 - 15.70 = \$4.30$$

28. c. Convert $9\frac{1}{4}$ to 9.25 and multiply by .82:

$$9.25 \times .82 = 7.585$$

Of the four choices, $7.60 is the closest to $7.585.

29. b. Use the formula *rate* $\times$ *time* = *distance* and input the known values:

$$rate \times 2.5 = 160$$
$$64 \times 2.5 = 160$$

Joan must average 64 mph during her trip.

30. d. Find the cost of the three day rental:

$$3 \times 27 = \$81$$

Find the mileage cost

$$.12 \times 111 = \$13.32$$

Add the rental and mileage costs to find the total cost:

$$\$81 + \$13.32 = \$94.32$$

31. d. Multiply the number of coins times their value in dollars: 11 quarters $\times$ \$0.25 = \$2.75; 6 dimes $\times$ \$0.10 = \$0.60; 15 nickels $\times$ \$0.05 = \$0.75; and 5 pennies $\times$ \$0.01 = \$0.05. Then add together the values to find the total, making sure to line up the decimals properly:

$$\begin{array}{r} \$2.75 \\ \$0.60 \\ \$0.75 \\ + \ \$0.01 \\ \hline \$4.15 \end{array}$$

32. d. Use the formula $\frac{part}{whole} = \frac{\%}{100}$ to find the percent discount.

Since the price was reduced by \$1, it represents *part* in the proportion.

$\frac{1}{4} = \frac{\%}{100}$

$1 \times 100 = 4 \times \%$

$100 = 4 \times \%$

$100 = 4 \times 25$

The price was reduced 25%.

33. d. Change $12\frac{1}{4}\%$ to a decimal and multiply it by 220 to find the interest charge.

$12\frac{1}{4}\% = 12.25\% = .1225$

$\$220 \times .1225 = \$26.95$

34. c. Subtract 15% from 100% to find the percent of the employees not hired this year:

$100\% - 15\% = 85\%$

Change 85% to a decimal and multiply it by 3,820:

$(.85)(3,820) = 3,247$

35. a. Use the formula $\frac{part}{whole} = \frac{\%}{100}$ to find the percentage of games won:

$\frac{12}{19} = \frac{\%}{100}$

$12 \times 100 = 19 \times \%$

$1,200 = 19 \times \%$

$1,200 = 19 \times 63.2$

Gilbert won 63.2% of his games. To find the percent of the games he did not win, subtract 63.2% from 100%:

$100 - 63.2 = 36.8\%$

To the nearest percent, 36.8% rounds to 37%.

36. b. Find 20% of 120 and subtract that amount from 120:

$\$120 \times .20 = \$24$

$\$120 - 24 = \$96$

Find 20% of \$96 and subtract that amount from 96:

$\$96 \times .20 = \$19.20$

$\$96 - \$19.20 = \$76.80$

37. d. To find the average of the three scores, find their sum and divide by 3.

Let x = the third exam score.

$\frac{75 + 65 + x}{3} = 80$

$\frac{140 + x}{3} = 80$

$3\left(\frac{140 + x}{3}\right) = (80)(3)$

$140 + x = 240$

$x = 100$

38. c. Count up all the marbles:

$$5 + 11 + 4 = 20$$

Use the formula $\frac{part}{whole} = \frac{\%}{100}$ and input the known values:

$$\frac{11}{20} = \frac{\%}{100}$$

Cross-multiply and solve for %:

$$11 \times 100 = \% \times 20$$

$$1{,}100 = \% \times 20$$

$$1{,}100 = 55 \times 20$$

55% of the marbles are green.

39. d. Change 40% to a decimal and multiply by 2:

$$40\% = .40 = .4$$

$$(.4)(2) = .8$$

40. b. Use the formula $\frac{is}{of} = \frac{\%}{100}$ and input the known values:

$$\frac{19}{25} = \frac{\%}{100}$$

Cross-multiply and solve for %:

$$19 \times 100 = 25 \times \%$$

$$1{,}900 = 25 \times \%$$

$$1{,}900 = 25 \times 76$$

19 is 76% of 25.

3

Reading Comprehension for the Paragraph Comprehension Subtest

Reading is a vital skill. Understanding written materials is critical for taking the ASVAB—after all, you can't understand the questions if you don't read well—but it is also critical for any military job. Memos, policies, procedures, reports—these are all things you will be expected to understand if you enlist in the armed services. That is why the ASVAB attempts to measure how well applicants understand what they read.

The Paragraph Comprehension subtest of the ASVAB contains multiple-choice questions based on brief passages. These questions test your ability to understand what you read. If you do not consider yourself a strong reader, take plenty of time to review the strategies in the following lessons. You should also complete all the practice exercises, so that you can increase your score on this important subtest.

Active Reading

Good readers are active readers. They see reading as an involved process. That's why they understand so much of what they read. To be an active reader you should:

1. **Write when you read.** Writing while you read can really help you absorb information better. Try to:
   - **underline key words and ideas** to identify important information stand out so that you can remember it later. This also helps you summarize it for yourself.
   - **circle and look up unfamiliar words and phrases**—you need to know what all the words in a sentence mean in order to completely understand what you are reading.
   - **list any questions and comments you might have.** As you read, you are bound to have questions about the meaning and purpose of the text. You're likely to have reactions to the reading as well. Writing down your questions and thoughts makes you think about what you read, and that means you will better understand the material.
2. **Pay close attention when you read.** Take note of details in sentences and passages to help you better understand the writer's ideas. Making observations and remembering these clues are essential because your observations are what lead you to logical inferences about what you have read. Inferences are conclusions based on reason, fact, or evidence. If you misunderstand what you read, it is often because you haven't looked closely enough at the text.

Types of Reading Comprehension Questions

You have probably encountered reading comprehension questions before, where you were given a passage to read and then required to answer relevant multiple-choice questions about it. This kind of question has an advantage for you as a test taker: you don't have to know anything about the topic of the passage because you're being tested only on the information the passage provides.

The disadvantage is that you have to know where and how to find that information quickly in an unfamiliar text. This makes it easy to select one of the wrong answer choices, especially since they're designed to mislead you.

The best way to do well on this passage/question format is to be very familiar with the kinds of questions that are typically asked on the test. The ASVAB Paragraph Comprehensive test will most frequently ask you to:

1. identify a specific fact or detail in the passage;
2. uncover the main idea of the passage;
3. make an inference based on the passage;
4. define a vocabulary word from the passage.

The following list of important words will help you to answer reading comprehension questions and analyze what you read more closely.

Reading Comprehension Glossary

Argument   a discussion aimed at supporting a claim by reasons or evidence

Basic Information   core facts or data; essential knowledge or ideas

Cause   a person or thing that makes something happen or creates an effect

Chronology   the order in which things happen

Compare   to examine in order to find similarities between two or more items

Conclusion   a belief or opinion based on reasoning

Connotation   the suggested or implied meaning of a word; its emotional impact

Context   the words and ideas surrounding a word that help give it its meaning

Contrast   to show the differences between two or more items

Effect   a change created by an action or cause

Emotional   based on strong mental feelings

Fact   something known for certain to be true

Formality   the quality of being proper, ceremonious

General   broad, wide, nonspecific; applying to most or all

Imply   to hint or suggest without stating directly

Indifferent   uncaring, showing no interest

Logical   according to reason; based on evidence or good common sense

Main Idea   the thought that holds a passage together

Narrator   the person who tells the story

Objective   unaffected by the thoughts, feelings, and experiences of the writer

Observant   paying careful attention

Observation   something seen or noticed

Opinion   something believed to be true, but that cannot be proven

Point of View   the person or position through which you see things

Rank   position or value in relation to others in a group

Reading Comprehension Glossary

Reason   a motive or grounds for something; good sense or judgment

Sentence Structure   the size and parts of a sentence

Specific   particular, exact

Style   the way of doing something, such as writing or speaking; the manner in which something is done

Subject   whom or what the passage is about

Subjective   based on the thoughts, feelings, and experiences of the writer

Tone   the mood or attitude conveyed by words or speech

Topic Sentence   the sentence that states the main idea

Transitions   words and phrases that link and relate the ideas to each other

8 ▶ Reading Comprehension Basics

In this lesson, you will master a few basic skills to build a strong reading foundation. By the end of this lesson (and with a little practice), you should be able to:

1. uncover the basic facts in a passage
2. find the main idea of a passage
3. decipher what words mean without a dictionary
4. recognize the difference between fact and opinion

Grasping Basic Information

The first thing you need to do when you read anything is to grasp the basic information. This includes the who, what, when, where, how, and why. What does the passage tell you? What happens? To whom? When? Where? How? Why?

The questions you ask yourself will change from reading to reading, but the idea is always the same: You need to find the basic information. Being observant while you read will help you.

The following short paragraph could be from a local newspaper article. Read it carefully and actively with a pencil in hand. As you read, look for the basic facts and think about the who, what, when, where, why, and how.

Yesterday the house of Mr. and Mrs. White was robbed. The thieves entered the house at 13 Elm Avenue around noon. Jason White and his wife, Alison, were not home. The house had an expensive security system linked to the local police station, but no alarms went off at the precinct. The robbery wasn't discovered until Mrs. White came home at 3:45 p.m. Police say that the thieves disconnected the security system. The thieves stole all of the Whites's furniture, jewelry, office equipment, and artwork. Mrs. White is an art appraiser. She values the stolen property at $1.6 million.

Reading actively should help you find the basic information in this passage. Here are some questions you could ask to find the facts:

1. What happened?
2. When did it happen?
3. Where did it happen?
4. How did it happen?
5. Who discovered the theft?
6. When was the theft discovered?
7. What was stolen?
8. How much is the stolen property worth?

Here's how this passage might look after an active reading. The basic facts have been underlined. There are notes in the margins. There is also a definition for the word *appraise*.

when · who · what happened— robbery

where

Yesterday the house of Mr. and Mrs. White was robbed. The thieves entered the house at 13 Elm Avenue around noon. Jason White and his wife, Alison, were not home. The house had an expensive security system linked to the local police station, but no alarms went off at the precinct. The robbery wasn't discovered until Mrs. White came home at 3:45 P.M. Police say that the thieves disconnected the security system. The thieves stole all of the Whites's furniture, jewelry, office equipment, and artwork. Mrs. White is an art appraiser. She values the stolen property at $1.6 million.

how

what was taken

noon–3:45 5 time gap between robbery & discovery

The thieves picked a good target!

appraise: to estimate the value or quality of

Here are the answers to the questions:

1. What happened? *The Whites' house was robbed.*
2. When did it happen? *Yesterday*
3. Where did it happen? *13 Elm Avenue*
4. How did it happen? *The thieves disconnected the security system.*
5. Who discovered the theft? *Mrs. White*
6. When was the theft discovered? *At 3:45 in the afternoon*
7. What was stolen? *Their furniture, jewelry, office equipment, and artwork*
8. How much is the stolen property worth? *$1.6 million*

This is the basic information in the paragraph. You could ask more questions—there is no maximum how many questions you should ask yourself. What you need to know depends on what kind of text you're reading. Are you reading a magazine article for pleasure about an athlete? Then just a handful of questions should do. On the other hand, a chapter in a history book or a passage on the ASVAB has important information that you will need to understand and remember. Prepared to be thorough.

Practice 1

In the following practice exercise, read the passage below carefully and actively. Then answer the questions that follow. Answers are found on page 135.

Remember to be an active reader. Circle and look up unfamiliar words, underline key words and ideas, and write questions and comments in the margins. Ask yourself questions as you read. When you are done, check your answers at the end of the lesson.

The U.S. Postal Service is more efficient than ever. Mail used to take months to arrive. It was delivered by horse or by foot. Now trucks, trains, and planes transport it around the country in days or hours. First-class mail arrives in three days or fewer. Urgent mail can move even faster. Priority Mail is guaranteed to go anywhere in the United States in three days or fewer. Express Mail will get your package there overnight.

Questions

1. What word is used to describe the current U.S. Postal Service? _____
   _____

2. How long did it take mail to arrive in the past?
   _____
   _____

3. Other than trucks and planes, how else is mail moved today? _____
   _____

4. Can urgent mail be sent in less than three days?
   _____
   _____

5. How long does Priority Mail take? _____
   _____

6. How long does Express Mail take? _____
   _____

Finding the Main Idea

The **main idea** is the thought that holds the passage together: the *why* of the passage. A good reader asks herself, "Why did the author write this? What idea does he or she want me to understand?" Asking yourself these questions will help lead you to the main idea of a passage.

The Difference between Subject and Main Idea

People often confuse the **subject** with the main idea, but there is an important difference. To see the difference, take another look at the passage about the postal system.

> The U.S. Postal Service is more efficient than ever. Mail used to take months to arrive. It was delivered by horse or by foot. Now trucks, trains, and planes transport it around the country in days or hours. First-class mail arrives in three days or less. Urgent mail can move even faster. Priority Mail is guaranteed to go anywhere in the United States in three days or less. Express Mail will get your package there overnight.

Reading tests often ask, "What is the main idea of this passage?" For the passage above, you might answer, "the post office." But you would be making a common mistake. The passage is *about* the post office, but the post office is not the main idea. Instead, the post office is the subject of the passage. The subject is who or what the passage is about. The main idea, on the other hand, says something about the subject.

Look back at the paragraph about the postal service, once again. The subject is the post office. Read the passage carefully and look for the idea that makes a claim about the subject. Remember, the idea should be general and it should hold together the whole paragraph. Now answer the following question:

> Which sentence best summarizes the main idea of the passage?
> **a.** Express Mail is a good way to send urgent mail.
> **b.** Mail service today is very effective.
> **c.** First-class mail usually takes three days or less.
> **d.** Mail used to take months to arrive.

All four options make a claim about mail services, but **a, c,** and **d** are too specific to be the main idea. None of these answers covers all of the ideas in the paragraph.

Only choice **b** is general enough to cover the whole paragraph. All of the other sentences support the idea that mail service is very effective. Each sentence offers proof for that idea. The writer's motive is to show that the post office is indeed better than ever. That main idea is stated in the first sentence, and the rest of the sentences support that idea.

The main idea of a passage makes a claim about its subject. But even more than that, it also holds the whole passage together. All of the other sentences in the passage must support that idea, usually with specific examples or explanations. In a way, the main idea is like a net over the passage.

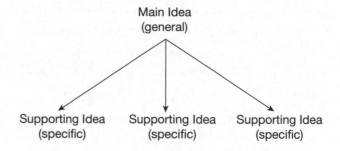

Main Idea (general) → Supporting Idea (specific), Supporting Idea (specific), Supporting Idea (specific)

The main idea is both a claim about the subject and the general idea that binds all of the ideas in the passage.

Topic Sentences

The **topic sentence** is a claim about the subject. It is usually a claim that needs support or proof. A topic sentence clearly states the main idea, and it must be general enough to cover all of the ideas in the passage.

Practice 2

Look at the following paragraph. Read it carefully and then underline the sentence that best states the topic sentence. You can check your answer at the end of the lesson on page 135.

> Erik always played cops and robbers when he was a boy. Now he's a police officer. Lauren always pretended to be a doctor as a little girl. Today she's a pediatrician. Kara always played store. Now she owns her own clothing store. Some lucky people have always known what they want to do with their lives.

Introducing Specific Examples

Readers need to see that the claim made in the topic sentence is true. That's what the other supporting sentences in the postal service paragraph do. They show readers that the postal service is more efficient than ever.

Supporting sentences often begin with signal words that introduce specific examples. Sentences that begin with these words and phrases are usually not topic sentences but rather supporting sentences, introducing specific examples. Here are some words and phrases that often introduce specific examples.

also	*for example*	*for instance*
for one thing	*furthermore*	*in addition*
in particular	*others*	*some*

Sometimes you might have trouble finding the main idea. You can try crossing out sentences (lightly) that begin with these specific signal words. Then you will have fewer sentences to choose from, and the topic sentences should be easier to find.

Defining Words in Context

As you read, you will often see unfamiliar words, or words you cannot define. You might have a dictionary to look up those words. But what if you don't have a dictionary? How can you understand what you're reading if you don't know what the words mean?

You can often figure out what a word means if you look at its **context**—the words and ideas surrounding a word that help supply its meaning. Reading comprehension tests often test your ability to find the meaning of words based on the context of the passage.

Finding Meaning in Context

Sometimes you can't understand an entire sentence, or group of sentences, if you don't understand one key word. For example, look at the following sentence.

> The new policy will *substantially* cut employee benefits.

Can you fully understand the sentence without knowing what *substantially* means? As an employee, you will want to know what *substantially* means. How much will your benefits be cut? Is *substantially* a little or a lot? There are not enough clues in this sentence; to figure out what the word means, you need more context.

Here's the same sentence in a paragraph.

> The new policy will substantially cut employee benefits. Employees will lose their dental coverage. Regular doctor check-ups will no longer be covered. In addition, psychiatric coverage will be cut from six visits to two.

You should be able to figure out what *substantially* means now.

    Substantially means

    a. just barely.

    b. a little, but not too much.

    c. small.

    d. a lot.

The answer is choice **d**, *a lot*. The paragraph describes a big cut in coverage. Both dental care and regular check-ups will no longer be covered and psychiatric care will be cut by two-thirds. These are serious cutbacks. You may have also noticed that *substantially* is similar to the word *substance*. Something that has substance is weighty or solid. Your knowledge of related words can also help you define words in context.

Practice 3

Read the following sentences carefully. Use context to determine what the italicized words mean. Then circle the correct meanings. Check your answers at the end of the lesson on page 135.

  1. I accidentally told Nell about her surprise party. What a stupid *blunder*!

    A *blunder* is

    a. a jerk.

    b. an idea.

    c. a mistake.

    d. a get-together.

  2. Our successful salespeople share one personality *trait*: honesty.

    A *trait* is

    a. an aspect.

    b. a disorder.

    c. a difference.

    d. a similarity.

  3. Please return the pink copy. *Retain* the yellow copy for your records.

    To *retain* means

    a. to copy.

    b. to throw away.

    c. to read.

    d. to keep.

Practice 4

Provide context for the words below. Write a sentence or two for each word. The sentences should show the reader what the words mean. Check your answers at the end of the lesson on page 135.

Example:

word:	glimpse
meaning:	to catch a quick view of
context:	I'm not sure what he looked like. I only glimpsed the man's face before he disappeared around the corner.

  1.

word:	mundane
meaning:	dull, boring, routine
context:	

  2.

word:	teem
meaning:	to be full of, to be present in large numbers
context:	

The Difference between Fact and Opinion

Sometimes people tell you what they *know* is true—they are telling you facts. Other times they tell you what they *think* is true—they are telling you opinions.

A **fact** is:

- something *known* for certain to have happened
- something *known* for certain to be true
- something *known* for certain to exist

An **opinion**, on the other hand, is:

- something *believed* to have happened
- something *believed* to be true
- something *believed* to exist

The key difference between fact and opinion is the difference between *knowing* and *believing*. Opinions are often based on facts, but opinions are still what people think or feel. They are not what people know. You can argue about an opinion, but you can't argue about a fact. In other words, opinions are debatable while facts are not.

Using Facts to Support Opinions

People can have opinions about almost anything. What's important is that they support their opinions. An opinion supported by facts is a reasonable opinion. In fact, that's mostly what you read about. Writers make a claim about their subject, and that claim is often an opinion. Then they offer facts to support their opinion.

Think about your own opinions. You could write a topic sentence about your friend Margarita:

Margarita is a good friend.

This is a good topic sentence. It makes a claim about its subject, Margarita, and it's also an opinion. It is something you could argue about. After all, someone could make an opposite claim:

Margarita is a bad friend.

This is another good topic sentence. It's also another opinion. A good writer will now show readers that this is a reasonable opinion. How? By offering supporting facts.

Margarita is a good friend. She always asks me how I am. If I have a problem, she is always willing to offer suggestions. For my last birthday, she organized a surprise party for me and invited all my friends. She even baked me a birthday cake.

The topic sentence states an opinion and the rest of the sentences support that opinion. They offer facts about Margarita. This makes it an effective paragraph. Now, here is a writer who doesn't support his opinion well:

Margarita is a bad friend. I don't think that she listens to me, and she doesn't seem to ever show up when I need her. And, she has stupid ideas about politics.

The first paragraph about Margarita is much better because it's not just an opinion. It's an opinion supported by facts. The second paragraph is all opinion. Every sentence is arguable, and the sentences show what the author *thinks* is true, not what is *known* to be true. The second paragraph doesn't include specific facts to show why Margarita is a bad friend, it includes only what the author *thinks* about Margarita.

Practice 5

Read the following claims carefully. Are they fact or opinion? Write an F in the blank if the claim is a fact and an O if it is an opinion. When you are done, you can check your answers at the end of the lesson on page 135.

_____ **1.** The World Series takes place every October.

_____ **2.** The World Series is fun to watch.

_____ **3.** The baseball season is too long; the World Series should be held earlier so fans don't have to sit outside in the cold.

_____ **4.** The 1969 New York Mets are the best team of all time.

_____ **5.** The team with the best record in the American League faces the top team in the National League.

Review

So far you know how to get the basic information from a passage. You know that asking *who*, *what*, *when*, *where*, *why*, and *how* will help you gather important information from what you are reading. You can also tell the difference between the subject—who or what the passage is about—and the main idea of a passage. The main idea makes a claim about the subject and is general enough to hold the passage together. The other sentences in the passage all support the main idea, which is often expressed in a topic sentence. In addition, you can decipher what words mean from the context. Finally, you learned that a fact is something *known* to be true, while an opinion is something *believed* to be true. Many main ideas are opinions. Good writers use facts to support their opinions.

Review Practice

Now you can combine the skills you just learned by reading longer passages. Read the passages carefully and answer the questions that follow. Check your answers at the end of the lesson.

BICYCLES

Today, bicycles are so common that it's hard to believe they haven't always been around. But two hundred years ago, bicycles didn't exist, and the first bicycle, invented in Germany in 1818, was nothing like our bicycles today. It was made of wood and did not even have pedals. Since then, however, numerous innovations and improvements in design have made the bicycle one of the most popular means of recreation and transportation around the world.

In 1839, Kirkpatrick Macmillan, a Scottish blacksmith, dramatically improved upon the original bicycle design. Macmillan's machine had tires with iron rims to keep them from getting worn down. He also used foot-operated cranks similar to pedals so his bicycle could be ridden at a quick pace. It didn't look much like a modern bicycle, though, because its back wheel was substantially larger than its front wheel. In 1861, the French Michaux brothers took the evolution of the bicycle a step further by inventing an improved crank mechanism.

Ten years later, James Starley, an English inventor, revolutionized bicycle design. He made the front wheel many times larger than the back wheel, put a gear on the pedals to make the bicycle more efficient, and lightened the wheels by using wire spokes. Although this bicycle was much lighter and less tiring to ride, it was still clumsy, extremely top-heavy, and ridden mostly for entertainment.

It wasn't until 1874 that the first truly modern bicycle appeared on the scene. Invented by another Englishman, H.J. Lawson, the "safety bicycle" would look familiar to today's cyclists. This bicycle had equal-sized wheels, which made it less prone to toppling over. Lawson also attached a chain to the pedals to drive the rear wheel. With these improvements, the bicycle became extremely popular and useful for transportation. Today they are built, used, and enjoyed all over the world.

1. The main idea of this passage is best expressed in which sentence?
   a. Today, bicycles are so common that it's hard to believe they haven't always been around.
   b. It wasn't until 1874 that the first truly modern bicycle appeared on the scene.
   c. Since 1874, however, numerous innovations and improvements in design have made the bicycle one of the most popular means of recreation and transportation around the world.
   d. Today bikes are built, used, and enjoyed all over the world.

2. Which of the following would be the best title for this passage?
   a. Bicycles Are Better
   b. A Ride through the History of Bicycles
   c. Cycle Your Way to Fitness
   d. The Popularity of Bicycles

3. Which sentence best expresses the main idea of the second paragraph?
   a. Macmillan was a great inventor.
   b. Macmillan's bike didn't look much like our modern bikes.
   c. Macmillan's bike could be ridden quickly.
   d. Macmillan made important changes in bicycle design.

4. An *innovation* is
   a. a new way of doing something.
   b. a design.
   c. a repair.
   d. a clever person.

5. Macmillan added iron rims to the tires of his bicycle to
   a. add weight to the bicycle.
   b. make the tires last longer.
   c. make the ride less bumpy.
   d. make the ride less tiring.

6. The first person to use a gear system on bicycles was
   a. H.J. Lawson.
   b. Kirkpatrick Macmillan.
   c. The Michaux brothers.
   d. James Starley.

The Chunnel

The Chunnel, or underwater tunnel that runs underneath the English Channel between England and France, is one of the most remarkable feats of architecture ever created. The incredible notion of connecting those two powerful countries that had been separated for more than 12,000 years was tossed around for more than two centuries. Everyone from engineers to architects to politicians had come up with a plan or a blueprint. The Chunnel is considered to be one of the true wonders of the modern world for its size and complexity and for the fact that it succeeded even though it was full of structural dilemmas like budget catastrophes and safety nightmares.

The idea for a connection between France and England was first mentioned at the end of the eighteenth century. Although frequently ignored, squashed, and thrown out, the idea just would not die. Both European countries were gaining in power and trade between them was on the rise. A century ago, the 20-plus miles that separated them made trade not only slow, but also quite dangerous. Under the best weather conditions, the trip from one coastline to the other took six to eight hours, and frequently, vicious storms delayed ships for days—even weeks. Frustration on both ends grew as shipments fell behind schedule and workers arrived at the docks too seasick to load or unload their cargo. Even later, when ferries and airplanes came along to make the trip faster and safer, passengers still had to put up with paying high transportation fees, standing in crowded airports and other inconveniences.

For decades, the debate had raged over the best way to link these two countries. Ideas ranged from sunken tubes to iron bridges. Which could be easiest and safest—a bridge, a tunnel, or some combination of the two? Every single plan posed unique problems. A bridge over 20 miles long was a nightmare to support. Experts argued that it would cause problems with the many ships that needed to pass through the Channel. Even the best of lighthouses, foghorns, and other precautions might not be enough to warn a ship that the bridge was ahead. That was asking for a real disaster.

7. Which of the following details from the passage is an opinion?
   a. The Chunnel is one of the most remarkable feats of architecture ever created.
   b. The idea for a connection between France and England was first mentioned at the end of the eighteenth century.
   c. For decades, the debate raged over the best way to link England and France.
   d. Experts argued that a bridge linking England and France would cause problems with the many ships that needed to pass through the Channel.

8. *Dilemmas* means
   a. theories
   b. improvements
   c. problems
   d. creations

9. The Chunnel was built to
  a. make the use of ships completely unnecessary.
  b. make trade between France and England easier.
  c. make France and England the most powerful countries in Europe.
  d. make lighthouses and foghorns more effective.

10. Which sentence best expresses the main idea of the second paragraph?
  a. Trade between France and England was once very dangerous.
  b. The Chunnel was necessary for a number of reasons.
  c. 20 miles separate France and England.
  d. There was much debate about the best way to link England and France.

11. Which of the following would be the best title for this passage?
  a. Visiting the Chunnel
  b. The Chunnel: Channel or Tunnel?
  c. The Great Chunnel Debate
  d. The Frustrations of the Chunnel

12. One reason experts argued against linking France and England with a bridge was
  a. crossing such a bridge would make people seasick.
  b. the difficulty of supporting such a long bridge.
  c. harsh weather conditions might damage a bridge.
  d. a bridge would result in high transportation fees.

13. *Precautions* are
  a. risky chances.
  b. unusual decisions.
  c. previous ideas.
  d. safety measures.

Exploring Genealogy

In a day and age where storytelling is beginning to be considered one of the lost arts and keeping records means booting up instead of writing down, families may find themselves wondering how to create and preserve their genealogy. Exploring and preserving the genealogy of ones family is an involved but rewarding project that serves several purposes. Perhaps they want to just save the family stories or trace the most recent generations. Others might want to explore their families' role in history or just put something together to commemorate an anniversary or other important event. A family tree is a chart detailing the relationships of a family over several generations. Putting together a family tree may sound like a great idea, but how do you even begin to make the first step, and how can it be a project that involves the whole family?

Investigating the many different people who came before you is an intricate task that involves asking questions, doing research, combing through real and virtual archives, and even taking field trips to places like cemeteries. After all, a graveyard is really a museum without walls; it contains fascinating historical artifacts, gravestones, some of which are hundreds of years old. Graveyards can be frightening places, but they're important resources for those interested in tracing their family history.

Another great source is the census records that can be found online, which might include birth and death records. Resources include the National Archives, as well as local family records. Your local library may connect you with basic genealogy guide-books and reference books as well.

Make sure not to overlook one of the best re-sources of all—your family. Grandparents, uncles, aunts, and cousins are often wonderful sources of sto-ries, traditions, facts, and other helpful information. Taking the time to talk to them about family stories can bring all of you closer—another side benefit from a project like this one.

14. One reason to explore your genealogy is to
   a. visit a graveyard.
   b. build a museum.
   c. dispose of family records.
   d. preserve family stories.

15. *Commemorate* means
   a. forget
   b. honor
   c. describe
   d. establish

16. Which of the following is the topic sentence of this passage?
   a. In a day and age where storytelling is begin-ning to be considered one of the lost arts and keeping records means booting up instead of writing down, families may find themselves wondering how to create and preserve their genealogy.
   b. Exploring and preserving the genealogy of ones family is an involved but rewarding project that serves several purposes.
   c. After all, a graveyard is really like a museum without walls because it contains fascinating historical artifacts in the form of gravestones, some of which are hundreds of years old.
   d. Taking the time to talk to them about family stories can bring all of you closer—another side benefit from a project like this one.

17. Which sentence best expresses the main idea of the fourth paragraph?
   a. Genealogy always makes families closer.
   b. Cousins always have the best stories.
   c. Census records contain valuable information about genealogy.
   d. Talking to family members can help you learn about your genealogy.

18. Which of the following details from the passage is an opinion?
   a. a family tree details the relationships of a family over several generations
   b. some gravestones are hundreds of years old
   c. graveyards are frightening places
   d. census records can be found on the Internet

19. *Intricate* means
   a. complex.
   b. simple.
   c. dull.
   d. strange.

20. Which detail in the second paragraph best sup-ports the idea that "a graveyard is really like a museum without walls"?
   a. graveyards are important resources for those interested in tracing their family history
   b. graveyards are places to which one might take a field trip
   c. graveyards contain fascinating historical ar-tifacts in the form of gravestones
   d. graveyards contain gravestones

Answers

Practice 1

1. efficient

2. months

3. trains

4. yes

5. three days or fewer

6. overnight

Practice 2

You should have underlined the last sentence: "Some lucky people have always known what they want to do with their lives." This sentence is a good topic sentence. It states the idea that holds the whole passage together. The first six sentences are specific examples of that idea. Thus, they all support the main idea. This time, the topic sentence is at the end of the paragraph.

Practice 3

1. **c.** The writer wasn't supposed to tell Nell about the surprise birthday party. Thus, a *blunder* is a mistake.

2. **a.** Honesty isn't a *problem*, so **b** can't be the answer. The passage says that the salespeople have this *trait* in common, so **c** can't be correct either. The only word that makes sense in the sentence is **a**, *aspect*.

3. **d.** You would want to keep a copy for your records.

Practice 4

Answers will vary. Here are some examples:

1. My job is very mundane. I do the same thing every day.

2. We left the picnic basket open. When we got back, it was teeming with ants.

Practice 5

1. **F**
2. **O.** This is clearly something arguable. Many baseball fans look forward to the World Series, but others find the game boring; it's a matter of opinion.
3. **O.** Even though this opinion is introduced with supporting evidence, it's still an opinion.
4. **O.** This is an opinion as well, since every baseball fan has a favorite team.
5. **F**

Review Practice

1. **c.** This is the only sentence general enough to encompass all of the ideas in the passage. Each paragraph describes the innovations that led to the modern design of the bicycle, and this design has made it popular around the world.

2. **b.** The essay describes the history of the bicycle, from its invention in 1818 to its modern design.

3. **d.** Macmillan may have been a great inventor, but this paragraph only describes his innovations in bicycle design. The first sentence in this paragraph expresses this main idea in a clear topic sentence. The rest of the paragraph provides specific examples of the improvements he made in bicycle design.

4. a. An innovation is a new way of doing something. The first clue is in the third sentence, which describes the first bicycle—"it was made of wood and did not even have pedals." Clearly, bicycles have changed dramatically. Other clues can be found in the following paragraphs, which describe the various changes made to bicycle design. Each bicycle designer devised a new way of building a bicycle.

5. b. Since the question is asking for a specific fact about Macmillan's design, you should know to look in the second paragraph. Then you can find the sentence with the key words, iron rims—the second sentence—to find the correct answer.

6. d. If you highlighted the various innovations, then all you have to do is scan the highlighted parts of the passage. Paragraph 3 states, "Starley . . . put a gear on the pedals . . ."

7. a. Some people may not consider the Chunnel to be among the most remarkable feats of architecture ever created, so this is an opinion rather than inarguable fact. Choices **b**, **c**, and **d** are facts.

8. c. The sentence mentions that some of the structural *dilemmas* were budget *catastrophes* and safety *nightmares*. Based on this context, you can conclude that *dilemmas* and *problems* share the same meaning.

9. b. The passage explains that "Both European countries were gaining in power and trade between them was on the rise" and that the trip between the two countries was difficult and unsafe before the Chunnel.

10. b. Paragraph two mentions several reasons why the Chunnel was necessary, including the danger, slowness, and inconvenience of making the trip between France and England over water. Choices **a** and **c** are incorrect because they are just details from the paragraph rather than the main idea. Choice **d** describes the main idea of paragraph three.

11. c. The passage describes the long and heated debate about whether or not the Chunnel should be built.

12. b. If you highlighted the various problems with linking France and England, then all you have to do is scan the highlighted parts of the passage. Paragraph three states that "A bridge over 20 miles long was a nightmare to support."

13. d. Things like foghorns and lighthouses are used to ensure the safety of ships. Based on the way *precautions* is used in this context, you can conclude that it means *safety measures*.

14. d. Paragraph 1 states that families may want to preserve their genealogy to "save the family stories."

15. b. The word *commemorate* is used to explain how people treat anniversaries and special events, which are things people *honor*.

16. b. Choice **b** makes several claims about the subject of the passage (exploring ones genealogy) that are supported by details throughout the passage.

17. d. The paragraph discusses using family members as resources for tracing your genealogy. Although the paragraph does suggest that a project such as this *can* bring a family together, it does not state that it *always* makes families closer, so choice **a** is incorrect. Choice **b** is incorrect because the paragraph does not suggest that certain family members tell better stories than others. Choice **c** describes an idea in the third paragraph, not the fourth one.

18. c. Not everyone agrees that "graveyards are frightening places," so this is an opinion rather than a fact. Choices **a**, **b**, and **d** are all facts.

19. a. After describing the investigation of family members who came before you as intricate, the author lists all of the parts such an investigation involves ("asking questions, doing research, combing through real and virtual archives, and even taking a field trip or two"). Something with so many parts is complex.

20. c. Museums contain historical artifacts, which is something they share with graveyards. Choice **a** is incorrect because simply stating that graveyards are important is not enough to support their similarity to museums. Although one might take a field trip to a museum, one might take a field trip nearly anywhere, so this is not strong enough to support the idea that graveyards are like museums. Therefore, choice **b** is incorrect.

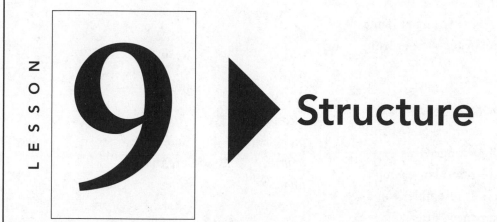

9 ▶ Structure

Understanding structure—how writers organize their ideas—will help you to comprehend what you read better. Writers must decide how to arrange their sentences and ideas. They choose the best places to put their ideas and how to move from one idea to another carefully. Most writers organize their ideas using these four patterns that help them effectively express their ideas:

1. Time Order
2. Order of Importance
3. Compare and Contrast
4. Cause and Effect

Reading will become easier for you as you learn to recognize these four patterns.

Time Order

There are many ways to tell a story. Often, stories begin with what happened first. The rest of the story follows the order in which the events occurred. Time order is also called **chronological order**—the order in which things happen.

Time Order and Transitions

Much of what you read is in time order. Newspaper and magazine articles are usually arranged this way—so are meeting minutes and directions. For example, look at the following paragraph. It resembles something you might see in a company newsletter:

> Our employee awards dinner was a success. To begin, President Mike Smith announced the award for Perfect Attendance. Carlos Feliciano and Yelena Grishov were the winners. The second award was for Most Dedicated Employee. Jennifer Steele received this award. Then Mr. Smith made an announcement. He and his wife are expecting their first child. Afterward, Vice President Jane Wu offered a toast. Next Mr. Smith gave the final award for Best New Idea. This award went to Karen Hunt. Finally, Mr. Smith ended the event with another surprise: He announced a 2% raise for all employees.

This paragraph describes what happened from start to finish. The writer used transitions to help you follow the order of events. **Transitions** allow writers to move from one idea to another. They also show readers the relationship between ideas. For example, transitions may show that one event came before another. That's how they work in this passage. Notice the transitions *to begin, second, then, afterward, next,* and *finally* in the paragraph. They keep the events in chronological order. Thus, transitions are important tools to help readers follow ideas in the paragraph.

These transitions signal the chronology in a paragraph:

first	*second*
third, etc.	*next*
now	*then*
when	*soon*
before	*after*
during	*while*
meanwhile	*in the meantime*
immediately	*suddenly*
at last	*eventually*
finally	*later*
before long	*shortly*
as soon as	*after a while*

Transitions help you figure out the order of events in a passage. These words also help readers understand the relationship between ideas.

Practice 1

The following is a list of transitions. Choose the ones that best fit into the paragraph. Write them in the blanks of the paragraph. Check your answers at the end of this lesson on page 148.

when

as soon as

yesterday

then

a moment later

right away

_____ I went to work early to get some extra filing done. _____ I got there, the phone started ringing. _____ my boss walked in. _____ he asked me to type a letter. _____ he asked me to set up a conference call. _____ I looked at my watch; it was already 11:00.

Order of Importance

Another way to present ideas is in order of importance. Once you understand this structure you will see which ideas are most important in what you read.

Ideas can be organized by rank. Using this method, the first idea listed isn't the one that happened first, but rather it's the idea that is the most, or least, important. If writers start with the most important idea, then they would continue to the least important one. Or they could do the reverse and start with the least important idea and build up to the idea that is most important. Writers usually choose their structure according to their purpose. And that structure affects how you understand what you read.

Most Important to Least Important

Sometimes passages begin with the most important idea. This often happens in newspaper articles when writers want readers to know the most important facts right away: "Student protesters shut down the campus at UCLA today" or "City officials approved a tax cut." This structure communicates main ideas clearly and directly, allowing readrs to skim passages and learn information quickly.

Here's a passage organized from the most important to the least important idea. Read it actively.

There are many ways to make tax time easier. The most important thing you can do is keep good records. Keep all of your pay stubs, receipts, and bank statements in a neat folder. When you're ready to prepare your tax forms, all of your paperwork will be in one place. The second thing you can do is start early. Start filling out the forms as soon as they arrive in the mail. If you run into problems, you'll have plenty of time to solve them. Finally, read the directions. This act can keep you from having to redo the form because you did it wrong the first time. It can also keep you from making mistakes.

The passage begins with a clear topic sentence. Then it offers three tax-time tips. The writer gives the most important tip first. "The most important thing you can do is keep good records."

What is the second-most important thing you can do to make tax time easier? The writer started with the most important thing, meaning that the ideas are organized from most to least important. Thus, the second most important tip should come right after the first. The second best thing to do is "start early."

Finally, what's the third-most important tip the writer offers? The answer, of course is the last tip. You should "read the directions."

Least Important to Most Important

Some writers organize ideas the opposite way. They don't start with the most important idea. Instead, they end with it. This order offers writers three advantages. First, readers are left with a strong conclusion. Second, this order makes use of what is called the *snowball effect*. Like a snowball rolling down a hill, the writer's ideas build and build. Each idea builds on the ones that come before it, growing more and more important. Third, starting with the least important idea creates suspense. Readers will be waiting to learn that final important idea.

You can often expect to see this structure in an argument. In an argument, the end is usually where the last point has the most impact.

Practice 2

Following is a list of reasons for reading more often. If you were to put these reasons in a paragraph, how would you organize them? First, rank the reasons in order of importance. Then rank them according to how *you* would present them. Check your answers on page 148.

Five Reasons to Read More Often:

- You will broaden your vocabulary.
- You will improve your reading comprehension.
- You will increase your reading speed.
- You will develop a better understanding of yourself and others.
- You will learn new information and ideas.

Order of Importance to You

1. _____
2. _____
3. _____
4. _____
5. _____

Order of Presentation

1. _____
2. _____
3. _____
4. _____
5. _____

In which order did you present your ideas? Most important to least important, or least important to most important? Either structure will work well with these ideas. Some writers want to hit their readers with what's most important at the beginning. Then they'll be sure to catch their readers' attention. Or they may want to save their best ideas for last. That way, readers build up to the most important idea.

Now that you've organized the ideas about reading, put them into a paragraph on a separate piece of paper. Add a topic sentence and transitions to the sentences listed.

Compare and Contrast

People spend a lot of time thinking about similarities and differences. When they want to explain similarities, they often compare the items. That will show how things are similar. Likewise, when they want to show how things are different, they contrast them to emphasize the differences between the items.

How Comparing and Contrasting Works

When writers **compare** and **contrast**, they help readers to judge the things that are being compared. For example, by comparing a cup of coffee to mud, you can give someone an idea how the coffee looks and tastes.

Writers use comparison and contrast for the same reason. When you read, you can see how two or more things measure up side by side. What do they have in common? What sets them apart?

Read the following passage carefully to see how the technique of compare and contrast works.

Being an assistant is a lot like being a parent. A child is dependent upon her parent. Your boss is dependent on you. Children must ask for permission before they go out. Similarly, your boss will come to you for permission, too. You keep track of her schedule. "Can I have a meeting on Tuesday at 3:30?" your boss might ask. You'll also clean up after your boss. Just as a parent tucks toys away at the end of the day, you'll file papers, put things back into drawers, and tidy up the office. A parent protects his or her children from danger. Likewise, you'll find yourself protecting your boss from dangers like angry callers and clients. But there is one big difference. Children grow more independent each year. Your boss will grow more dependent on you as the years pass.

Two things are being compared and contrasted here: a parent and an assistant. The writer lists four similarities between parents and assistants:

1. Bosses depend upon assistants like children depend upon their parents.
2. Bosses ask permission from their assistants to do certain things just as children ask permission from their parents.
3. Assistants clean up after their bosses like parents clean up after children.
4. Assistants protect their bosses like parents protect their children.

Then the writer points out one difference between assistants and parents: children grow less and less dependent upon their parents. Meanwhile, bosses grow more and more dependent upon their assistants.

Remember, writers always have a motive. So when you come across compare and contrast passages, ask yourself why the author is comparing those items. What does the writer want you to get from the comparison? This comparison makes readers see assistants in a new way. That's one of the values of this structure.

Transitions in Comparison and Contrast

Did you notice the transitions in the paragraph about assistants and parents? Some transitions told you that the writer was comparing (showing a similarity). Others told you that the writer was contrasting (showing a difference). Read the passage again. As you read it this time, underline the transitions.

There are several transitions that show comparison and contrast. You should have underlined *like, similarly, also, just as, likewise,* and *but.* Here is a more complete list of transitional words and phrases.

WORDS THAT HELP YOU COMPARE	
similarly	in the same way
likewise	in a like manner
like	just as, just like
also	much as, much like

WORDS THAT HELP YOU CONTRAST	
but	on the contrary
however	on the other hand
yet	nevertheless
conversely	instead

Practice 3

Compare and contrast the two items below. List three ways the two items are alike. Then list three ways they are different. One similarity is listed to get you started. You can check your answers at the end of the lesson on page 149.

Item A: movies
Item B: live theater

Comparisons (similarities)

1. Both provide entertainment
2. _____
3. _____

Contrasts (differences)

1. _____
2. _____
3. _____

Cause and Effect

A **cause** is something that makes something else happen. On the other hand, an **effect** is what happens *after* something takes place. Many reading passages incorporate cause and effect. For example, a passage could explain the *cause* for increased electricity costs and the *effect* these rising costs have on small businesses. A passage may also be limited to discussing only a cause (for example, increased electricity costs) or only an effect (small businesses struggle to pay high electricity bills). It's the writer's choice.

Transitions for Cause and Effect

Just as certain transitions tell readers whether two things are similar or different, or in what order events occur, other words tell readers whether things are causes or effects. Watch for these transitions as you read.

WORDS THAT SHOW CAUSE	
because (of)	created (by)
since	caused (by)
led (to)	due (to)

WORDS THAT SHOW EFFECT		
since	therefore	hence
so	consequently	as a result

Opinions about Cause and Effect

Sometimes, writers offer their opinions about why something happened (cause). Or they might explain what they think will happen because of a certain event (effect). As a reader, you need to consider how reasonable those opinions are. Are the writer's ideas logical? Does the writer support the conclusions offered?

You will also have to decide which opinions make more sense to you. Is the cause likely to have that result? Does the author's argument make sense?

Practice 4

The following two paragraphs consider how a no-smoking policy would affect an office. Read them carefully. Then answer the questions that follow. You can check your answers at the end of the lesson on page 149.

PARAGRAPH A

A no-smoking policy would be disastrous. More than one-third of our employees smoke half a pack a day. If they can't smoke in the office, they will have to leave the building. As a result, they will have to take longer breaks. This will interrupt their work. They will also have to take fewer breaks, farther apart. This means longer stretches of time between cigarettes. Furthermore, long-time smokers may quit work, rather than adhere to this strict policy.

PARAGRAPH B

A no-smoking policy would be a great benefit to all of us. We would be able to breathe smoke-free air. Furthermore, cigarette odor and smoke would no longer bother sensitive clients. In addition, smokers may find it easier to quit since they can't smoke as often during the day. Finally, we will be able to save employees money by cutting the cost of healthcare coverage due to cigarette-related health problems.

1. What effects does Paragraph A say the no-smoking policy will have? _____ _____

2. What effects does Paragraph B say the no-smoking policy will have? _____ _____

3. Which passage do you think sounds most reasonable? Why? _____ _____ _____

Review Practice

By now, you should have a good idea about the way writers organize their ideas. This new understanding should help you determine more easily what a passage is conveying. Don't forget to use skills you learned in Lesson 8 as well.

Read the following passages carefully and actively. Don't look up any unfamiliar words yet. First, try to decipher their meaning from context. Then answer the questions that follow.

PARAGRAPH 1

There are many fatal mistakes businesses can make. The Right Stuff was a toy store. It sold stuffed animals. It closed after it made a promise it couldn't keep. The Right Stuff had only been open a few weeks. It ordered a large shipment of Wilbur, the popular stuffed dog. Then The Right Stuff ran an ad in the newspaper. The ad claimed that The Right Stuff had Wilbur in-stock and on-sale starting Sunday.

But by Friday, the Wilburs hadn't arrived. The Right Stuff called the warehouse. They learned the toys were on back order. They wouldn't even ship until the next Thursday. What could The

Right Stuff do? On Sunday, employees had to tell customers that there were no Wilbur dolls. They offered I.O.U. coupons, but customers were mad. The sale was supposed to boost the store's business. Instead, it was a disaster. Two months later, The Right Stuff permanently closed its doors.

1. Which two organizing strategies does this writer use? Select two answer choices.
   a. time order
   b. order of importance
   c. compare and contrast
   d. cause and effect

2. *Fatal* means
   a. big.
   b. ruinous.
   c. obvious.
   d. minor.

3. What started the trouble for The Right Stuff? _____ _____

4. What is the main idea of this paragraph? _____ _____

PARAGRAPH 2

Milton Hershey was born near the small village of Derry Church, Pennsylvania, in 1857.

It was a humble beginning that did not foretell his later success. Milton only attended school through the fourth grade; at that point, he was apprenticed to a printer in a nearby town. Fortunately for all chocolate lovers, Milton did not excel as a printer. After a while, he left the printing business to take a position for which he was better suited. He apprenticed to a Lancaster, Pennsylvania candy maker. It was apparent he had found his calling in life, and at the age of 18, he opened his own candy store in Philadelphia. In spite of his talents as a candy maker, the shop failed after six years.

It may come as a surprise to current Hershey fans, but his first candy success was with the manufacture of caramel. After the failure of his Philadelphia store, Milton headed for Denver, where he learned the art of making caramels. There he took a job with a local manufacturer who made the finest caramels in the United States by using fresh milk in his recipe. Fresh milk made Milton's caramels especially tasty. After a time in Denver, Milton next attempted to open his own candy-making businesses, in Chicago, New Orleans, and New York City. Finally, he went back to Lancaster, Pennsylvania, where he raised the money necessary to try again. This company—the Lancaster Caramel Company—established Milton's reputation as a master candy maker.

5. Which organizing strategy does this writer use in the second paragraph?
  a. time order
  b. order of importance
  c. compare and contrast
  d. cause and effect

6. *Excel* means
  a. disappoint.
  b. fail.
  c. shine.
  d. understand.

7. What caused Milton to move to Denver?

_____

8. What is an opinion in this passage?

_____

_____

PARAGRAPH 3

There are two types of diabetes, insulin-dependent and non-insulin-dependent. Both types affect the body's ability to use food for energy. Diabetes does not interfere with digestion, but it does prevent the body from using glucose, (an important product of digestion commonly known as sugar), for energy. After a meal, the normal digestive system breaks some food down into glucose. The blood carries the glucose or sugar throughout the body, causing blood glucose levels to rise. In response to this rise, the hormone insulin is released into the bloodstream and signals the body tissues to metabolize or burn the glucose for fuel, which causes blood glucose levels to return to normal. The glucose that the body does not use right away is stored in the liver, muscle, or fat.

In both types of diabetes, however, this normal digestive process malfunctions. A gland called the *pancreas*, found just behind the stomach, makes *insulin*. In people with insulin-dependent diabetes, the pancreas does not produce insulin at all. This condition usually begins in childhood and is known as Type I (formerly called juvenile-onset) diabetes. These patients must have daily insulin injections to survive. However, people with non-insulin-dependent diabetes usually produce some insulin in their pancreas, but their bodies' tissues do not respond well to the insulin signal and, therefore, do not metabolize the glucose properly, a condition known as insulin resistance.

9. Which organizing strategy does this writer use in the second paragraph?
  a. time order
  b. order of importance
  c. compare and contrast
  d. cause and effect

10. Which word in the second paragraph is a clue to how the passage is organized?
a. usually
b. however
c. properly
d. and

11. What is a trait specific to non-insulin-dependent diabetes?

_____

_____

12. What is a similarity between insulin-dependent and non-insulin-dependent diabetes in the second paragraph?

_____

_____

PARAGRAPH 4

The post-World War II era marked a period of unprecedented energy against the second-class citizenship accorded to African Americans in many parts of the nation. Resistance to racial segregation and discrimination with strategies like civil disobedience, nonviolent resistance, marches, protests, boycotts, "freedom rides," and rallies received national attention as newspaper, radio, and television reporters and photographers documented the struggle to end racial inequality.

When Rosa Parks refused to give up her seat to a white person in Montgomery, Alabama, and was arrested in December 1955, she took her place in a train of events that generated a momentum the civil rights movement had never before experienced. Local civil rights leaders were hoping for such an opportunity to test the city's segregation laws. Deciding to boycott the buses, the African-American community soon formed a new organization to supervise the boycott, the Montgomery Improvement Association (MIA). The young pastor of the Dexter Avenue Baptist Church, Reverend Martin Luther King, Jr., was chosen as the first MIA leader. The boycott, more successful than anyone hoped, led to a 1956 Supreme Court decision banning segregated buses.

In 1960, four black freshmen from North Carolina Agricultural and Technical College in Greensboro strolled into the F. W. Woolworth store and quietly sat down at the lunch counter. They were not served, but they stayed until closing time. The next morning they came with twenty-five more students. Two weeks later, similar demonstrations had spread to several cities. Within a year, similar peaceful demonstrations took place in over a hundred cities throughout the country. At Shaw University in Raleigh, North Carolina, the students formed their own organization, the Student Non-Violent Coordinating Committee (SNCC, pronounced "Snick"). The students' bravery in the face of verbal and physical abuse led to integration in many stores even before the passage of the Civil Rights Act of 1964.

13. Which two organizing strategies does this writer use? Select <u>two</u> answer choices.
a. time order
b. order of importance
c. compare and contrast
d. cause and effect

14. When was the Civil Rights Act passed?
a. 1955
b. 1956
c. 1960
d. 1964

15. What started the formation of the Montgomery Improvement Association (MIA)?

_____

16. What is the topic sentence of this passage?

_____

PARAGRAPH 5

The vast majority of schools entered the high-tech age years ago by installing computers throughout their libraries and classrooms. All administrative offices were equipped with computer systems as well. However, an innovative school in Arizona is taking this trend one step further, providing an all new way for students to do their homework. They provide them with their own laptop!

Instead of using money to buy all new textbooks for Empire High School, laptop computers were bought by the administration with the funds. The teachers commonly select educational materials on the Internet for students to consult to complete homework assignments. To make the laptops feel more personal, students are allowed to store their own music collections on them. Empire High School has clearly improved on the old model of education.

Instead of handing in handwritten reports and homework on paper, these Arizona students just email it into their individual teachers. So much for that old excuse that the dog ate your homework!

17. Which organizing strategy does this writer use in the second paragraph?
   a. time order
   b. order of importance
   c. compare and contrast
   d. cause and effect

18. Which of the following details from the passage is an opinion?
   a. Empire High School in Arizona is providing each of its students with a new laptop.
   b. Empire High School has clearly improved on the old model of education.
   c. At Empire High School, teachers select educational materials on the Internet.
   d. At Empire High School, students email their homework to their teachers.

19. Why are students at Empire High School allowed to store music on their laptops?

   _____

20. What is a good title for this passage?

   _____

Check your answers to see how you did. Could you see how each cause led to an effect? Could you see how each effect then caused another effect?

Answers

Practice 1

There are several ways to fill in the blanks. One option is below. Notice how much more fluid the paragraph is with transitions.

Yesterday, I went to work early to get some extra filing done. As soon as I got there, the phone started ringing. A moment later, my boss walked in. Right away he asked me to type a letter. Then, he asked me to set up a conference call. When I looked at my watch, it was already 11:00.

Practice 2

There are many ways to organize these ideas. Here is one example:

Order of Importance to You

1. You will develop a better understanding of yourself and others.
2. You will learn new information and ideas.
3. You will improve your reading comprehension.
4. You will broaden your vocabulary.
5. You will increase your reading speed.

Order of Presentation

  5. You will develop a better understanding of
     yourself and others.
  4. You will learn new information and ideas.
  3. You will improve your reading comprehension.
  2. You will broaden your vocabulary.
  1. You will increase your reading speed.

The way your paragraph turns out depends on how you decided to order the ideas. The following are two sample paragraphs ordered from most to least important and from least to most important. The main idea is stated in the first sentence in each paragraph. The topic sentence is in boldface type and the transitions are underlined.

Most to Least Important

There are many benefits to reading more often. <u>First and foremost</u>, reading more will give you a better understanding of yourself and others. You will <u>also</u> learn new information and ideas. <u>Furthermore</u>, you will improve your reading comprehension. You will begin to understand more of what you read. <u>In addition</u>, you will increase both your vocabulary and your reading speed.

Least to Most Important

There are many benefits to reading more often. <u>First of all</u>, by reading more, you will increase your reading speed. You will be able to read more in less time. <u>Second</u>, you will broaden your vocabulary. <u>Third</u>, you will improve your reading comprehension. You will understand more of what you read. <u>Furthermore</u>, you will learn new information and ideas. <u>Most importantly</u>, you will develop a better understanding of yourself and others.

Practice 3

Answers will vary. Here is one possibility.

Comparisons (similarities)

  1. Both provide entertainment.
  2. Both use actors.
  3. Both can be comedy or drama.

Contrasts (differences)

  1. Movies are prerecorded; theater is live.
  2. Movies require electricity to be displayed; theater does not necessarily require electricity.
  3. Movies can be shown several times per a day, while live theater is performed usually only once or twice per day.

Practice 4

  1. Paragraph A says that the no-smoking policy will have the following effects:
   - Smokers will take longer breaks. This will interrupt their work.
   - Smokers will have to take fewer breaks.
   - Smokers' irritability will affect their coworkers.
   - Long-time smokers may quit work.
  2. Paragraph B says the no-smoking policy will have the following effects:
   - Everyone will be able to breathe smoke-free air.
   - Cigarette odor and smoke would no longer bother sensitive clients.
   - Healthcare coverage would cost less.
  3. Answers will vary.

Review Practice

1. The writer uses **a** and **d**—time order and cause and effect.

2. *Fatal* means bringing about misfortune, or *ruinous* (**b**). The main clue is that The Right Stuff closed down just two months after the incident.

3. The trouble was started by the ad. The first event in this chain reaction was ordering the Wilbur dogs, but that didn't cause the problem. The problem began with the ad. It promised that the dogs would be in stock.

4. The main idea of this paragraph is stated in the first sentence: "There are many fatal mistakes businesses can make." The rest of the passage gives a specific example of such mistakes.

5. Words such as *after*, *next*, and *finally* should help you to figure out that this paragraph is organized using time order, choice **a.**

6. *Excel* means to perform extremely well, or *shine*, (choice **c**). The main clue that Milton did not shine as a printer is that he quit printing to do something for which "he was better suited"—making candy.

7. Hershey moved to Denver because his candy store in Philadelphia failed.

8. There are a couple of opinions in this passage. The idea that Milton's failure as a printer was fortunate "for all chocolate lovers" is an opinion because some chocolate lovers might not like the chocolate Milton made. The idea that "Fresh milk made Milton's caramels especially tasty" is also an opinion because not everyone will agree it is true.

9. The passage is organized using compare and contrast structure, choice **c**, as it discusses the similarities and differences between insulin-dependent and non-insulin-dependent diabetes.

10. However, choice **b** helps create a contrast between ideas, indicating the passage's compare and contrast structure.

11. The second paragraph states that "people with non-insulin-dependent diabetes usually produce some insulin in their pancreas." This is a trait that distinguishes it from insulin-dependent diabetes.

12. The second paragraph begins by stating that with "both types of diabetes . . . [the] normal digestive process malfunctions." The rest of the paragraph describes differences between the two types.

13. That this passage was composed using time order, choice **a**, structure can be determined because the writer distinguishes each detail according to the date it happened. The dates follow the order in which they occurred. The writer also uses cause and effect, choice **d**, as Rosa Parks's arrest caused the civil rights movement to gain momentum. The ultimate effect of this and the actions of the four black freshmen from North Carolina Agricultural and Technical College was the passage of the Civil Rights Act.

14. The final sentence of the passage states that the Civil Rights Act was passed in 1964, choice **d.**

15. According to the second paragraph, the MIA was formed because an organization was needed to supervise the boycott of buses in Montgomery, Alabama. The need for a supervisor was the cause and the MIA was the effect.

16. The topic sentence of this paragraph is its first one: "The post-World War II era marked a period of unprecedented energy against the second-class citizenship accorded to African Americans in many parts of the nation." The rest of the passage develops this topic sentence by giving specific examples of the activities of African-Americans who fought against their second-class citizenship.

17. Multiple uses of the contrasting word *instead* is a clue to figuring out this passage's structure. It is organized using compare and contrast structure, choice **c**, as it compares the old model of teaching using textbooks and handwritten reports with the modern model using computers.

18. Some people may not agree with the statement that "Empire High School has clearly improved on the old model of education," thinking that printed textbooks and handwritten homework is better than computer and email. Therefore, choice **b** is an opinion.

19. The second paragraph states that students are allowed to store music on their laptops "to make the laptops feel more personal." The need to personalize their laptops is the cause, and the effect is students being allowed to store music on them.

20. Answers will vary, but the title should acknowledge the innovative nature of Empire High School's use of computers as teaching aids. Two such titles might be "Technology as Teaching Tool" and "The Computerized Classroom."

10 ▶ Language and Style

The language and style a writer uses can give readers even more clues about the text. Sometimes, the main idea won't be stated directly, and you will have to use these clues to understand what the author is trying to convey. This lesson will show how understanding the language and style of a paragraph can improve your reading comprehension skills.

Point of View

Point of view is the position from which one sees things. People can look at an object from many different points of view. You can look at it from above, below, behind, beside, and so on. How you see the object depends on your point of view. A situation can be viewed from many different points of view, as well. In writing, the point of view is like a filter. It's the voice the writer uses to share his or her ideas. What readers learn from a text depends on who is speaking to them. Thus, point of view is important in writing. Who will tell the readers the writer's ideas? Who will narrate the story?

Three Points of View

There are three points of view writers can use: **first person**, **second person**, and **third person**. A writer chooses the point of view depending upon the particular topic and purpose of the passage. The point of view helps a writer create a particular effect because each point of view works differently; each creates a different relationship between a reader and writer.

First-Person Point of View

The first-person point of view is a personal one. The writer uses the pronouns *I* or *we* and thus shares his or her own feelings, experiences, and ideas with readers.

> *Example:*
> I knew I was going to be late, but there was no way to get in touch with my boss.

This point of view creates a closeness between the reader and writer. By using the pronouns *I, my, mine, we, our,* or *us*, the relationship between reader and writer has a feeling of confidentiality because the writer is talking directly to the reader.

Second-Person Point of View

In the second-person point of view, writers use the pronoun *you*. The writer addresses the reader directly and makes the reader feel involved in the action.

> *Example:*
> You knew you were going to be late, but there was no way to get in touch with your boss.

The second-person point of view singles you (as the reader) out as an individual and encourages an interactive relationship with the text.

Third-Person Point of View

The third-person point of view offers readers the voice of an "outsider." There are no direct references to the writer or the reader. The writer uses the pronouns *he, she, it,* or *they.*

> *Example:*
> He knew he was going to be late. But there was no way to get in touch with his boss.

Third-person creates a distance between the reader and the writer (or narrator). There's no direct person-to-person contact (me to you). Rather, someone else is speaking to the reader.

Practice 1

Change the point of view from third person to first person. Check your answers at the end of the lesson on page 162.

1. They decided it would be best for them not to join the others.

2. The babysitter was annoyed by the last-minute cancellation.

3. People enjoy meals at nice restaurants.

Subjective versus Objective

The first person point of view is **subjective** (based on the thoughts, feelings, and experiences of the speaker or writer). However, ideas often carry more weight if they are **objective** (unaffected by the thoughts, feelings, and experiences of the speaker or writer). An objective person is outside of the action. He or she isn't personally involved; therefore, his or her ideas are likely to be more fair to everyone.

Example:

Subjective: I don't like the biweekly pay period. Why should I have to wait two weeks to get paid?

Objective: The biweekly pay period is a problem. It's unfair to make employees wait two weeks to get paid.

Most people would say that the second passage makes a better argument. The subjective passage doesn't sound like a thoughtful argument. Instead, it sounds like a complaint. The first-person, or subjective, point of view can create a wonderful closeness between writer and reader, but it's often less effective in an argument.

Word Choice

You already know that being observant is an important part of reading. Writers have made a lot of decisions by the time their writing reaches you. They decided what to say and how to say it. They chose to use particular points of view and particular words for a reason. Some authors choose to clearly state their ideas; some *suggest* their ideas instead. They don't make explicit statements; rather they leave clues to tell the reader what the writer is saying. That's why it's important for readers to be observant.

Looking closely at what you read helps you see the writer's strategies. This will help you understand the text. You've already learned many of these strategies. For example, you know to look for the way writers arrange ideas. It's also helpful to look for:

- particular words and phrases the writer uses;
- how those words and phrases are arranged in sentences;
- word patterns or sentence patterns that are repeated;
- important details about people, places, and things.

The Importance of Word Choice

Even words that meant almost the same thing can make a different impression on a reader. For example, look at *brusque* and *assertive*. If you say your aunt is *brusque*, that means one thing; if you say she is *assertive*, it's another, because brusque and assertive have different **connotations** (a meaning suggested or implied by a word) and make you feel or think distinct things when you hear them. Their **denotation** (how they'd be defined in a dictionary) is not very different. Both *brusque* and *assertive* can mean *direct* or to the *point*. However, *brusque* is a negative word. To use it implies you think your aunt can be too short with people, or speak roughly. *Assertive* is a positive word—it suggests your aunt stands up for herself and knows how to take charge. The **connotations** of the words authors choose can tell their readers as much as the words themselves.

Noticing word choice is especially important when the main idea of a reading passage isn't clear. For example, look at the following paragraph. It's a letter of recommendation. There's no topic sentence. Use your powers of observation to uncover the writer's message.

This letter regards my former office assistant, Jane Rosenberg. Jane usually completed her work on time. She proofread it carefully. She is an able typist. She is familiar with several word processing programs. She also knows some legal terms and procedures, which was helpful. Jane was always punctual. She always asked if she had a question.

Think about what message this letter sends to its reader:

a. Jane Rosenberg is a great office assistant. Hire her right away!

b. Jane Rosenberg is an average employee. She doesn't do outstanding work, but she's capable and reliable.

c. Jane Rosenberg is a bad worker. Don't even think about hiring her.

Clearly, the writer does not think that Jane is an outstanding employee, or that Jane is a bad employee. The words used suggest that Jane is an average employee.

OBSERVATION	CONCLUSION
The first sentence is neutral. The writer doesn't say, "I'm happy to recommend" or "my wonderful office assistant." The sentence is flat, without emotion.	The writer doesn't feel strongly about Jane. She doesn't want to suggest that Jane is a great employee. At the same time, she doesn't want to suggest that Jane would be a bad hire.
The writer uses "usually" in the second sentence.	Jane is good about meeting deadlines but not great. She may not always get work done on time.
The writer says that Jane proofreads her work carefully.	Jane makes sure she does quality work. She's not sloppy.
The writer calls Jane an "able" typist.	*Able* is a neutral word; it suggests that Jane types well enough, but that she could do better.
The writer says that Jane is "familiar with" several word processing programs.	Jane knows a little about the programs but isn't an expert. She can probably do a few basic things in each program, but she would have trouble doing complex projects.
The writer says that Jane knows "some legal terms and procedures."	Jane's knowledge of legal terms and procedures is limited. She knows a little, but not a lot. She's better than someone who knows nothing, but she's no expert.
The writer says Jane "was always punctual."	Jane is a reliable employee.
The writer says that Jane "always asked if she had a question."	Jane won't assume things. If she's unsure, she'll ask because she wants to be sure she has it right, which can be both a positive and a negative depending on how independent an employer wants his or her assistant to be.

Practice 2

Now it's your turn. Read another letter about Jane carefully. Then, fill in the chart on the next page. What do you observe? What can you conclude from what you notice? Once you fill in the chart, answer the question that follows. When you are done, check your answers at the end of the lesson.

I am pleased to recommend my former office assistant, Jane Rosenberg. I could always count on Jane to get her work done on time. I also knew she would proofread it very carefully. In addition, she is an outstanding typist and has also mastered several word processing programs. Furthermore, she knows legal terms and procedures inside and out. That was a tremendous help. I could always count on Jane to be prompt, and I knew she would check with me if she had any questions.

OBSERVATION	CONCLUSION

Look at your observations and conclusions. What message is this writer sending?

a. Jane is a great office assistant. Hire her right away.

b. Jane is an average employee. She doesn't do outstanding work, but she is capable and reliable.

c. Jane is a bad worker. Don't even think about hiring her.

Style

Understanding **style** is important to reading success. Writers use different structures to organize their ideas. They also use different styles to express those ideas. Being aware of style helps you see what writers are trying to convey.

Style is also important for another reason. It's often what makes readers like or dislike certain writers or types of writing. You may not change your taste after this lesson, but you will probably be able to appreciate and understand many different kinds of writers and styles. Style consists of three elements:

1. sentence structure
2. level of detail and description
3. level of formality

Sentence Structure

Sentences can vary greatly. They can be short and simple. They can also be long and complex, with lots of ideas packed together. Writers can use mostly one kind of sentence, or they can use a variety of sentence sizes. Sometimes sentences will all sound the same. Other times sentences will vary in word order, syntax choice, and structure.

1. I had a terrible commute home today.
2. My commute home was plagued by slow drivers, faulty traffic lights, and a disruptive street demonstration.
3. This commute! I can't stand it!

Notice how distinct the "voice" is in each sentence, depending on whether the structure is straightforward, includes a detailed list, or features short exclamatory bursts.

Level of Detail and Description

The level of description and detail has an effect on the reader. Some writers are quite descriptive. Others offer only a few details. Here are two things to consider:

1. How specific is the writer? Does he write, "dog" (general) or "Labrador retriever" (specific)? Does he write "some" (general) or "three and a half pounds" (specific)?
2. How much description does the writer provide? Does she write, "Ms. Zee is my manager" (non-descriptive)? Or does she offer some description: "Ms. Zee, my manager, is a tall woman with piercing eyes and a firm handshake"? Or does she go even further: "Ms. Zee, my manager, is five-foot-ten with eyes that pierce like knives and a vise-like grip." (very descriptive)?

Notice the increasing level of detail in the following examples. The first sentence is very general. The second sentence adds some detail. The third sentence gets even more specific.

1. Charles is a bank teller.
2. Charles is a bank teller at Pennview Savings.
3. Charles is a bank teller at Pennview Savings, the first bank in this city.

1. Let's meet after work on the corner.
2. Let's meet after work on the corner of 58th and Broadway.
3. Let's meet at 6:15 P.M., on the corner of 58th and Broadway.

Practice 3

Change the style of the following sentences. Add specific description and detail. When you are done, check your answers at the end of the lesson on page 163.

1. She ate a huge breakfast this morning.
Descriptive Version:

_____

_____

_____

_____

2. Please dress up for the party.
Descriptive Version:

_____

_____

_____

_____

3. The new gym has lots of equipment.
Descriptive Version:

_____

_____

_____

Level of Formality

Writers must decide how **formal** or **informal** they should be when they write. In correspondence, they decide the level of formality based on their audience and their purpose.

Writers can use slang (which is informal), proper language, or anything in between. In correspondence, they can address readers by their first names (casual)

or by their title (formal). For example, the following sentences use two different levels of formality.

Let's get together after work on Thursday.

We invite you to join us for a social gathering at the close of business on Thursday.

Notice the drastic difference in style. The first sentence, likely directed at a friend, is casual and informal. The second sentence is formal. Yet, both sentences send the same message; they just do it in different styles.

Practice 4

Rank the following sentences from 1 to 3 (1 is the most formal and 3 is the least formal). When you are done, check your answers on page 163.

1. _____ Sales have improved.
_____ These figures show that sales have increased.
_____ Sales are up!

2. _____ You're doing great work, O'Brien.
_____ Nice job, O'Brien.
_____ Your performance is above our expectations, O'Brien.

So far you have learned that style is one thing writers use to express their ideas. Style consists of three elements: sentence structure, level of description and detail, and level of formality. Some writers use a very formal style while others are more casual. Remember, style depends on the writer's audience and purpose.

Review Practice

Read the following passages carefully and answer the questions that follow. When you are done, check your answers at the end of the lesson on page 164.

Use the following passage to answer questions 1 through 6

Our company plans to merge with A+ Systems, but the merger will have dire consequences for employees. First, the merger will force many of us to relocate. Second, many of us will be transferred to new departments. But most importantly, a merger means that hundreds of us will lose our jobs.

1. Which sentence states the main idea of this passage?
   a. The merger would be great for the company.
   b. The merger wouldn't change things too much.
   c. The merger would be bad for employees.
   d. The merger will benefit employees.

2. Which structure does this writer use to organize his ideas?
   a. time order
   b. cause and effect
   c. order of importance
   d. both **b** and **c**

3. Which point of view does the writer use in this passage?
   a. first person
   b. second person
   c. third person
   d. fourth person

4. Based on the point of view, you can conclude that the writer is
   a. an employer.
   b. an employee.
   c. an outside consultant.
   d. a business journalist.

5. The word *dire* means
   a. minimal.
   b. expected.
   c. disastrous.
   d. tranquil.

6. How would you describe the writer's tone or message?
   a. objective
   b. positive
   c. subjective
   d. indifferent

Use the following passage to answer questions 7 through 13

Bentley's Paints is ecstatic to announce their nationwide Presidents' Day sale! This Monday, February 15th, is the day to take advantage of amazing deals offered at each of their 62 locations throughout the United States! Bentley's will be slashing prices on rollers, brushes, pans, and drop cloths! But most impressive is their astounding 50% discount on their entire line of interior and exterior paints—275 distinctive shades in all! This Presidents' Day, go to Bentley's and save!

7. Which point of view does the writer use in this passage?
   a. first person
   b. second person
   c. third person
   d. fourth person

8. Based on the point of view, you can conclude that the writer is
   a. the owner of Bentley's Paints.
   b. an employee of Bentley's Paints.
   c. a journalist writing a story about Bentley's Paints.
   d. an outside contractor of Bentley's Paints.

9. Which of the following details from the passage is an opinion?
   a. Bentley's Paints is having a sale on Presidents' Day.
   b. Bentley's Paints is offering amazing deals during its sale.
   c. Bentley's Paints has 62 locations throughout the United States.
   d. Bentley's Paints is offering a 50% discount on its line of paints.

10. Which structure does this writer use to organize her ideas?
    a. time order
    b. cause and effect
    c. order of importance
    d. compare and contrast

11. How would you describe the writer's tone or message?
    a. objective
    b. positive
    c. negative
    d. indifferent

12. Which of the following is the topic sentence of this passage?
    a. Bentley's Paints is proud to announce their nationwide Presidents' Day sale!
    b. Bentley's will be slashing prices on rollers, brushes, pans, and drop clothes!
    c. But most impressive is their astounding 50% discount on our entire line of interior and exterior paints—275 distinctive shades in all!
    d. There is no topic sentence.

13. The word *ecstatic* means
    a. happy.
    b. concerned.
    c. tired.
    d. serious.

Use the following passage to answer questions 14 through 20

Dear Candice,

Long time no see! What have you been up to since abandoning New York for Los Angeles to mold young minds? Those students are lucky to have you. Are you still digging the change of scenery since your relocation, or are you simply dying for a ride on the subway and a crush of tourists around the Empire State Building (ha ha)? Anyway, I'm not just writing to see how you're doing . . . I have some awesome news. Guess who's coming to visit you in the City of Lights this July . . . me! That's right, Sal and I are going to be in L.A. for five fabulous days and we'd love to drop by, see your new home, and meet your new pup (the photos of Reggie that you posted on Facebook are simply adorable!!). So, keep your schedule open from July 15th through the 20th, because Sal and I are hoping to see lots of you (and Reggie!).

Love,
Tony

14. Which point of view does the writer use in this passage?
   a. first person
   b. second person
   c. third person
   d. fourth person

15. Candice moved to Los Angeles mainly to
   a. get a new dog.
   b. enjoy the scenery.
   c. ride on the subway.
   d. take a job as a teacher.

16. The word *relocation* means
   a. plan.
   b. move.
   c. suggest.
   d. fight.

17. Which structure does this writer use to organize his ideas?
   a. time order
   b. cause and effect
   c. order of importance
   d. compare and contrast

18. The level of formality of this passage can best be described as
   a. informal.
   b. slightly informal.
   c. formal.
   d. very formal.

19. Based on the level of formality, you can conclude the writer is
   a. an acquaintance.
   b. a friend.
   c. a business associate.
   d. an employer.

20. How would you describe the writer's tone or message?
   a. indifferent
   b. negative
   c. positive
   d. objective

You should be able to apply what you have learned to all that you read. Now you know how authors write—you see how the words they use, their point of view and the types of sentences they choose influence your understanding of a passage. You also understand how authors use style to convey meaning.

Answers

Practice 1

The changed pronouns are italicized below.

1. *I/We* decided it would be best for *me/us* not to join the others.
2. *I* was annoyed by the last-minute cancellation.
3. *I/We* enjoy meals at nice restaurants.

Practice 2

OBSERVATION	CONCLUSION
The first sentence is positive. The writer "is pleased" to recommend Jane.	The writer was happy with Jane's work.
The writer says she could "always" count on Jane to get work done "on time."	Jane is a dependable worker. She meets deadlines.
The writer says she "knew" Jane would proofread "carefully."	Jane is always careful about her work.
She calls Jane an "outstanding" typist.	Jane types quickly and correctly.
She says that Jane has "mastered" several word processing programs.	Jane knows those programs inside and out. She can create all kinds of documents with them.
She says that Jane knows legal terms and procedures "inside and out."	Jane really knows legal terms and procedures.
The writer "could always count on Jane" to be prompt.	Jane is never late.

2. **a.** Based on the high praise that Jane received, she will most likely be a great employee.

Practice 3

Answers will vary. Here are some examples.

1. Cedric ate two scrambled eggs, three slices of bacon, and four pieces of buttered toast for breakfast this morning.
2. Please wear an evening gown or tuxedo for Thursday's holiday party.
3. The brand new gym has seven Stairmasters, twenty stationary bikes, twenty-five treadmills, three sets of Nautilus equipment, four racquetball courts, and an Olympic-sized pool.

Practice 4

1. 2, 1, 3
2. 2, 3, 1

Review Practice

1. c. The first sentence in the passage is the topic sentence. It states that the merger will be bad for employees. The other sentences in the paragraph support that idea.

2. d. The writer describes the effects of the merger (which is the cause) on the employees. She lists these effects in order of importance. She saves the most important effect for last.

3. a. The writer uses the first-person pronouns *our*, *us*, and *we*. Also, there is no such thing as a fourth-person point of view.

4. b. The writer uses the first-person point of view. Thus, you can conclude that the author is an employee.

5. c. The consequences are all serious. They are all very negative. Thus, dire can't mean *minimal*. These effects may be *expected* (choice **b**), but the focus of the paragraph is the negative results.

6. c. The first-person point of view is based on the feelings and opinions of the narrator. Personal experiences are subjective.

7. c. The writer uses the third-person pronoun *their*. There is no such thing as fourth-person point of view.

8. d. Because the passage is written using the third person point of view, you can conclude that it was written by an outside contractor, such as an advertising agency. The passage is an advertisement, not a journalistic news story, so choice **c** is incorrect.

9. b. Not everyone might agree that the deals Bentley's Paints is offering during its Presidents' Day sale are *amazing*. Whether or not something is amazing is an arguable opinion, not an inarguable fact. The other answer choices all describe inarguable facts.

10. c. That the writer puts the sentence beginning with "most impressive" at the end of the passage is a tip that it is written in order of importance.

11. b. Key words such as *amazing, impressive,* and *astounding* indicate that the writer's message is intended to be a positive one.

12. a. The first sentence of the passage is the topic sentence because it establishes the main topic that Bentley's Paints is having a sale on Presidents' Day. Choices **b** and **c** support this topic with additional details.

13. a. Based on the positive tone of the passage, you can conclude that Bradley's Paints is *happy* to announce its Presidents' Day sale. Therefore, *ecstatic* most likely means *happy*.

14. a. The writer uses the first-person pronouns *I'm, I, me,* and *we'd*. There is no such thing as a fourth-person point of view.

15. d. In the second sentence of the passage, the writer says, "What have you been up to since abandoning New York for Los Angeles to mold young minds? Those students are lucky to have you." Although Candice has gotten a new dog since moving to Los Angeles, there is no evidence to support the idea this is why she moved. Therefore, choice **a** is incorrect.

16. b. If you were to substitute each answer choice for the word *relocation* in the sentence "Are you still digging the change of scenery since your relocation," the only one that would make sense is *move*.

17. c. That the writer saves the main point of his letter—his visit to Los Angeles—after small talk about how Candice is enjoying L.A. indicates it is written using order of importance structure.

18. a. The writer uses informal wording and slang in this passage, such as "Long time no see," "Are you still digging the change of scenery," "ha ha," and "we'd love to drop by."

19. b. The informal tone of the passage suggests it was written by a close friend.

20. c. Key words such as *awesome, fabulous,* and *adorable* indicate that the writer's message is intended to be a positive one.

11 ▶ Drawing Conclusions

So far, you have studied how writers use structure and language to convey meaning to readers. Now it's time to put your new knowledge to work. In this lesson, you will look at passages that don't have a clear main idea. You will have to look carefully for clues. Then you can read between the lines to see what the author means.

Finding an Implied Main Idea

When the main idea is **implied** (hinted at), there is not necessarily any topic sentence, so finding the main idea can be a challenge. But, you already know about the importance of word choice and style. You know how to look carefully at the text to find clues that will help you figure out the main idea.

To find an implied main idea, you have to find an idea that is general enough to cover the whole paragraph. Choices that are too specific and do not include all of the ideas in the paragraph obviously cannot be the main idea of the paragraph. You must ask yourself which idea is supported by all of the sentences in the paragraph. You also need to look for words and phrases that point to this main idea.

Practice Passage 1

Read the following paragraph actively. Look for clues that suggest the main idea. Pay close attention to language. Notice how the writer describes Mr. Wilson. Then answer the questions that follow. Check your answers at the end of the lesson on page 174.

> At 9:00 every morning, my boss, Mr. Wilson, invades the office. He marches straight to my desk and demands his reports. He spends the day looking over my shoulder and barking orders. And he blames every mistake—even if it's *his* fault—on me.

1. Which sentence states the main idea of the passage?
   a. It's a pleasure to work for Mr. Wilson.
   b. Mr. Wilson is a good manager.
   c. Mr. Wilson is brusque and unfair.
   d. Mr. Wilson is always on time.

2. How did you figure out the main idea? List some of the clues you found.

   _____

   _____

   _____

   _____

   _____

   _____

There are a lot of clues in this practice passage. They probably helped you determine the implied main idea. Perhaps you also noticed something else while studying the passage. What point of view does the writer use? She uses the first person. Her description is based on her personal experience and feelings. Thus, her view is subjective. An outsider might have a different opinion of Mr. Wilson.

Inference

Inferences are conclusions that we draw based on the clues the writer has given us or implied. When you draw inferences, you must look for the clues (word choice, details, and so on) that suggest a certain conclusion, attitude, or point of view. You have to read between the lines in order to make a judgment about what an author was implying in the passage.

Questions that ask you about the meaning of a vocabulary word in the passage and those that ask what the passage suggests or implies are different from detail or main idea questions. Inference questions can be the most difficult to answer because they require you to draw meaning from the text when that meaning is implied rather than directly stated.

A good way to test whether you have drawn an acceptable inference is to ask yourself what evidence you have to support your conclusion. If you can't find any, you probably have the wrong answer. You need to be sure that your inference is logical and based on something suggested or implied in the passage—not by an opinion that you, or others, hold. You need to base your conclusions on evidence—facts, details, and other information—not on random guesses.

Practice Passage 2

Solidify what you have learned about reading comprehension questions by writing similar test questions. After reading the passage on the next page, write one question for each of the following four question types that you will find on the Paragraph Comprehension portion of the ASVAB: fact or detail, main idea, inference, and vocabulary.

For or Against?—That Is the Question

Andy is the most unreasonable, pigheaded, subhuman life-form in the entire galaxy, and he makes me so angry I could scream! Of course, I love him like a brother. I sort of have to because he is my brother. More than that, he's my twin! That's right. Andy and Amy (that's me) have the same curly hair and dark eyes and equally stubborn temperaments. Though we may look alike, we usually take diametrically opposite positions on most issues. If I say, "day," you can count on Andy to say, "night."

Just this week, the big buzz in school was all about the PTA's proposal to adopt a school dress code. Every student would be required to wear a uniform. Uniforms! Can you imagine? Oh, they won't be military-style uniforms, but the clothes would be uniform in color. The dress style would be sort of loose and liberal.

Boys would have to wear white or blue button-down shirts, a school tie, blue or gray pants, and a navy blue blazer or cardigan sweater. Girls would wear white or blue blouses or sweaters, blue or gray pants or skirts, along with a navy blue blazer or cardigan sweater. Socks or tights could be black, gray, blue, or white. The teachers are divided: Some are in favor of the uniforms, others are opposed. The principal has asked the students to express their opinion by voting on the issue before the final is made decision, though Principal Diaz has the final word on the dress code.

I think a dress code is a good idea. The reason is simple. School is tough enough without worrying about looking cool every single day. The fact is, the less I have to decide in the morning, the better. I can't tell you how many mornings I look into my closet and just stare, unable to decide what to wear. Of course, there are other mornings when my room looks like a cyclone had hit it, with bits and pieces of a dozen different possible outfits on the bed, on the floor, or dangling from the lamps. I also wouldn't mind not seeing guys with oversized jeans and shirts so huge they would fit a sumo wrestler. And, I certainly would welcome not seeing kids showing off designer-labeled clothes.

Andy is appalled at my opinion. He says he can't believe that I would be willing to give up my all-American teenage birthright by dressing like—well, like a typical teenager. "Kanye West never wore a school uniform. Jay-Z wouldn't have been caught dead in a school uniform!" he declared. Andy was now on his soapbox. "When I am feeling political, I want to be able to wear clothes made of natural, undyed fibers, sewn or assembled in countries that do not pollute the environment or exploit child labor. If I have to wear a uniform, I won't feel like me!"

To which I replied, "So your personal heroes didn't wear school uniforms. Big deal! They went to high school about a million years ago! I feel sorry for you, brother dear. I had no idea that your ego is so fragile that it would be completely destroyed by gray or blue pants, a white or blue shirt, a tie, and a blazer."

That really made him angry. Then he said, "You're just mimicking what you hear that new music teacher saying."

"Is that so? Anyone who doesn't agree with you is automatically stupid. And that's the stupidest thing of all!" I said.

Fortunately, the bell rang ending the argument, and we went (thankfully) to our separate classes.

The vote for or against uniforms took place later that day. The results of the vote and the principal's decision will be announced next week. I wonder what it will be? I know how I voted, and I'm pretty sure I know how Andy voted.

How would you vote—for or against?

Questions

1. Detail Question: _____

_____

   a. _____

   b. _____

   c. _____

   d. _____

2. Main Idea Question: _____

   a. _____

   b. _____

   c. _____

   d. _____

3. Inference Question: _____

_____

   a. _____

   b. _____

   c. _____

   d. _____

4. Vocabulary question: _____

_____

   a. _____

   b. _____

   c. _____

   d. _____

Implied Information

Often writers have thoughts that they don't want to say directly. So, they use **suggestion** to get their ideas across. They suggest things in many ways. Some clues are action clues—what people said and did. Clues can also come in the form of details, word choice, and style. For example, look at the following passage.

Dennis was scared. His knees were weak. He looked down. The water was 20 feet below. He looked up again, quickly. He tried to think of something else. He tried to reassure himself. "It's only 20 feet!" he said aloud. But that only made it sound worse. Twenty feet! He felt dizzy and hot.

The writer could have said, "Dennis was scared. He was afraid of heights." Instead the writer *suggests* this information. The author *shows* you how Dennis feels. You see what he thinks and feels. Through these details, you can guess that Dennis is up somewhere high, like a cliff, a ledge, or a bridge, and that he is afraid of heights. The repetition of "20 feet" is another clue, so is the sentence structure. Notice that the sentences are short and choppy. In fact, they sound a little panicky. This helps show how Dennis felt.

Practice Passage 3

Here is an excerpt from a short story. Read the passage carefully. Then answer the questions that follow.

Anne tensed when she heard the front door open. She waited in the kitchen near the dirty dishes in the sink. She knew her neat-freak roommate, Chandra, would look there first. Taking a deep breath, Anne thought about what she would say to her. She waited.

A moment later, Chandra stepped into the kitchen. Her face dropped immediately when she saw the dishes piled high in the sink. Pointing angrily at them, Chandra asked, "What are those filthy things still doing in the sink?"

"Uh, I haven't gotten to them yet," Anne replied. She tried to remain calm.

Chandra yelled, "How many times have I told you that I like to have my house clean at all times?"

"Well, you say that every time I leave any kind of mess, no matter how small. You have to understand that I have an important exam this week and can't spend all my free time cleaning," Anne replied.

"Then you should hire a maid to do it for you!" shouted Chandra.

Anne could only walk out of the room in response. She knew Chandra was not the perfect roommate, but right now, Anne was more worried about her exam.

1. Why does Chandra get mad?
a. because Anne didn't greet her at the door
b. because she had a bad day
c. because Anne didn't do the dishes
d. because Anne is lazy

2. Why didn't Anne do the dishes?
a. because she just returned home
b. because she wanted to start a fight
c. because she isn't a maid
d. because she had to study

3. Why is Anne upset with Chandra?
a. because Chandra pays less rent than Anne
b. because Chandra wants to hire a maid
c. because Chandra never cleans up
d. because Chandra expects Anne to clean up even small messes immediately

Writers often suggest ideas and other information. You have to read between the lines to identify them. Look for clues in the action. What do people say and do? Look for more clues in details, word choice, and style. Use your sense of logic to answer questions and think about what the clues mean.

Review Practice

Read the passages and answer the questions. Then check your answers at the end of the lesson on page 175.

PARAGRAPH 1

Dealing with irritable patients is a great challenge for healthcare workers. It is critical that you do not lose your patience when confronted by such a patient. When handling irate patients, remember that they are not angry with you; they are simply projecting their anger at something else onto you. If you respond to these patients as irritably as they act with you, you will only increase their hostility, making it much more difficult to give them proper treatment. The best thing to do is to remain calm, and ignore any imprecations patients may hurl your way. Such patients may be irrational and may not realize what they are saying. Often, these patients will purposely try to anger you to get some reaction out of you. If you react to this behavior with anger, they win by getting your attention, but you both lose because the patient is less likely to get proper care.

1. The word *irate* as it is used in the passage most nearly means
a. irregular.
b. cheerful.
c. ill tempered.
d. lazy.

2. The passage suggests that healthcare workers
a. easily lose control of their emotions.
b. are better off not talking to their patients.
c. must be careful when dealing with irate patients because the patients may sue the hospital.
d. may provide inadequate treatment if they become angry at patients.

3. An *imprecation* is most likely
   a. an object.
   b. a curse.
   c. a joke.
   d. a medication.

4. Which of the following best expresses the writer's views about irate patients?
   a. Some irate patients just want attention.
   b. Irate patients are always miserable.
   c. Irate patients should be made to wait for treatment.
   d. Managing irate patients is the key to a successful career.

PARAGRAPH 2

Both year-round school and regular school schedules are found throughout the United States. With year-round school schedules, students attend classes for nine weeks, and then have three weeks of vacation. This continues all year long. The regular school schedule requires students to attend classes from September to June, with a three-month summer vacation at the end of the year. This schedule began because farmers needed their children at home to help with crops during the summer. Today, most people work in businesses and offices. Year-round school is easier for parents who work in businesses and don't have the summer to be with their children. While educational systems around the world have modified their schedules to keep up with their population, others still use the old agrarian calendar.

5. The writer suggests that
   a. the regular school schedule is preferred by parents who have to work through the summer.
   b. the United States places too much of an emphasis on education.
   c. year-round school is better than the regular school schedule.
   d. establishing a school schedule is extremely difficult.

6. Which point of view does the writer use in this passage?
   a. first person
   b. second person
   c. third person
   d. fourth person

7. The regular school schedule was first established because
   a. students preferred it to the year-round schedule.
   b. teachers wanted to have their summers off from work.
   c. parents liked to spend their summers with their children.
   d. farmers needed their children to help with their crops during the summer.

8. The word *modified* as it is used in the passage nearly means
   a. changed.
   b. continued.
   c. deleted.
   d. strengthened.

PARAGRAPH 3

In her lecture "Keeping Your Heart Healthy," Dr. Miranda Woodhouse challenged Americans to join her in the fight to reduce the risks of heart disease. Her plan includes four basic strategies meant to increase public awareness and prevent heart disease. The following is a brief outline of each of the four strategies.

Eating a healthy diet that contains nine full servings of fruits and vegetables each day can help lower your cholesterol levels. More fruits and vegetables means less dairy and meat, which, in turn, means less cholesterol-boosting saturated fat. Do not smoke. Cigarette smoking increases the risk of heart disease, and when it is combined with other factors, that risk is even greater. Smoking increases blood pressure, increases the tendency for blood to clot, decreases good cholesterol, and decreases tolerance for exercise. Ask about your blood pressure and cholesterol levels at every medical appointment or checkup. Because there are often no symptoms, many people don't even know that they have high blood pressure. This is extremely dangerous since uncontrolled high blood pressure can lead to heart attack, kidney failure, and stroke. Finally, relax and be happy. Studies show that being constantly incensed or depressed can increase your risk of heart disease so you should take a deep breath, smile, and focus on the positive things in life.

9. Which sentence states the main idea of this passage?
   a. "Keeping Your Heart Healthy" outlines four basic strategies for increasing public awareness about and preventing heart disease.
   b. Every person should eat nine full servings of fruits and vegetables each day to help lower their cholesterol levels.
   c. You should not smoke because cigarettes increase the risk of heart disease.
   d. Being aware of your blood pressure level to help avoid heart attack, kidney failure, and stroke.

10. The word *incensed* as it is used in the passage nearly means
    a. glad.
    b. angry.
    c. calm.
    d. suspended.

11. The passage suggests that
    a. milk is essential to good health.
    b. a heart attack is worse than kidney failure.
    c. deep breathing will ensure a healthy heart.
    d. meat contains saturated-fat.

12. Which point of view does the writer use in this passage?
    a. first person
    b. second person
    c. third person
    d. fourth person

PARAGRAPH 4

Police officers must read suspects their Miranda rights upon taking them into custody. Before being interrogated, suspects must know that they have the right to remain silent to avoid incriminating themselves. When a suspect who is merely being questioned incriminates himself, he might later claim to have been in custody and seek to have the case dismissed on the grounds of not having been apprised of his Miranda rights. In such cases, a judge must make a determination as to whether or not a reasonable person would have believed himself to have been in custody, based on certain criteria. The judge must ascertain whether the suspect was questioned in a threatening manner (threatening could mean that the suspect was seated while both officers remained standing). Officers must be aware of these criteria and take care not to give suspects grounds for later claiming they believed them-selves to be in custody. If the suspect success-fully argues his belief, the case would have to be dismissed.

13. The word *apprised* as it is used in the passage nearly means
  a. controlled.
  b. listened.
  c. informed.
  d. studied.

14. Which of the following is the topic sentence of this passage?
  a. Police officers must read suspects their Miranda rights upon taking them into custody.
  b. In such cases, a judge must make a determination as to whether or not a reasonable person would have believed himself to have been in custody, based on certain criteria.
  c. Officers must be aware of these criteria and take care not to give suspects grounds for later claiming they believed themselves to be in custody.
  d. If the suspect successfully argues his belief, the case would have to be dismissed.

15. Based on information in the passage, you can infer that a suspect who has been questioned in a threatening manner
  a. will sue the police department.
  b. might believe himself to be in custody.
  c. does not have to be read his Miranda rights.
  d. has committed a terrible crime.

16. When must suspects be told that they have the right to remain silent?
  a. before being interrogated
  b. after being interrogated
  c. while being interrogated
  d. both **a** and **b**

PARAGRAPH 5

It is clear that the United States is a nation that needs to eat healthier and slim down. A step in the right direction would be for school cafeterias to provide healthy, low-fat lunch options for students.

School cafeterias need to make money. So, in an effort to provide food that is appetizing to young people, their menus often mimic fast-food menus, serving items such as burgers, pizza, hot dogs, and fried chicken. While these high-protein foods do provide some nutritional value, they are relatively high in fat.

According to nutritionist Elizabeth Warner, many of the lunch selections currently offered by school cafeterias could be made healthier with a few simple and inexpensive substitutions. "Veggie burgers offered alongside beef burgers would be a positive addition," says Warner. "A salad bar would also serve the purpose of providing a healthy and satisfying meal. And grilled chicken sandwiches, which can be very tasty, would be a far better option than fried chicken. Additionally, the beverage case should be stocked with containers of low-fat milk."

17. The word *appetizing* as it is used in the passage most nearly means
  a. appealing.
  b. uninteresting.
  c. unusual.
  d. awful.

18. Which of the following details from the passage is a fact?

   a. a salad is a satisfying meal

   b. burgers, pizza, hot dogs, and fried chicken provide some nutritional value

   c. the lunch substitutions Elizabeth Warner suggests are inexpensive

   d. grilled chicken sandwiches can be very tasty

19. Which of the following best expresses the writer's views of young Americans?

   a. Too many of them are unhealthy and overweight.

   b. They would rather eat salads than hamburgers.

   c. Too many of them cannot afford school lunches.

   d. They would buy more school lunches if cafeterias offered low-fat milk.

20. Which of the following best states the main idea of this passage?

   a. All school cafeterias throughout the United States need to eliminate burgers, pizza, hot dogs, and fried chicken from their menus.

   b. Nutritionist Elizabeth Warner is an expert on nutrition and has excellent ideas about how to improve the health of Americans.

   c. The United States would be a healthier, slimmer country if school cafeterias offered low-fat lunches.

   d. School cafeterias make their menus mimic fast-food menus in order to sell more food to young people.

By now, you should know what you need to pass the Paragraph Comprehension subtest. If you still want more practice, try these additional resources:

- *Reading Comprehension Success in 20 Minutes a Day*, 3rd Ed. (LearningExpress)
- *501 Reading Comprehension Questions*, 3rd Ed. (LearningExpress)

Answers

Practice 1

1. **c.** The main idea is that Mr. Wilson is brusque and unfair.

2. There are lots of clues in the passage. First, the writer uses the word "invades." This word suggests that Mr. Wilson is trying to take over something that isn't his. It suggests that he isn't wanted. Second, Mr. Wilson spends the day "barking orders." He doesn't ask. He doesn't consider feelings. He just demands that things get done. Furthermore, the last sentence shows you that Wilson is unfair—*his* mistakes get blamed on someone else.

Practice 2

Here is one question of each type based on the passage. Your questions may be different, but these will give you an idea of the kinds of questions that could be asked.

1. Detail question: Amy and Andy fight because
   a. neither one is able to convince the other to change his or her point of view.
   b. they are twins.
   c. they always take the opposite view on issues.
   d. they don't like each other.

2. Main idea question: Which of the following is the best statement of Andy's position on the issue presented in the story?
   a. School clothing should reflect parents' values.
   b. Wearing school uniforms means one less decision every morning.
   c. How one dresses should be an expression of one's personality.
   d. Teenagers should never follow the latest fashion trends.

3. Inference question: Amy's position on school uniforms is most likely based on
   a. logical conclusions drawn from her own observation and personal experience.
   b. an emotional response to what she has been told by people in authority.
   c. her preference for designer-labeled clothes.
   d. not liking anything her brother likes.

4. Vocabulary question: Read the following sentences from the story:
   Andy is <u>appalled</u> at my opinion. He says he can't believe that I would be willing to give up my all-American teenage birthright by dressing like— well, like a typical teenager.
   As it is used in these sentences, what does *appalled at* mean?
   a. angry
   b. in denial
   c. supportive of
   d. horrified by

Practice 3

1. **c.** Chandra is a neat freak and expects Anne to clean up messes immediately, even if Anne is preparing for an important exam.

2. **d.** Anne says that she has an important exam this week, which implies that she has to study. The other choices are not implied in the story.

3. **d.** Anne is upset because Chandra is not reasonable in her expectations of cleanliness. Chandra expects Anne to keep the apartment spotless no matter what.

Review Practice

1. c. This is a vocabulary question. Irate means *ill-tempered*. It should be clear that choice **b**, *cheerful*, is not the answer; dealing with happy patients is normally not "a great challenge." Patients that are choice **a**, *irregular*, or choice **d**, *lazy*, may be a challenge in their own way, but they aren't likely to rouse healthcare workers to anger. In addition, the passage explains that irate patients are not "angry at you," and irate is used as a synonym for *irritable*, which describes the patients in the first sentence.

2. d. This is an inference question, as the phrase "the passage suggests" might have told you. The idea that angry healthcare workers might give inadequate treatment is implied by the passage as a whole, which seems to be an attempt to prevent angry reactions to irate patients. Furthermore, the last sentence in particular makes this inference possible: "If you react to this behavior with anger . . . you both lose because the patient is less likely to get proper care." Choice **c** is not correct, because while it may be true that some irate patients have sued hospitals in the past, there is no mention of lawsuits anywhere in this passage. Likewise, choice **b** is incorrect; the passage does suggest ignoring patients' insults, but it does not recommend not talking to patients—it simply recommends not talking angrily. And while it may be true that some healthcare workers may lose control of their emotions, the passage does not provide any facts or details to support choice **a**, that they "easily lose control." Watch out for key words like *easily* that may distort the meaning of the passage.

3. b. If you didn't know what an imprecation is, the context should reveal that it's something you can ignore, so neither choice **a**, an *object*, nor choice **d**, a *medication*, is a likely answer. Furthermore, choice **c** is not likely either, since an irate patient is not likely to be making jokes.

4. a. The writer seems to believe that some irate patients just want attention, as is suggested when the writer says, "Often these patients will purposely try to anger you to get some reaction out of you. If you react to this behavior with anger, they win by getting your attention." It should be clear that choice **b** cannot be the answer because it includes an absolute: "Irate patients are always miserable." Perhaps some of the patients are often miserable, but an absolute like *always* is wrong. Besides, this passage refers to patients who may be irate in the hospital, but we have no indication of what these patients are like at other times, and miserable and irate are not exactly the same thing. Choice **c** is also incorrect because the purpose of the passage is to ensure that patients receive "proper treatment" and that irate patients are not discriminated against because of their behavior. Thus, "irate patients should be made to wait for treatment" is not a logical answer. Finally, choice **d** cannot be correct because, although it may be true, there is no discussion of career advancement in the passage.

5. c. The only preference the writer expresses in this passage is when she writes, "Year-round school is easier for parents who work in businesses and don't have the summer to be with their children." Because her statement is a positive one about year-round school schedules, you can infer that she prefers such schedule to the regular school schedule.

6. c. The writer does not use personal pronouns, such as *I*, *me*, and *mine*, so you can eliminate first person, **a**. The writer does not use the second person pronoun *you*, either, so you can eliminate choice **b**, as well. Since there is no such thing as fourth-person point of view, **d**, the only possible correct answer choice is third person, **c**.

7. d. Choice **d** is directly stated in the fifth sentence of the passage. Choices **a**, **b**, and **c** are not suggested anywhere in the passage.

8. a. If you didn't know what *modified* means, the context should help you to figure out its definition. The writer contrasts the statement that "some educational systems have modified their schedules," with the statement that "others still use the old agrarian calendar." This contrast should lead you to understand that *modified* is the opposite of *still* doing something, which is to *change*. Choices **b**, **c**, and **d** do not make sense in this context.

9. a. The passage's main purpose is to describe the four strategies for heart health in Dr. Woodhouse's lecture "Keeping Your Heart Healthy," **a**. Choices **b**, **c**, and **d** are just details that support this main idea.

10. b. The passage states the importance of being relaxed and happy before stating the risk of being *incensed*. Therefore, you can infer that being *incensed* is unlike being relaxed or happy and that the best answer choice is *angry*, **b**. Since *glad*, **a**, is a synonym of happy and *calm*, **c**, is a synonym of relaxed, you can eliminate these answer choices. You can also eliminate *suspended*, **d**, because that word does not make any sense in the context in which *incensed* is used.

11. d. Although the writer does not directly state "meat contains saturated fat," he does state that eating less meat "means less cholesterol-boosting saturated fat," so you can infer that choice **d** is correct. Choice **a** is wrong because the writer suggests milk contains dangerous saturated fat, as well. The writer states that both heart attacks and kidney failure are "extremely dangerous" conditions, and does not suggest that one is worse than the other. Therefore, there is no evidence to infer that choice **b** is correct. Although the writer recommends deep-breathing as a way to stay relaxed and happy, which reduces the risk of heart problems, he does not suggest that this will ensure a healthy heart. The writer describes too many other factors for keeping a heart healthy to infer that choice **c** is correct.

12. b. The writer addresses the reader directly by using the second-person pronouns *you* and *your*.

13. c. In the passage, a suspect is *apprised* of his rights. Saying that someone has been "controlled of his Miranda rights" does not make sense, so choice **a** is incorrect. One also would not be "listened of his Miranda rights," which eliminates choice **b**. To be "studied apprised of his Miranda rights" does not make sense either, so choice **d** is wrong, as well. However, a suspect could be "informed of his Miranda rights," so choice **c** is the only possible correct answer.

14. a. The topic of the passage is the fact that police officers must read suspects their Miranda rights. Choices **b**, **c**, and **d** go into deeper detail about this topic without stating the overall topic in a clear manner.

15. b. After stating that a judge "must make a determination as to whether or not a reasonable person would have believed himself to have been in custody," the writer states "The judge must ascertain whether the suspect was questioned in a threatening manner." Because this second idea follows the one about determining whether or not someone might believe himself to be in custody immediately, you can infer that the two ideas are related. Therefore, choice **b** is the one that makes the most sense. Suing the police department is never mentioned in the passage, so there is no evidence to support choice **a**. All suspects have to be read their Miranda rights, so choice **c** is wrong, too. The actions of police who question a suspect in a threatening manner do not guarantee that the suspect has committed the crime. Therefore, choice **d** is incorrect.

16. a. The second sentence of the passage directly states "Before being interrogated, suspects must know that they have the right to remain silent to avoid incriminating themselves." The passage never states nor suggests that these rights must also be read to the suspect after interrogation, so choice **d** is incorrect.

17. a. The context provides import clues that should help you choose the correct answer. School cafeterias would not want to provide food that young people do not like, so any negative answer choices can be eliminated. The cafeteria would not sell much food if that food was *uninteresting*, **b**, or *awful* **d**. Perhaps some young people might appreciate food that is *unusual*, **c**, but a more sensible choice is *appealing*, **a**.

18. b. Choice **b** is the only inarguable fact among the answer choices. Not everyone might agree that a salad is a satisfying meal, so choice **a** is an opinion, not a fact. Whether or not something is expensive is always a matter of opinion, so you can eliminate choice **c**. The tastiness of a grilled chicken sandwich is also a matter of opinion. Therefore, choice **d** is incorrect.

19. a. The writer begins the passage by stating that "It is clear that the United States is a nation that needs to eat healthier and slim down." If people need to "eat healthier and slim down," one can reasonably infer that such people are "unhealthy and overweight," choice **a**. The writer suggests that young people in America like to eat hamburgers, and says nothing about their enjoyment of salads. Therefore, there is no evidence to support the inference that Americans "would rather eat salads than hamburgers," choice **b**. There is no evidence to support choices **c** and **d** either.

20. c. The passage is mainly about how school cafeteria lunch menus should be changed to offer lunch options that will improve the health and weight of Americans, choice **c**. The writer never makes a sweeping statement about eliminating certain foods from school lunch menus, so choice **a** is incorrect. Elizabeth Warner is not introduced until the third and final paragraph of the passage, so she can't be the main focus of the overall passage. Therefore, choice **b** is incorrect. Choice **d** is a single detail in the passage and not the main idea.

4

Vocabulary for the Word Knowledge Subtest

Effective communication skills—including vocabulary and spelling—are essential to everything you do. A good vocabulary increases your ability to understand reading material and express yourself in both speaking and writing. Without a broad vocabulary, your ability to learn is limited. The good news is that vocabulary can be developed with practice.

The Word Knowledge portion of the ASVAB is basically a vocabulary test. Combined with the Paragraph Comprehension score, Word Knowledge helps make up your Verbal Equivalent score—it's one of the all-important subtests that determine whether you will be allowed to enlist. Your ability to understand your training materials depends in part on your reading comprehension and vocabulary skills

There are two different kinds of questions on the Word Knowledge subtest:

1. **Synonyms:** Identifying words that mean the same as the given words.
2. **Context:** Determining the meaning of a word or phrase by noting how it is used in a sentence or paragraph.

You already have had some practice identifying the meanings of words by examining their context in Section 3: Reading Comprehension for the Paragraph Comprehension subtest. You will get some more practice in this section, and you will also learn about synonyms and word parts, including word roots, prefixes, and suffixes. These lessons will help you improve and develop your vocabulary skills, teaching you how to break down words into parts you recognize so that you can decipher their meanings. Remember, you are not penalized for guessing on the ASVAB, so these methods will help you improve your guessing power when you encounter unknown words on the Word Knowledge subtest.

There are three ways we learn vocabulary:

- from the **sound** of words
- from the **structure** of words
- from the **context**; how the word is used

Learning words is therefore a three-step process.

1. Ask yourself, "Does this word **sound** like anything I've ever heard?"
   If not, ask
2. "Does any part of the word **look** familiar?"
   If not, then ask
3. "How is this word **used** in the sentence I read or heard?"

Try asking yourself this sequence of questions with each unfamiliar word you encounter. As you learn more about how vocabulary works, you will find that you already know some of the words, and you can use your new knowledge to figure out the others.

12▶ Word Parts

Learning word parts is valuable because they clue you into other words in the same family. If you encounter words you don't know on the ASVAB, don't panic. You've practiced reading in context and you're about to acquire another set of tools to help you establish meaning. Plus, many of them you already know by sight! **Roots**, **prefixes**, and **suffixes** are word elements that inpart shared characteristics.

English words share many traits because they descend from a long line of intermingled Indo-European languages. Many English words come from Greek and Latin, and learning word parts gives you access to whole groups of words once you know a few language families.

You may already know a given root, prefix, or suffix that can guide you in determining the meaning of an unfamiliar word. For example, you may know that the root *hydro* suggests water. Therefore, if you came across the word *hydrotherapy*, you would figure it is a treatment that uses water.

If you don't know the part by itself, you may recognize it from a word you know. By association, then, you link the known meaning to that of an unfamiliar word. For example, you know that a fire hydrant stores water. Therefore, when you read (*hydrotherapy*), you can recognize the (*hyd*) root and deduce the meaning.

Roots

Roots are the pieces of words that carry direct meaning. Generally, roots of English words are derived from ancient Greek and Latin words. Because so many English words have their source in certain recurring roots, knowing some of the most commonly used ones gives you access to the meaning of many words at once. When you combine your knowledge of roots with your knowledge of **prefixes** and **suffixes**—the small parts of words that go at the beginning or end of words to change their meanings—you have the tools to decipher the meanings of words from their structure.

Definitions and Roots

Following are the definitions and roots of some words, along with other words that share their roots.

agoraphobic: fear of open spaces (*phobe* = fear)
  phobia, claustrophobia, xenophobia

ant**agon**ize: to struggle against (*agon* = struggle)
  protagonist, agony, agonize

as**simil**ate: to fit in (*simul* = copy)
  similar, simile, facsimile, simulate

at**trib**ute a special quality (*trib* = to give)
  tributary, contribution, tribunal

audible: (*aud* = hear) able to be heard
  audition, audience, auditorium

belligerent: warlike (*bell* = war)
  bellicose, antebellum

benevolent: kind (*ben* = good)
  benefactor, beneficiary, benign, benediction

biodegradable: able to be broken down by living things (*bio* = life)
  bionic, biology, antibiotic

chronic: occurring over time (*chron* = time)
  chronological, chronometer, chronicle

con**spic**uous: highly visible (*spic, spec* = see)
  spectacle, spectator, inspection, introspection

contradict: the act or state of disagreeing (*contra* = against, *dict* = say)
  contrary, contrast, dictate, dictionary, interdict, dictation

credence: belief, believability (*cred* = believe)
  creed, credulous, credit, incredible

demographic: a measurement of populations (*demo* = people)
  democracy, demagogue

evident: obvious (*vid* = see)
  video, evidence, visible, provident

fidelity: faithfulness (*fid* = faith)
  fiduciary, infidel, infidelity

fluctuate: to rise and fall (*flux, flu* = to flow)
  fluid, fluidity, superfluous, influx

gregarious: sociable (*greg* = crowd, herd)
  egregious

im**ped**iment: a barrier or hindrance (*ped, pod* = foot)
  pedestal, pedestrian, pediment

in**cis**ive: penetrating, clear cut (*cis* = to cut)
  incision, precise, scissors

in**cog**nito: unrecognizable (*cog, gno* = to know)
  diagnosis, recognize, cognition, cognitive

in**duc**ement: leading to an action (*duc* = to lead)
  induction, reduction, introduction, reduce

in**fer**ence: guess or surmise (*fer* = bear or carry)
  transfer, refer, reference, interfere

inter**rog**ate: to question (*rog* = to ask)
  surrogate, derogatory, arrogant

loquacious: talkative (*loq* = speak)
  eloquent, soliloquy

mediocre: of medium quality, (*med* = middle)
  median, intermediate, mediator

nominal: in name only (*nom, nym* = name)
  nominate, nomenclature, synonym, anonymous

pathos: feeling of sympathy or pity (*path* = feeling)
  pathetic, empathy, sympathy, apathy

philanthropy: giving generously to worthy causes
(*phil* = love)
philosophy, Philadelphia, bibliophile

pre**ced**ent: a prior ruling or experience (*ced* = go)
intercede, procedure, succeed

pro**tract**ed: dragged out (*tract* = draw, pull)
tractor, distracted, attraction, subtracted

re**cap**itulate: to review in detail (*cap* = head)
capital, caption, captain, decapitate

re**ject**ed: sent back (*ject* = to throw or send)
subject, dejected, interjected, projectile

re**mit**tance: to send back (*mit, mis* = to send)
submit, commission, permission

sophisticated: having knowledge (*soph* = wisdom)
sophomore, sophistry, philosopher

tangential: touching slightly (*tang, tac, tig* =
touch)
tangent, tactical, tactile, contiguous

tenacious: unwilling to let go (*ten, tain* = hold)
tenacity, contain, tenable

urbane: polished, sophisticated (*urb* = city)
urban, suburban, urbanite

verify: to establish as truth (*ver* = truth)
verity, veritable, veracious, aver

vivacious: lively in manner (*viv, vit* = life)
vivid, vital

Practice 1

Fill in the blanks with words from the previous list. Check your answers at the end of the lesson on page 192.

1. His remarks were _____ and cut right to the heart of the subject.

2. It doesn't pay to _____ the opinions of those who are in authority.

3. His _____ arose from his deep desire to help those less fortunate than himself.

4. The store demanded the _____ of the required payment to clear the debt.

5. One of her best _____ is her clear-eyed wisdom.

6. Over the years, people from many countries have come to _____ into American life.

7. Public works projects in the 1930s set a _____ for social legislation for the next 60 years.

8. After the game, the commentators continued to _____ the key plays for those who had been unable to watch.

9. By wearing a wig and glasses, Shana believed she was going _____.

10. It was the principal's duty to _____ the students and find out who was responsible for the vandalism.

11. The _____ time it took to receive my test results was torturous.

12. The story about the homeless man stirred strong feelings of _____ in me.

13. He tends to dominate conversations because he is _____.

14. She likes to stay indoors because she is severely _____.

15. Compared to the high-quality book I read last week, this one is unfortunately _____.

16. Although she is the one who made the most important decisions in our club, he is our _____ president.

17. Plastic lasts forever because it is not _____.

18. She prefers _____ humor to silly, childish jokes.

19. The police had to _____ whether or not the suspect was actually at home last Sunday night.

20. The manager _____ my job application because I failed to include any references on it.

Practice 2

Answer the following with words from the previous list. Check your answers at the end of the lesson on page 192.

1. Which word stems from a root that means *good*? _____

2. Which word stems from a root that relates to *hearing*? _____

3. Which word stems from a root that means *to cut*? _____

4. Which word stems from a root that means to *bear* or *carry*? _____

5. Which word stems from a root than means a *fear*? _____

6. Which word stems from a root that means *crowd*? _____.

7. Which word stems from a root that suggests *touching*? _____

8. Which word stems from a root that means *belief*? _____

9. Which word stems from a root that suggests *to lead*? _____

10. Which word stems from a root that means *middle*? _____

11. Which word stems from a root that means *war*? _____

12. Which word stems from a root that means *faith*? _____

13. Which word stems from a root that means *people*? _____

14. Which word stems from a root that means *go*? _____

15. Which word stems from a root that means *life*? _____

16. Which word stems from a root that relates to *the city*? _____

17. Which word stems from a root that means *to hold*? _____

18. Which word stems from a root that means *love*? _____

19. Which word stems from a root that means *to give*? _____

20. Which word stems from a root that means *to struggle*? _____

Prefixes

Prefixes are word parts at the beginning of a root word that alter to the word's meaning in some way. They have different forms and may fundamentally change the meaning of a root word—making it an opposite, for example. Or, a prefix may only remotely affect meaning. The point of working with prefixes is not to memorize a batch of disconnected word parts but to become familiar with the most common examples. Then you may be able to figure out how a word's meaning may have been affected by a prefix.

For example, the Latin root *vert* means to turn. Look at what happens when you add different prefixes in front of that root:

- *con* (with or together) + *vert* = convert (think turn together—transform)
  She wanted to **convert** the old barn into a studio.
- *di* (two) + *vert* = divert (turn aside)
  He wanted to **divert** attention from the spectacle.
- *ex* (out of, away from) + *vert* = extrovert (an outgoing individual)
  He was an **extrovert** who was the life of every party.
- *in* (opposite) + *vert* = invert (turn over)
  He **inverted** the saucer over the cup.
- *intro* (inside) + *vert* = introvert (an inwardly directed person)
  She was an **introvert** who generally shied away from company.
- *re* (back or again) + *vert* = revert (turn back)
  She **reverted** to speaking Spanish with her grandmother.

Definitions and Prefixes

Following are some words with their prefixes and meanings, as well as other words that use the prefix.

antecedents: something that comes before, especially ancestors (*ante* = before)
antenatal, antebellum, anteroom

antipathy: hatred, feelings against (*anti* = against)
antiwar, antibiotic, antidote

circumvent: to get around (*circum, circ* = around)
circumscribe, circulate, circumference

consensus: agreement on a course of action (*con* = with, together)
congress, convivial, congregate

controversy: public dispute (*contr* = against)
contrast, contrary

decimate: to destroy or kill a large portion of something (*dec* = ten)

decimal, decibel

demote: to lower in grade or position (*de* = down, away from)

decline, deflate

disinterested: not having selfish interest in (not the same as uninterested) (*dis* = not, opposite of)

disappointed, disabled, disqualified

euphemism: a more pleasant term for something distasteful (*eu* = good, well)

euphonious, eugenic, eulogy

exorbitant: excessive (literally, out of orbit) (*ex* = out of, away from)

exhume, extort, exhale, export

illegible: not readable (*il* = not, opposite)

illegal, illegitimate, illicit

intermittent: occurring from time to time, occasional (*inter* = between)

intermediate, interlude, intermission

malevolent: cruel, evil (*mal* = bad)

malady, malefactor, malice, malignant

precursor: a form that precedes a current model (*pre* = before)

premeditate, premature, prevent, preview

prognosis: opinion about the future state of something (*pro* = before)

provide, professional, produce

retrospect: hindsight (*retro* = back, again)

retroactive, retrograde

subordinate: ower in rank(*sub* = under) l

subterranean, substrate, subscription

synthesis: the combination of many things into one (*syn, sym* = with or together)

synthetic, symphony, symbiotic

transcend: to go beyond (*trans* = across)

transfer, transportation, transatlantic

trivial: unimportant (*tri* = three)

tripod, triangle, triennial

Note that some words translate very neatly into their components:

- Antipathy literally means feelings against (*anti* = against, *path* = feelings).
- Retrospect literally means looking back (*retro* = back, *spect* = to look or see).

But beware, in some cases, the connection between the meaning of the prefix and the meaning of the word is much less obvious. For instance, the word *trivial* comes from the place where, in ancient times, the three (**tri**) caravan routes (or **via**, "way") met and people exchanged gossip and bits of information. Today we use trivial to refer to small items of information that are relatively unimportant.

Practice 3

Complete each of the following sentences with a word from the previous list. In some cases you may have to change the tense of a word as it appears in the list. Check your answers at the end of the lesson on page 192.

1. The manager threatened to _____ the head cashier if he came to work late one more time.

2. The union leaders finally reached a(n) _____ over the salary package.

3. The Civil War _____ both the land and the population of the South.

4. Because the signature was _____, no one knew who wrote the letter.

5. The choice had to be made by a(n) _____ person who would not benefit from the outcome.

6. Using too many _____ to avoid distasteful subjects weakens our ability to express ourselves clearly.

7. The boy always found a way to _____ authority and get his own way.

8. The photography exhibition showed the _____ between images and color.

9. Many people focus on the _____ things in life and ignore the more important matters.

10. Every January, the president of the club offers her _____ on the coming year.

11. I set the windshield wipers to _____ so they would not run constantly.

12. My grandparents are _____ of my parents.

13. The villain in the novel had completely _____ intentions.

14. Matters that affect the entire world _____ ones personal problems.

15. The silent film was a _____ to the modern sound film.

16. The private was _____ to his sergeant in the army.

17. There is a huge _____ about whether or not a highway should be built through that forest.

18. In _____, I realize I should have been more careful about where I parked my car.

19. The environmentalists had _____ for anyone who would pollute the ocean.

20. She decided to start taking the bus rather than pay the _____ gas prices to fill up her car.

Practice 4

Mark the following statements as true or false according to the meaning of the underlined word. Check your answers at the end of the lesson on page 192.

_____ **1.** Most people would want to pay an <u>exorbitant</u> sum for a theater ticket.

_____ **2.** An <u>intermittent</u> action does not happen once.

_____ **3.** A <u>retrospective</u> exhibition shows only recent works by an artist.

_____ **4.** A <u>disinterested</u> person is bored with her work.

_____ **5.** To <u>circumvent</u> an issue is to address it directly.

_____ **6.** A <u>malevolent</u> character in a movie is usually the hero.

_____ **7.** One's children are one's <u>antecedents</u>.

_____ **8.** The bicycle is a <u>precursor</u> to a motorcycle.

_____ **9.** If you have <u>antipathy</u> toward someone, you have little or no feeling at all.

_____ **10.** We use <u>euphemisms</u> when we want to soften the meaning of what we say.

_____ **11.** A major fire is capable of <u>decimating</u> a forest.

_____ **12.** Two parties are in complete disagreement when they reach a <u>consensus</u>.

_____ **13.** An <u>illegible</u> note is neatly and clearly written.

_____ **14.** A perfect essay displays a <u>synthesis</u> of style and ideas.

_____ **15.** A <u>prognosis</u> relates to a future matter.

_____ **16.** Your <u>subordinate</u> gives you orders.

_____ **17.** To think about something in <u>retrospect</u> is to think about something from the past.

_____ **18.** A boss would <u>demote</u> her best employee.

_____ **19.** Nobody wants to be ruled by a <u>malevolent</u> leader.

_____ **20.** A <u>trivial</u> thing is very important.

Suffixes

Words are divided into something called parts of speech—primarily nouns (people, places, and things), verbs (action or existence words), and adjectives and adverbs (words which describe other words). **Suffixes** are word endings that often change the word's part of speech.

Thus, adding a suffix often changes the function of the word in a sentence without fundamentally changing the word's meaning. You can think of a suffix as the hat a word wears for a particular job in the sentence.

For example, take the word *devote*, meaning to dedicate time to the care of someone or something. Suffixes change the way the word works in a sentence.

- As a **verb**, it appears as it is:

  I will *devote* my time to my family.
- As a **noun**, it takes the *-tion* suffix and becomes devotion:

  His *devotion* to his family was well known.
- As an **adjective** modifying a noun, it takes the *-ed* suffix:

  He is a *devoted* family man.
- As an **adverb** modifying a verb, it takes the *-ly* suffix:

  He *devotedly* served his family for many years.

The table that follows shows commonly used suffixes. They are divided into the parts of speech they suggest for the words. Other words that contain those suffixes are listed. In the last column, you can add at least one other word you already know that uses the same suffix.

SUFFIX	MEANING	EXAMPLES	YOUR EXAMPLE
Noun Endings			
-tion	act or state of	retraction, contraction	
-ment	quality of	deportment, impediment	
-ian	one who is or does, relating to	tactician, patrician	
-ist	one who	feminist, philanthropist	
-ism	state or doctrine of	barbarism, materialism	

SUFFIX	MEANING	EXAMPLES	YOUR EXAMPLE
Noun Endings			
-ity	state of being	futility, civility	
-ology	study of	biology, psychology	
-escence	state of	adolescence, convalescence	
-y, -ry	state of	mimicry, trickery	
Adjective Endings			
-able	capable of	perishable, flammable	
-ic	causing, making	nostalgic, fatalistic	
-ile	pertaining to	senile, servile	
-ious	having the quality of	religious, glorious	
-ive	having the nature of	sensitive, divisive	
-less	without	guileless, reckless	
Verb Endings			
-ize	to bring about	colonize, plagiarize	
-ate	to make	decimate, tolerate	
-ify	to make	beautify, electrify	

Definitions and Suffixes

Following are some words with their suffixes and meanings. The words contain boldfaced suffixes that identify the word's part of speech. As you look at the words, think about words you already know that contain the same suffix.

agrar**ian**: having to do with agriculture or farming
The farmer loved his agrarian life.

bigot**ry**: narrow-minded intolerance
We must guard against bigotry wherever it exists.

consumm**ate**: to make complete
The deal was consummated after long negotiations.

cop**ious**: plentiful
She received copious praise for her excellent work.

cryp**tic**: mysterious, hidden
Her cryptic comment was unclear to everyone.

defer**ment**: delay
He wanted a deferment on paying his student loans.

etym**ology**: study of word origins
The scholar was an authority on the etymology of words.

furt**ive**: underhanded and sly
He had a furtive manner.

laud**able**: praiseworthy
He had laudable intentions to do good in his community.

muta**tion**: a change in form
The scientist found a significant mutation in the gene.

obsol**escence**: the state of being outdated
The new designs were already headed for obsolescence.

parity: equality

He wanted parity with the other employees.

pragmatism: faith in the practical approach

His pragmatism helped him run a successful business.

protagonist: one who is the central figure in a drama

The protagonist was played by a great actor.

provocative: inciting to action

The actions of a few demonstrators were provocative.

puerile: childish

The father's actions were puerile; his five-year-old was more mature.

rectify: to correct

He wanted to rectify the misunderstanding.

relentless: unstoppable

He was relentless in his search for knowledge.

satirize: to use humor to expose folly in institutions or people

Comedians like to satirize politicians.

venerate: to respect or worship

He venerated his parents and protected their interests.

Practice 5

Mark the following statements as true or false according to the meanings of the underlined words. Check your answers at the end of the lesson on page 193.

_____ **1.** A <u>deferment</u> allows immediate action.

_____ **2.** The <u>protagonist</u> is usually the most important person in a play.

_____ **3.** People <u>venerate</u> things they respect.

_____ **4.** <u>Obsolescence</u> adds value to merchandise.

_____ **5.** <u>Etymology</u> is the study of insect life.

_____ **6.** A <u>mutation</u> can be a change of form.

_____ **7.** A <u>relentless</u> search is over quickly.

_____ **8.** If there is a <u>copious</u> amount of something, you are likely to run out of it quickly.

_____ **9.** A <u>furtive</u> glance is sly and secretive.

_____ **10.** <u>Agrarian</u> life is found in the country.

_____ **11.** To <u>satirize</u> a man is to demonstrate your faith in his abilities.

_____ **12.** Volunteering at an animal shelter is a <u>laudable</u> activity.

_____ **13.** All people deserve <u>parity</u> regardless of their race or gender.

_____ **14.** A <u>puerile</u> television show is intended for a sophisticated audience.

_____ **15.** <u>Pragmatism</u> often leads to illogical decisions.

_____ **16.** A <u>cryptic</u> message is difficult to understand.

_____ **17.** A <u>provocative</u> statement is not meant to stir a strong reaction.

_____ **18.** <u>Bigotry</u> is a trait of a close-minded person.

_____ **19.** The protagonist is the least important character in a play.

_____ **20.** To consummate an essay is to leave out many important details in it.

Practice 6

Complete the following sentences. Check your answers at the end of the lesson on page 193.

1. If you venerate something, you _____ _____.

2. If you request a deferment, you want _____ _____.

3. If you want to rectify a situation, you must ___ _____.

4. If you are a relentless person, you _____ _____.

5. If your motives are laudable, they are _____ _____.

6. If you satirize something, you _____ _____.

7. If you behave in a puerile manner, you are_____ _____.

8. If you behave in a furtive way, you are being __ _____.

9. If you want parity at work, you want _____ _____.

10. If you consummate arrangements for a trip, you _____.

11. If you make something cryptic, you make it __ _____.

12. If you observe a mutation, you notice _____ _____.

13. If you are the protagonist, you are _____ _____.

14. If you are being provocative, you are trying to _____.

15. If you are displaying bigotry, you are displaying _____.

16. If you have copious amounts of something, you have _____.

17. If you are approaching a problem with pragmatism, you are approaching it _____.

18. If you have an agrarian job, you work _____ _____.

19. If your car is headed for obsolescence, it will soon be _____.

20. If you are trying to find the etymology of the word "guitar," you are trying to find its _____ _____.

By now you should be familiar with many word parts, from roots, to prefixes, to suffixes. You have not only learned new words, but you have also learned how to identify unfamiliar words by identifying parts of the word that you already know.

Answers

Practice 1

1. incisive
2. contradict
3. philanthropy
4. remittance
5. attributes
6. assimilate
7. precedent
8. recapitulate
9. incognito
10. interrogate
11. protracted
12. pathos
13. loquacious
14. agoraphobic
15. mediocre
16. nominal
17. biodegradable
18. sophisticated
19. verify
20. rejected

Practice 2

1. benevolent
2. audible
3. incisive
4. inference
5. agoraphobia
6. gregarious
7. tangential
8. credence
9. inducement
10. mediocre
11. belligerent
12. fidelity
13. demographic
14. precedent
15. vivacious
16. urbane
17. tenacious
18. philanthropy
19. attribute
20. antagonize

Practice 3

1. demote
2. consensus
3. decimated
4. illegible
5. disinterested
6. euphemisms
7. circumvent
8. synthesis
9. trivial
10. prognosis
11. intermittent
12. antecedents
13. malevolent
14. transcend
15. precursor
16. subordinate
17. controversy
18. retrospect
19. antipathy
20. exorbitant

Practice 4

1. false
2. true
3. false
4. false
5. false
6. false
7. false
8. true
9. false

10. true
11. true
12. false
13. false
14. true
15. true
16. false
17. true
18. false
19. true
20. false

Practice 5

1. false
2. true
3. false
4. false
5. false
6. true
7. false
8. false
9. true
10. false
11. false
12. true
13. true
14. false
15. false
16. true

17. false
18. true
19. false
20. false

Practice 6

Your anwers may not match the following answers exactly, but their meanings should be the same.

1. respect it
2. a postponement
3. correct it
4. don't give up
5. praiseworthy
6. make fun of it
7. childish
8. sly and sneaky
9. equal treatment
10. finalize them
11. mysterious
12. a change in form
13. the central figure in a drama
14. incite an action
15. narrow-minded intolerance
16. a lot of it
17. practically
18. on a farm
19. outdated
20. origin

13 ▶ Words in Context

Since you have already learned about context in Lesson 8 of the Reading Comprehension section, this lesson is mostly practice questions similar to those on the ASVAB.

Remember, **context** is the surrounding text in which a word is used. Most people use context to help them determine the meaning of an unknown word. A vocabulary question that gives you a sentence around the vocabulary word is usually easier to answer than one with little or no context. The surrounding text can help you as you look for synonyms in the sentences.

The best way to take meaning from context is to look for key words in sentences or paragraphs that convey the meaning of the text. If nothing else, the context will give you a means to eliminate wrong answer choices that clearly don't fit. The process of elimination will often leave you with the correct answer.

Remember, there's no penalty for guessing on the ASVAB, so you should use your best judgment to deduce which answer is most likely.

Practice 1

Choose the word that best fills the blank in the following sentences. Check your answers at the end of the lesson on page 206.

1. The main _____ Jim had was too many parking tickets.
   a. disaster
   b. search
   c. request
   d. problem

2. While trying to _____ her pet iguana from a tree, Tanya fell and broke her ankle.
   a. examine
   b. transfer
   c. rescue
   d. pardon

3. The brand new sports car cost a(n) _____ amount of money.
   a. considerate
   b. conscientious
   c. lucrative
   d. considerable

4. We knew nothing about Betty, because she was so _____
   a. expressive
   b. secretive
   c. emotional
   d. artistic

5. We were tired when we reached the _____, but the spectacular view of the valley below was worth the hike.
   a. circumference
   b. summit
   c. fulcrum
   d. nadir

6. The _____ of not turning in your homework is after-school detention.
   a. reward
   b. denial
   c. consequence
   d. cause

7. His suit had a(n) _____ odor, as if it had been closed up for a long time in an old trunk.
   a. aged
   b. dried-up
   c. musty
   d. decrepit

8. Every day, she had to deal with crowds of noisy, demanding people, so she longed most of all for _____.
   a. solitude
   b. association
   c. loneliness
   d. irrelevancy

9. Julia was blamed for the town's bad fortune, and so she was _____ by everyone.
   a. regarded
   b. shunned
   c. neglected
   d. forewarned

10. When Doug described the blackbird as black, the teacher reminded him that his description was _____.

   a. animated

   b. redundant

   c. inconsequential

   d. typical

11. His _____ nature meant that he never showed emotion even when terrible things kept happening to him.

   a. upsetting

   b. prestigious

   c. stoic

   d. sympathetic

12. The teacher put the crayons on the bottom shelf to make them _____ to the young children.

   a. accessible

   b. receptive

   c. eloquent

   d. ambiguous

13. My computer was state-of-the-art when I bought it five years ago, but now it is _____.

   a. current

   b. dedicated

   c. unnecessary

   d. outmoded

14. Lola had been traveling for weeks; she was on a _____ to find the perfect hotel.

   a. surge

   b. quest

   c. discovery

   d. cadence

15. Roland developed an _____ plan to earn extra money to buy the car he had always wanted.

   a. elitist

   b. irrational

   c. aloof

   d. ingenious

16. Julia is _____ because she is the only one on staff who knows how to use this computer program.

   a. frustrated

   b. prudent

   c. indispensable

   d. creative

17. Selling ice-cold lemonade during a heat wave can be very _____.

   a. lucrative

   b. spiteful

   c. irrelevant

   d. revered

18. I do not like your negative attitude, and it has _____ affected our working relationship.

   a. favorably

   b. adversely

   c. shamelessly

   d. candidly

19. Saul's first step onto the high wire was very _____.

   a. scarce

   b. terrified

   c. tentative

   d. fascinated

20. The field remained _____ until the farmer decided to plant strawberry plants in it.
a. fallow
b. lush
c. tasteless
d. disturbed

Practice 2

Choose the word that best fills the blank in the following sentences. Check your answers at the end of the lesson on page 206.

1. It's easy to take care of my cousin's dog Sparky; he's a _____ and obedient pet.
a. delectable
b. commonplace
c. meddlesome
d. docile

2. I had no trouble finding your house; your directions were _____.
a. priceless
b. arduous
c. explicit
d. embodied

3. Though the principal had expected an uproar when he canceled the senior class trip, both parents and students seemed _____.
a. enraged
b. apathetic
c. suspicious
d. evasive

4. Make sure that drinking water is _____; otherwise, you could get sick.
a. valid
b. quenchable
c. impure
d. potable

5. I will vote in favor of the new city ordinance because it _____ many of the points we discussed earlier this year.
a. encompasses
b. releases
c. reminisces
d. disperses

6. Rachel _____ a plan to become a millionaire by age thirty.
a. devised
b. conformed
c. decreased
d. condoned

7. Juana was known as a _____ person; she was always worrying about something.
a. loquacious
b. illogical
c. fretful
d. shrewd

8. The famous celebrity expected _____ treatment wherever he went.
a. tepid
b. consoling
c. exorbitant
d. preferential

9. Jessica needs an A in her class, so studying for exams takes _____ over watching television.
a. precedence
b. conformity
c. perplexity
d. endeavor

10. My mother was _____ when she discovered I broke her favorite vase.
a. irate
b. ironic
c. indifferent
d. obscure

11. Whitney fell asleep during the movie because it had a(n) _____ plot.
a. monotonous
b. torrid
c. ample
d. vital

12. Barney _____ to go back to school to study dog grooming.
a. relied
b. surmised
c. presumed
d. resolved

13. Your drawing is a fair _____ of my family as the infamous Doppler gang.
a. portrayal
b. council
c. desolation
d. degeneration

14. When Marty let go of the handlebars, his bike _____ down the hill and splashed into a duck pond.
a. dissented
b. ventilated
c. careened
d. agitated

15. My sister decided to switch to pancakes when the sour milk on her cereal gave off a _____ odor.
a. pungent
b. virtuous
c. fraudulent
d. frugal

16. The 5:00 whistle _____ announces the end of the workday at the largest toothpaste factory in town.
a. approvingly
b. significantly
c. symbolically
d. audibly

17. Jade was so hungry after her workout that she _____ gobbled up the fruit salad.
a. dynamically
b. voraciously
c. generously
d. beneficially

18. A small _____ occurred when my car door nicked the fender of a neighboring motor scooter.
a. mishap
b. attraction
c. reflex
d. duplicate

19. A hot cup of tea and a comfortable pair of slippers provided Aaron with some much needed _____ after a hard day or work.
  a. trauma
  b. solace
  c. distinction
  d. productivity

20. The artist molded the _____ lump of clay into a beautiful sculpture with great ease.
  a. lumpy
  b. torrential
  c. stiff
  d. malleable

Practice 3

Choose the word that best fills the blank in the following sentences. Check your answers at the end of the lesson on page 207.

1. José rose to a(n) _____ sales position when he helped the company double its profits.
  a. average
  b. prominent
  c. prudent
  d. objective

2. Jeffrey was visibly nervous and spoke _____ about his upcoming appointment with his lawyer.
  a. warily
  b. luxuriously
  c. measurably
  d. narrowly

3. The painter was a(n) _____ artist who was hardly known outside his native city.
  a. infamous
  b. stubborn
  c. eminent
  d. obscure

4. When Wayne learned that he had won the contest, he developed an _____ attitude, and we all had to listen to him crow about his accomplishments.
  a. arrogant
  b. achievable
  c. enlightened
  d. objective

5. Andrew showed _____ disregard for his pickup when he neglected to replenish the oil after the warning light came on.
  a. wanton
  b. admissive
  c. pretentious
  d. eloquent

6. Denise showed great _____ when she refused to discuss what was on the final exam in her economics class.
  a. substance
  b. generosity
  c. obligation
  d. integrity

7. The hail _____ the corn until the entire crop was lost.
  a. belittled
  b. pummeled
  c. rebuked
  d. commended

8. One of Angelo's _____ is collecting antique lemon juicers.
   a. eccentricities
   b. disappointments
   c. admonitions
   d. idioms

9. The motel offered a _____ after our long drive in the Grand Canyon.
   a. relapse
   b. respite
   c. brevity
   d. median

10. Margot brought large garbage bags to _____ our cleanup along Route 66.
   a. confound
   b. pacify
   c. integrate
   d. facilitate

11. Sandy's excellent bobsledding skills during the competition _____ what we all hoped to master.
   a. prevailed
   b. diverged
   c. exemplified
   d. varied

12. The _____ of sunshine and warm weather made for a happy vacation at the beach.
   a. assumption
   b. confluence
   c. seclusion
   d. treatise

13. Do you have the _____ papers to apply for this job?
   a. punitive
   b. grandiose
   c. restorative
   d. requisite

14. Don't _____ yourself: You must pass that exam to graduate.
   a. delude
   b. depreciate
   c. relinquish
   d. prohibit

15. When you write your paper about *The Catcher in the Rye*, please be sure to give a _____ description of the main character.
   a. principled
   b. determined
   c. comprehensive
   d. massive

16. Although Maria was _____ when we first met her, she soon came to talk more than any of us.
   a. customary
   b. reticent
   c. animated
   d. voluntary

17. Viola thought that comparing fingerprints would be exciting work, but she actually found it quite _____ .
   a. glamorous
   b. tedious
   c. dynamic
   d. prestigious

18. In some countries during the winter months, there is _____ darkness; the sun never rises.
   a. blinding
   b. brief
   c. perpetual
   d. offending

19. In an attempt to _____ my work, Marjorie claimed I did not perform adequate research while writing my book.
   a. discredit
   b. corroborate
   c. associate
   d. empathize

20. My mother was so proud of me after winning the poetry contest that she showered me with _____ praise.
   a. negligible
   b. flimsy
   c. profuse
   d. anguished

Practice 4

Choose the word that best fills the blank in the following sentences. Check your answers at the end of the lesson on page 207.

1. After an hour of heavy rain, the storm _____ and we were able to get back out on the golf course.
   a. abated
   b. germinated
   c. constricted
   d. evoked

2. After years of experience, Layna became the _____ veterinarian, performing surgery with ease.
   a. acute
   b. superficial
   c. consummate
   d. ample

3. Anthony tended his neighbors' goldfish _____ while they were on vacation.
   a. terminally
   b. perpendicularly
   c. assiduously
   d. essentially

4. Her _____ business sense meant that she always made the best and most profitable decisions.
   a. erring
   b. radical
   c. shrewd
   d. subjective

5. My friend _____ me by hugging me and making sure I was okay.
   a. intimidated
   b. consoled
   c. alienated
   d. stunned

6. The two cats could be _____ only by the number of rings on their tails; otherwise, they were exactly alike.
   a. separated
   b. divided
   c. disconnected
   d. differentiated

7. The room was _____, the bed unmade, and the dishes dirty; mice and cockroaches were everywhere.
   a. squalid
   b. squeamish
   c. queasy
   d. licentious

8. The drive was dangerous because of the rain; on each slick, wet curve I was afraid we would _____ into a ditch.
   a. operate
   b. hydroplane
   c. submerge
   d. reconnoiter

9. Eduardo liked to _____ his younger sister and make her upset.
   a. provoke
   b. upgrade
   c. spoil
   d. heave

10. Yelena was always _____ with her money; she preferred to save it than spend it.
   a. wistful
   b. desultory
   c. expository
   d. prudent

11. The tiny boat spun into the _____, and we were sure that all hope was lost.
   a. matrix
   b. paradox
   c. vector
   d. vortex

12. The old man was _____; he refused to leave his home, even when told the volcano was about to erupt.
   a. recitative
   b. redundant
   c. repatriated
   d. recalcitrant

13. The project seemed _____, so we all applied ourselves to it with enthusiasm.
   a. implacable
   b. feasible
   c. incorrigible
   d. irreparable

14. The many colors in the swarm of butterflies seemed to create a(n) _____ cloud.
   a. incandescent
   b. iridescent
   c. luminescent
   d. cumulous

15. Mike and Jamal had a perfect _____, each seeming to know, without being told, what the other felt.
   a. stability
   b. equilibrium
   c. rapport
   d. symmetry

16. I always relied on the manager to _____ a new project when productivity was low.
   a. oppose
   b. induct
   c. instigate
   d. transpose

17. Now that she is a teenager, my daughter is
_____ when I ask about virtually all personal topics—she simply sits and stares at me.
   a. synchronous
   b. unanimous
   c. indentured
   d. taciturn

18. *The New York Times* printed an erroneous
report about New York City student scores
on standardized tests, so the school board
demanded a(n) _____.
   a. abolition
   b. invalidation
   c. retraction
   d. annulment

19. I expected the so-called bully to be mean, but
he was actually quite _____.
   a. acerbic
   b. amiable
   c. vitriolic
   d. caustic

20. After running around in the yard all day, the
exhausted dog became decidedly _____.
   a. stimulated
   b. segregated
   c. scintillating
   d. sedate

Practice 5

Choose the word that best fills the blank in the following sentences. For each sentence you will have a pair
of words to choose from. The pairs contain words that
are easily confused and commonly misused.

Check your answers at the end of the lesson on
page 208.

1. Janelle _____ first aid to the child with the
broken arm.
   a. administered
   b. ministered

2. Enrique was _____ to see his kids after his
long vacation.
   a. eager
   b. anxious

3. The judge set a huge amount for bail to
_____ that the man would return to court.
   a. ensure
   b. insure

4. I am going to _____ an article by Jacques
Cousteau in my report about dolphins.
   a. site
   b. cite

5. She looks fabulous in that dress; it fits
_____.
   a. good
   b. well

6. The United States is _____ of 50 states.
   a. composed
   b. comprised

7. If I lose all of my savings, I will be profoundly
_____.
   a. discomfited
   b. discomforted

8. All of the police officers were _____
witnesses because they actually saw the
accident.
   a. credible
   b. credulous

9. When I cheat on my diet by eating chocolate cake, I have a guilty _____ .
   a. conscious
   b. conscience

10. Dogs _____ to the cold weather when their fur grows thick.
    a. adapt
    b. adopt

11. A vitamin a day is part of a _____ diet.
    a. healthy
    b. healthful

12. After his amazing career, it seemed time to _____ him into the hall of fame.
    a. deduct
    b. induct

13. This book is an _____ study of the Mayan culture.
    a. exhaustive
    b. exhausting

14. Because she lived across the globe, it was not _____ for Latania to attend her high school reunion.
    a. feasible
    b. possible

15. The mail carrier _____ puts my neighbor's mail in my box.
    a. continuously
    b. continually

16. We will _____ with the plan we made earlier this month.
    a. proceed
    b. precede

17. Before buying a house, you should seek the _____ of a qualified attorney.
    a. counsel
    b. council

18. In most classes, homework is _____ .
    a. compulsive
    b. compulsory

19. Her students appreciate Professor Diamond's _____ grading system.
    a. judicial
    b. judicious

20. He spoke _____ so everyone could hear.
    a. aloud
    b. allowed

Answers

Practice 1

1. **d.** The word *problem* in this context means a source of distress.
2. **c.** *Rescue* in this context implies freeing from danger.
3. **d.** *Considerable* means large. You would expect a brand new sports car to cost a lot of money.
4. **b.** The context clue is "we knew nothing." *Secretive* means having the habit of keeping secrets.
5. **b.** *Summit* means the highest point, where the hikers would have a view.
6. **c.** A *consequence* is the result of something.
7. **c.** A *musty* odor is one that is stale or moldy.
8. **a.** *Solitude*, unlike *loneliness* (choice **c**), can be a desirable thing.
9. **b.** To be *shunned* is to be avoided deliberately, usually as a punishment.
10. **b.** *Redundant* means repetitive. It is repetitive to describe a blackbird as black.
11. **c.** *Stoic* means not affected by emotion.
12. **a.** *Accessible* means capable of being reached; being within reach.
13. **d.** *Outmoded* means no longer in style or no longer usable.
14. **b.** A *quest* is a search or pursuit of something.
15. **d.** *Ingenious* means marked by originality, resourcefulness, and cleverness in conception; clever.
16. **c.** To be *indispensable* is to be essential or necessary.
17. **a.** *Lucrative* means profitable.
18. **b.** *Adversely* means acting against or in a contrary direction.
19. **c.** The word *tentative* means cautious. Although Saul may have been scared, the word *terrified* does not describe a step well, so choice **b** is incorrect. Choices **a** and **d** do not make sense.

20. **a.** The context clue is "until the farmer decide to plant." The word *fallow* means unplanted and neglected. Choice **b** is incorrect because a *lush* field would be full of plants and not require new ones. Choices **c** and **d** do not make sense in this context.

Practice 2

1. **d.** *Docile* means easily led or managed.
2. **c.** *Explicit* means clearly defined.
3. **b.** *Apathetic* means having little or no concern. (The principal expected an uproar, but that never happened.)
4. **d.** *Potable* means fit for drinking.
5. **a.** *Encompasses* in this context means includes.
6. **a.** *Devised* means to form in the mind by new combinations or applications of ideas or principles; to plan to obtain or bring about.
7. **c.** *Fretful* means worried.
8. **d.** *Preferential* means special.
9. **a.** *Precedence* means priority of importance—i.e., studying is more important to Jessica than watching television.
10. **a.** *Irate* means upset or angry. You would expect someone to be irate if a favorite possession were destroyed.
11. **a.** *Monotonous* means having a tedious sameness.
12. **d.** *Resolved* means having reached a firm decision about something.
13. **a.** *Portrayal* means representation or portrait.
14. **c.** *Career* means to rush headlong or carelessly; to lurch or swerve while in motion.
15. **a.** *Pungent* implies a sharp, stinging, or biting quality, especially of an odor.
16. **d.** *Audibly* means the manner of being heard.
17. **b.** *Voraciously* means ravenously.
18. **a.** *Mishap* means an unfortunate accident.
19. **b.** *Solace* means comfort. Choice **a** can be eliminated because one would not seek *trauma*,

a physical or psychological injury, after suffering a hard day at work. Choice **d** is incorrect, because the sentence suggests that Aaron wanted a change of pace after his hard day at work, which was probably *productive*. Choice **c** does not make sense.

20. **d.** *Malleable* means capable of being shaped. Choice **a** is incorrect, because describing a lump of clay as *lumpy* is redundant. Choice **c** can be eliminated because a *stiff* lump of clay probably could not be molded with great ease. Choice **b** does not make sense; *torrential* means violently copious.

Practice 3

1. **b.** *Prominent* means important or leading.
2. **a.** *Warily* means in a manner marked by keen caution, cunning, or watchful prudence. The context clue in this sentence is Jeffrey's nervousness.
3. **d.** *Obscure* means unknown.
4. **a.** *Arrogant* means exaggerating or disposed to exaggerate one's own worth or importance in an overbearing manner.
5. **a.** *Wanton* means being without check or limitation.
6. **d.** *Integrity* means firm adherence to a code of moral values; honesty.
7. **b.** To *pummel* means to pound or beat.
8. **a.** An *eccentricity* is something that deviates from the norm. (Antique lemon juicers are not a commonplace item.)
9. **b.** *Respite* means an interval of rest and relief.
10. **d.** *Facilitate* means to make easier or to help bring about.
11. **c.** *Exemplify* means to be an instance of or serve as an example.
12. **b.** *Confluence* means a coming or flowing together, meeting, or gathering at one point.
13. **d.** *Requisite* means essential or necessary.

14. **a.** *Delude* means to mislead the mind; to deceive.
15. **c.** *Comprehensive* means covering completely. (*Massive,* choice **d**, refers to a large or bulky size.)
16. **b.** *Reticent* means inclined to be silent or uncommunicative; reserved. Maria was silent at first, but then talked more than anyone else.
17. **b.** *Tedious* means tiresome or boring.
18. **c.** *Perpetual* means unending.
19. **a.** To *discredit* something is to damage its reputation or validity. Claiming a book was not well-researched is a way of saying it is invalid.
20. **c.** The context clue is "showered." *Profuse* means abundant.

Practice 4

1. **a.** *Abated* means to decrease in force or intensity.
2. **c.** *Consummate* (adj.) means extremely skilled and experienced.
3. **c.** *Assiduously* means in a careful manner or with unremitting attention.
4. **c.** *Shrewd* means clever.
5. **b.** *Console* means to comfort.
6. **d.** To *differentiate* between two things is to establish the distinction between them. The other choices, although somewhat related, make no sense.
7. **a.** Something *squalid* has a dirty or wretched appearance. The other adjectives, though somewhat related, can properly be applied to a person but not to a place.
8. **b.** When a car goes out of control and skims along the surface of a wet road, it is called *hydroplaning.*
9. **a.** *Provoke* means to cause anger.
10. **d.** *Prudent* means cautious.
11. **d.** A *vortex* is a whirlpool and so fits the sentence. The other choices do not make sense.
12. **d.** To be *recalcitrant* is to be stubbornly resistant.

13. b. To be *feasible* is to be practicable, so this word best fits the sentence. The other three choices would not apply to projects that are possible (note that they all begin with prefixes generally meaning "not").

14. b. Something that is *iridescent* displays lustrous, rainbow colors. Choices **a** and **b** are somewhat close, but neither necessarily includes color as a necessary property. *Cumulous* (choice **d**) is a scientific name for a type of cloud.

15. c. To have *rapport* is to have mutual trust and emotional affinity. The other words do not necessarily imply trust.

16. c. *Instigate* means to cause or start.

17. d. To be *taciturn* is to be disinclined to speak out. The other choices make no sense in this context.

18. c. To *retract* something is to take it back or disavow it. This is the term usually applied to disavowing something erroneous or libelous printed in a newspaper. The other choices are somewhat similar in meaning but do not normally apply to newspaper errors.

19. b. *Amiable* means friendly. Although the sentence is talking about a bully, the key word *but* indicates that the quality he has is not expected.

20. d. An exhausted dog would likely be *sedate*, which means calm and composed.

Practice 5

1. a. To *administer* means to give something remedially (transitive verb). To *minister* means to aid or give service to people (intransitive verb).

2. a. *Eager* implies enthusiastic or impatient desire or interest. *Anxious* implies a more negative feeling: an extreme uneasiness of mind, or worried.

3. a. *Ensure* means to make a future occurrence certain or reliable; *insure* means protecting the worth of goods.

4. b. *Cite* means to quote or document. A *site* is a position or place.

5. b. *Well* should be used as an adverb to modify verbs (how does it fit?). *Good* is an adjective often used with linking verbs (*be, seem,* or *appe*ar).

6. b. *Comprised* means to consist of—it expresses the relation of the larger to the smaller (think of this larger sense by remembering that *comprised* is a longer word than composes). *Composed* means to make up the parts of.

7. a. *Discomfit* means to wholly undo or defeat. *Discomfort* means to deprive of comfort or to distress.

8. a. *Credible* means offering reasonable grounds for being believed; *credulous* means ready to believe, especially on slight or uncertain evidence.

9. b. *Conscience* means a sense of moral goodness. *Conscious* means alert or aware.

10. a. *Adapt* implies a modification according to changing circumstances. *Adopt* means accepting something created by another or foreign to one's nature.

11. b. *Healthful* implies a positive contribution to a healthy condition, or beneficial to health. *Healthy* implies full of strength and vigor as well as freedom from signs of disease.

12. b. *Induct* means to introduce or initiate. *Deduct* means to take away from a total.

13. a. *Exhaustive* means treating all parts without omission. *Exhausting* means tiring.

14. a. *Feasible* means logical or likely. *Possible* means capable of happening or existing.

15. b. *Continually* means recurring regularly. *Continuously* means uninterrupted in time.

16. a. *Proceed* means to go forward in an orderly way; *precede* means to come before.

17. a. *Counsel* means advice or guidance. A *council* is an assembly of people called together for consultation.

18. b. *Compulsory* means obligatory or required. *Compulsive* means having the capacity to compel.

19. b. *Judicious* is having or exhibiting sound judgment. *Judicial* is of, or relating to, courts of law.

20. a. *Aloud* means able to be heard. *Allowed* means permitted.

14 ▶ Synonyms and Antonyms

A word is a **synonym** of another word if it has *the same or nearly the same* meaning as the word to which it is being compared. An **antonym** is a word that means *the opposite* of the word to which it is being compared. Questions on the ASVAB often ask you to find the synonym or antonym of a word. Sometimes the word will be in context—surrounded by a sentence that helps you guess what the word means. Other times, you will be provided with only the word and will have to decipher what the word means without any context.

Synonyms

Questions that ask for synonyms can be tricky because they require you to recognize the meanings of several words that may be unfamiliar to you—not only the words in the question, but also the words in the answer choices. Usually, the best strategy is to look at the structure of the word and listen for its sound. See if a part of a word looks familiar. Think of other words you know that may have similar key elements, and then think about how those words could be related.

Practice 1

For each question, choose the synonym. Check your answers at the end of the lesson on page 227.

1. Which word means the same as ENTHUSIASTIC?
   a. available
   b. cheerful
   c. eager
   d. relevant

2. Which word means the same as ADEQUATE?
   a. sufficient
   b. awful
   c. proficient
   d. stupendous

3. Which word means the same as ECSTATIC?
   a. inconsistent
   b. positive
   c. wild
   d. thrilled

4. Which word means the same as AFFECT?
   a. accomplish
   b. conflict
   c. sicken
   d. influence

5. Which word means the same as CONTINUOUS?
   a. intermittent
   b. adjacent
   c. uninterrupted
   d. contiguous

6. Which word means the same as COURTESY?
   a. civility
   b. congruity
   c. conviviality
   d. rudeness

7. Which word means the same as DAINTY?
   a. vivid
   b. delicate
   c. robust
   d. adaptable

8. Which word means the same as RECUPERATE?
   a. mend
   b. endorse
   c. persist
   d. worsen

9. Which word means the same as PEACEFUL?
   a. majestic
   b. scarce
   c. tranquil
   d. adequate

10. Which word means the same as COMPOSURE?
    a. agitation
    b. poise
    c. liveliness
    d. stimulation

11. Which word means the same as STRIFE?
    a. remove
    b. strange
    c. conflict
    d. achieve

12. Which word means the same as COMMENDABLE?
    a. admirable
    b. accountable
    c. irresponsible
    d. noticeable

13. Which word means the same as PASSIVE?
    a. inactive
    b. emotional
    c. lively
    d. woeful

14. Which word means the same as VAST?
   a. attentive
   b. immense
   c. steady
   d. slight

15. Which word means the same as COMPLY?
   a. subdue
   b. entertain
   c. flatter
   d. obey

16. Which word means the same as WILL?
   a. resolve
   b. spite
   c. sanity
   d. idleness

17. Which word means the same as ENLIGHTEN?
   a. relocate
   b. confuse
   c. comply
   d. teach

18. Which word means the same as RIGOROUS?
   a. demanding
   b. tolerable
   c. lenient
   d. disorderly

19. Which word means the same as OBLIVIOUS?
   a. visible
   b. sinister
   c. conscious
   d. unaware

20. Which word means the same as VERIFY?
   a. disclose
   b. confirm
   c. refute
   d. unite

Practice 2

For each question, choose the synonym. Check your answers at the end of the lesson on page 227.

1. Which word means the same as ERRONEOUS?
   a. digressive
   b. confused
   c. impenetrable
   d. incorrect

2. Which word means the same as GROTESQUE?
   a. extreme
   b. frenzied
   c. hideous
   d. typical

3. Which word means the same as GARBLED?
   a. lucid
   b. unintelligible
   c. devoured
   d. outrageous

4. Which word means the same as PUNGENT?
   a. odorous
   b. puerile
   c. aware
   d. sharp

5. Which word means the same as COERCE?
   a. force
   b. permit
   c. waste
   d. deny

6. Which word means the same as ABRUPT?
   a. interrupt
   b. sudden
   c. extended
   d. corrupt

7. Which word means the same as APATHY?
   a. hostility
   b. depression
   c. indifference
   d. concern

8. Which word means the same as DISPARAGE?
   a. disparate
   b. degrade
   c. dispose
   d. parry

9. Which word means the same as CONTEMPTUOUS?
   a. respectful
   b. unique
   c. scornful
   d. insecure

10. Which word means the same as TOTE?
   a. acquire
   b. carry
   c. tremble
   d. abandon

11. Which word means the same as DISTINCT?
   a. satisfied
   b. frenzied
   c. uneasy
   d. separate

12. Which word means the same as FLAGRANT?
   a. secret
   b. worthless
   c. noble
   d. glaring

13. Which word means the same as ORATION?
   a. nuisance
   b. independence
   c. address
   d. length

14. Which word means the same as LIBEL?
   a. description
   b. praise
   c. destiny
   d. slander

15. Which word means the same as PHILANTHROPY?
   a. selfishness
   b. fascination
   c. disrespect
   d. generosity

16. Which word means the same as PROXIMITY?
   a. distance
   b. agreement
   c. nearness
   d. intelligence

17. Which word means the same as NEGLIGIBLE?
   a. insignificant
   b. delicate
   c. meaningful
   d. illegible

18. Which word means the same as VIGILANT?
   a. nonchalant
   b. watchful
   c. righteous
   d. strenuous

19. Which word means the same as ASTUTE?
   a. perceptive
   b. inattentive
   c. stubborn
   d. elegant

20. Which word means the same as COLLABORATE?
   a. cooperate
   b. coordinate
   c. entice
   d. elaborate

Practice 3

For each question, choose the word that has the same or nearly the same meaning as the capitalized word. Check your answers at the end of the lesson on page 228.

1. SUBSCRIBE
   a. sign
   b. read
   c. divide
   d. support

2. OPPORTUNITY
   a. sensitivity
   b. arrogance
   c. chance
   d. reference

3. INVENT
   a. insert
   b. discover
   c. apply
   d. allow

4. SPHERE
   a. air
   b. spread
   c. globe
   d. enclosure

5. REFINE
   a. condone
   b. provide
   c. change
   d. purify

6. NARRATE
   a. tell
   b. story
   c. concede
   d. participate

7. NULLIFY
   a. numb
   b. delete
   c. negate
   d. petrify

8. SAGE
   a. wise
   b. obnoxious
   c. conceited
   d. heartless

9. URBANE
   a. city
   b. sophisticated
   c. unnerved
   d. rural

10. DORMANT
    a. hidden
    b. slumbering
    c. rigid
    d. misplaced

11. BANISH
    a. exile
    b. decorate
    c. succumb
    d. encourage

12. TAILOR
    a. measure
    b. construct
    c. launder
    d. alter

13. WAIVE
    a. merge
    b. relinquish
    c. destroy
    d. hinder

14. EVADE
   a. cause
   b. avoid
   c. remind
   d. destroy

15. ETERNAL
   a. timeless
   b. heavenly
   c. loving
   d. wealthy

16. TIMID
   a. shy
   b. terrific
   c. terrified
   d. forgetful

17. STOW
   a. pack
   b. curtsy
   c. fool
   d. trample

18. REVOKE
   a. affect
   b. condone
   c. condemn
   d. annul

19. COVERT
   a. change
   b. hidden
   c. movement
   d. mission

20. FALTER
   a. falsify
   b. determine
   c. stumble
   d. plague

Practice 4

Choose the word that means the same or nearly the same as the underlined word. Check your answers at the end of the lesson on page 228.

1. its <u>inferior</u> quality
   a. noted
   b. distinguished
   c. lower
   d. questionable

2. in a <u>curt</u> manner
   a. gruff
   b. careful
   c. devious
   d. calm

3. their <u>perilous</u> journey
   a. dangerous
   b. doubtful
   c. adventurous
   d. thrilling

4. the <u>precise</u> amount
   a. fair
   b. exact
   c. undetermined
   d. valuable

5. to <u>commence</u> the meeting
   a. begin
   b. leave
   c. disclose
   d. terminate

6. a <u>humble</u> person
   a. common
   b. tolerant
   c. conceited
   d. unassertive

7. a <u>jubilant</u> graduate
   a. charming
   b. joyful
   c. stubborn
   d. scholarly

8. created a <u>replica</u>
   a. portion
   b. masterpiece
   c. prompt
   d. copy

9. a <u>temperate</u> climate
   a. moderate
   b. harsh
   c. warm
   d. cold

10. a <u>destitute</u> person
   a. poor
   b. wise
   c. traveling
   d. large

11. the <u>agile</u> dancer
   a. proud
   b. nimble
   c. humble
   d. talented

12. acted <u>brazenly</u>
   a. boldly
   b. blissfully
   c. brutally
   d. broadly

13. the <u>unique</u> individual
   a. rigorous
   b. admirable
   c. unparalleled
   d. remarkable

14. the <u>prerequisite</u> number of items
   a. optional
   b. preferred
   c. advisable
   d. required

15. <u>alleviate</u> the pain
   a. ease
   b. tolerate
   c. stop
   d. intensify

16. an <u>ample</u> supply
   a. meager
   b. archaic
   c. generous
   d. paltry

17. the <u>unanimous</u> decision
   a. uniform
   b. divided
   c. adamant
   d. clear-cut

18. the <u>proficient</u> worker
   a. inexperienced
   b. unequaled
   c. sufficient
   d. skilled

19. <u>obstinately</u> refused
   a. repeatedly
   b. reluctantly
   c. angrily
   d. stubbornly

20. to <u>rectify</u> the situation
   a. correct
   b. forget
   c. alter
   d. abuse

Practice 5

Choose the word that means the same or nearly the same as the underlined word. Check your answers at the end of the lesson on page 228.

1. expedite the process
   a. accelerate
   b. evaluate
   c. reverse
   d. justify

2. a fictitious character
   a. evil
   b. imaginary
   c. prominent
   d. colorful

3. to absolve a person
   a. convict
   b. accuse
   c. forgive
   d. exclude

4. to hoist the flag
   a. lower
   b. destroy
   c. salute
   d. raise

5. to disrupt an event
   a. interrupt
   b. invent
   c. organize
   d. host

6. to sustain a cause
   a. demolish
   b. renovate
   c. support
   d. remodel

7. simmering anger
   a. unacknowledged
   b. diminishing
   c. righteous
   d. seething

8. to initiate a campaign
   a. support
   b. begin
   c. sabotage
   d. run

9. ravenous hunger
   a. natural
   b. ungratified
   c. voracious
   d. satisfied

10. uninhabitable island
    a. deserted
    b. unlivable
    c. remote
    d. uncivilized

11. suppressed anger
    a. explosive
    b. repressed
    c. minimized
    d. expressed

12. to be immersed in study
    a. trapped
    b. absorbed
    c. held
    d. enriched

13. to detract from something
    a. destroy
    b. break
    c. obliterate
    d. diminish

14. to <u>haggle</u> over the price
   a. bargain
   b. complain
   c. worry
   d. cheat

15. <u>palpable</u> tension
   a. rising
   b. understated
   c. nervous
   d. tangible

16. a <u>solemn</u> ceremony
   a. impudent
   b. serious
   c. religious
   d. marriage

17. urban <u>sprawl</u>
   a. decay
   b. construction
   c. growth
   d. crime

18. an <u>ingenious</u> invention
   a. worthwhile
   b. credible
   c. clever
   d. desolate

19. a <u>meandering</u> stream
   a. clear
   b. flowing
   c. polluted
   d. winding

20. a <u>precarious</u> situation
   a. joyous
   b. dangerous
   c. unforgettable
   d. secure

Antonyms

Many antonyms seem obvious—good and bad, night and day—but others are not as easily recognizable. This is because many words have more than one meaning. For example, the word *clear* could mean cloudless, transparent, or unmistakable. For each of those meanings, clear has an opposite. If an antonym isn't obvious, think about other possible meanings of the word. Also, do not be fooled by answer choices that are synonyms. Remember that you are looking for a word that means the closest to the question word's *opposite*, not a word that means the same. You can check your answers at the end of the lesson on page 229.

Practice 6

1. Which word means the *opposite* of UNITY?
   a. discord
   b. stimulation
   c. consent
   d. neglect

2. Which word means the *opposite* of DETEST?
   a. prohibit
   b. hate
   c. examine
   d. admire

3. Which word means the *opposite* of VALIANT?
   a. instinctive
   b. cowardly
   c. cynical
   d. worthy

4. Which word means the *opposite* of LENIENT?
   a. capable
   b. impractical
   c. merciful
   d. domineering

5. Which word means the *opposite* of TARNISH?
   a. absorb
   b. endure
   c. shine
   d. sully

6. Which word means the *opposite* of CREDIBLE?
   a. unimportant
   b. conventional
   c. comparable
   d. unbelievable

7. Which word means the *opposite* of YIELD?
   a. merge
   b. offer
   c. resist
   d. provide

8. Which word means the *opposite* of COMMENCE?
   a. initiate
   b. adapt
   c. harass
   d. terminate

9. Which word means the *opposite* of CONSCIENTIOUS?
   a. careless
   b. apologetic
   c. diligent
   d. boisterous

10. Which word means the *opposite* of DEFICIENT?
   a. necessary
   b. complete
   c. flawed
   d. simple

11. Which word means the *opposite* of CLARIFY?
   a. explain
   b. dismay
   c. obscure
   d. provide

12. Which word means the *opposite* of GRANT?
   a. deny
   b. consume
   c. allocate
   d. provoke

13. Which word means the *opposite* of LUCID?
   a. ordinary
   b. turbulent
   c. implausible
   d. unclear

14. Which word means the *opposite* of IMPARTIAL?
   a. complete
   b. prejudiced
   c. unbiased
   d. erudite

15. Which word means the *opposite* of JUDICIOUS?
   a. partial
   b. litigious
   c. imprudent
   d. unrestrained

16. Which word means the *opposite* of SHALLOW?
   a. profound
   b. proficient
   c. ignorant
   d. malicious

17. Which word means the *opposite* of ERUDITE?
   a. uneducated
   b. polite
   c. unknown
   d. agitated

18. Which word means the *opposite* of AMIABLE?
   a. dangerous
   b. permissive
   c. aloof
   d. congenial

19. Which word means the *opposite* of COMPETENT?
   a. incomplete
   b. intense
   c. inept
   d. massive

20. Which word means the *opposite* of PROMOTE?
   a. explicate
   b. curtail
   c. concede
   d. retain

Practice 7

Choose the word that means the OPPOSITE or most nearly the opposite of the word in capitals. You can check your answers at the end of the lesson on page 229.

1. DEPLETE
   a. remove
   b. replace
   c. diminish
   d. add

2. IRRITATE
   a. soothe
   b. drain
   c. resist
   d. solve

3. DECEITFUL
   a. honest
   b. deceptive
   c. misleading
   d. decrepit

4. VIRTUE
   a. reality
   b. fact
   c. vice
   d. amateur

5. HARMONY
   a. noise
   b. brevity
   c. safety
   d. discord

6. INSULT
   a. compliment
   b. contempt
   c. argument
   d. attitude

7. THRIVE
   a. divide
   b. fail
   c. recant
   d. diminish

8. SERENE
   a. severe
   b. diplomatic
   c. chaotic
   d. academic

9. DILIGENT
   a. serious
   b. sloppy
   c. elusive
   d. incredible

10. DEMOLISH
   a. attend
   b. consider
   c. create
   d. stifle

11. NOTABLE
   a. oral
   b. graceful
   c. legal
   d. ordinary

12. BERATE
   a. tear
   b. replace
   c. inspect
   d. compliment

13. PROSPEROUS
   a. affluent
   b. destitute
   c. cowardly
   d. receptive

14. CONVENE
   a. scatter
   b. organize
   c. remit
   d. ignore

15. CRITICAL
   a. inimical
   b. judgmental
   c. massive
   d. trivial

16. NIMBLE
   a. sturdy
   b. sluggish
   c. thoughtless
   d. relaxed

17. TRANQUIL
   a. agitated
   b. explicit
   c. slow
   d. composed

18. SPRIGHTLY
   a. eagerly
   b. loftily
   c. dully
   d. locally

19. GENERATE
   a. elongate
   b. electrify
   c. destroy
   d. dignify

20. IMPULSIVE
   a. secure
   b. mandatory
   c. rash
   d. cautious

Practice 8

Choose the word that means the OPPOSITE or most nearly the opposite of the word in capitals. You can check your answers at the end of the lesson on page 230.

1. PRUDENT
   a. hasty
   b. licentious
   c. libertine
   d. demonstrative

2. RETAIN
   a. withhold
   b. release
   c. succumb
   d. incise

3. SCANT
   a. pellucid
   b. meager
   c. copious
   d. vocal

4. KNOWLEDGEABLE
  a. bookish
  b. stubborn
  c. ignorant
  d. implied

5. STRINGENT
  a. obese
  b. lax
  c. obtuse
  d. fluid

6. COMMONPLACE
  a. incredulous
  b. mysterious
  c. boring
  d. solemn

7. SUCCINCT
  a. distinct
  b. laconic
  c. unpersuasive
  d. verbose

8. TIRESOME
  a. stimulating
  b. alarming
  c. intemperate
  d. tranquil

9. UNIFORM
  a. dissembling
  b. diverse
  c. bizarre
  d. slovenly

10. WARY
  a. alert
  b. leery
  c. worried
  d. careless

11. NOVEL
  a. dangerous
  b. unsettled
  c. suitable
  d. old

12. FALLACY
  a. truth
  b. blessing
  c. weakness
  d. fable

13. PERMANENT
  a. solid
  b. sober
  c. fleeting
  d. indifferent

14. SUBSEQUENT
  a. necessary
  b. insignificant
  c. primary
  d. previous

15. NONCHALANT
  a. intelligent
  b. popular
  c. concerned
  d. reckless

16. EXCISE
  a. sleep
  b. retain
  c. organize
  d. staple

17. DISPERSE
  a. gather
  b. agree
  c. praise
  d. satisfy

18. PRESSING
   a. composed
   b. unimportant
   c. unlimited
   d. strong

19. MIRTH
   a. height
   b. solemnity
   c. expense
   d. preparation

20. SENSIBLE
   a. foolhardy
   b. replenished
   c. severe
   d. religious

Practice 9

Choose the word that means the OPPOSITE or most nearly the opposite of the word in capitals. You can check your answers at the end of the lesson on page 230.

1. ORIENT
   a. confuse
   b. arouse
   c. deter
   d. simplify

2. LEVITATE
   a. plod
   b. undulate
   c. whisper
   d. sink

3. PACIFY
   a. complicate
   b. dismiss
   c. excite
   d. atomize

4. PLAUSIBLE
   a. insufficient
   b. apologetic
   c. unbelievable
   d. credible

5. AVIDLY
   a. partially
   b. unenthusiastically
   c. equally
   d. unkindly

6. MEEKLY
   a. mildly
   b. painfully
   c. forcefully
   d. politely

7. COMPLACENT
   a. concerned
   b. pleasant
   c. happy
   d. convinced

8. AMBIGUOUS
   a. apathetic
   b. certain
   c. equivocal
   d. indefinite

9. SPONTANEOUS
   a. serious
   b. intimidated
   c. declarative
   d. prepared

10. ELOQUENT
   a. shabby
   b. fluent
   c. inarticulate
   d. plain

11. DETERRENT
   a. encouragement
   b. obstacle
   c. proponent
   d. discomfort

12. ENTANGLE
   a. involve
   b. replace
   c. subject
   d. separate

13. IMPERTINENT
   a. animated
   b. rude
   c. relentless
   d. polite

14. LUDICROUS
   a. absurd
   b. somber
   c. reasonable
   d. charitable

15. ARCHAIC
   a. tangible
   b. modern
   c. ancient
   d. haunted

16. SULLEN
   a. morose
   b. impetuous
   c. provocative
   d. jovial

17. AWE
   a. contempt
   b. reverence
   c. valor
   d. distortion

18. TAUT
   a. neutral
   b. relaxed
   c. rigid
   d. vague

19. RILE
   a. appease
   b. prosper
   c. oppress
   d. irk

20. MAR
   a. delineate
   b. bolster
   c. clarify
   d. repair

Practice 10

Choose the word that means the OPPOSITE or most nearly the opposite of the word in capitals. You can check your answers at the end of the lesson on page 231.

1. INTREPID
   a. belligerent
   b. consistent
   c. chivalrous
   d. fearful

2. METHODICAL
   a. erratic
   b. deliberate
   c. hostile
   d. deformed

3. LATENT
   a. slow
   b. tardy
   c. dormant
   d. active

4. AFFABLE
  a. disagreeable
  b. hollow
  c. simple
  d. eager

5. TREPIDATION
  a. distribution
  b. agitation
  c. fearlessness
  d. uniformity

6. AUSPICIOUS
  a. unpromising
  b. repulsive
  c. jealous
  d. inattentive

7. IDLE
  a. slow
  b. illegible
  c. busy
  d. lucky

8. FURTIVELY
  a. silently
  b. openly
  c. mildly
  d. quickly

9. ENTICE
  a. excite
  b. tempt
  c. express
  d. repel

10. ORNATE
  a. simple
  b. gorgeous
  c. dirty
  d. pleased

11. OSTENTATIOUS
  a. hilarious
  b. humble
  c. careful
  d. obnoxious

12. ENDORSE
  a. condemn
  b. recommend
  c. announce
  d. adopt

13. ACCEDE
  a. excel
  b. retard
  c. disapprove
  d. increase

14. FRAIL
  a. scared
  b. hardy
  c. child-like
  d. attentive

15. AMBIVALENCE
  a. compensation
  b. decisiveness
  c. enthusiasm
  d. devotion

16. DIVERGENT
  a. persuasive
  b. identical
  c. incomplete
  d. malicious

17. PENSIVE
  a. nervous
  b. prejudiced
  c. dizzy
  d. thoughtless

18. DISCERNIBLE
 a. invisible
 b. recognizable
 c. paradoxical
 d. scornful

19. BLEMISHED
 a. speckled
 b. flawless
 c. productive
 d. absent

20. ABHOR
 a. scare
 b. surprise
 c. desire
 d. inspire

Answers

Practice 1

 1. c. *Enthusiastic* means eager or excited.
 2. a. If something is *adequate,* it is sufficient.
 3. d. A person who is *ecstatic* is thrilled or exhilarated.
 4. d. To *affect* means to influence.
 5. c. *Continuous* means marked by uninterrupted extension in space and time.
 6. a. A *courtesy* implies being courteous or mannerly; it is civility.
 7. b. A *dainty* person is delicate.
 8. a. *Recuperate* means to heal; to mend.
 9. c. *Peaceful* and *tranquil* both mean calm.
 10. b. If you maintain your *composure,* you have poise.
 11. c. *Strife* means a struggle or conflict.
 12. a. *Commendable* is the same as admirable.
 13. a. *Passive* means not active.
 14. b. *Vast* means very great in size; immense.
 15. d. To *comply* is the same as to obey.

 16. a. *Will* and *resolve* share the same meaning.
 17. d. If you *enlighten* someone, you have taught them something.
 18. a. If something is *rigorous,* it is demanding.
 19. d. If you are *oblivious* to your surroundings, you are unaware of them.
 20. b. To *verify* means to establish the truth or accuracy; to confirm.

Practice 2

 1. d. *Erroneous* means inaccurate, or incorrect.
 2. c. *Grotesque* means distorted, or hideous.
 3. b. If something is *garbled,* it is jumbled or unintelligible.
 4. d. *Pungent* means caustic or sharp. Do not be tempted by choice **a**—*pungent* is a word used to describe an odor, while *odorous* means something that has an odor.
 5. a. To *coerce* means to dominate by force.
 6. b. *Abrupt* means sudden, quick, or hasty.
 7. c. *Apathy* means a lack of interest or concern; indifference.
 8. b. *Disparage* means to lower in rank or degrade.
 9. c. A *contemptuous* person is full of scorn.
 10. b. To *tote* means to carry.
 11. d. If something is *distinct* it is distinguishable, or separate.
 12. d. *Flagrant* means glaring.
 13. c. An *oration* is a speech; an address.
 14. d. *Libel* and *slander* both refer to defaming someone.
 15. d. *Philanthropy* is a noun that means good-will toward fellow men; humanitarianism; generosity.
 16. c. *Proximity* means nearness.
 17. a. *Negligible* means of little consequence; insignificant.
 18. b. *Vigilant* means watchful, especially to danger.
 19. a. *Astute* and *perceptive* both mean having or showing a keen awareness.

20. **a.** To *collaborate* means to work jointly with others; to cooperate.

Practice 3

1. **d.** One meaning of *subscribe* is to support.

2. **c.** An *opportunity* to do something is the same as a *chance* to do it.

3. **b.** *Invent* means to create or to *discover*.

4. **c.** *Sphere* and *globe* both mean ball or orb.

5. **d.** To *refine* and to *purify* both mean to remove impurities.

6. **a.** *Narrate* means to tell. Do not be fooled by choice **b**—you narrate a story, but narrate does not mean story.

7. **c.** *Nullify* means to *negate*.

8. **a.** *Sage* and *wise* both mean intelligent, perceptive.

9. **b.** *Urbane* means *sophisticated*.

10. **b.** *Dormant* and *slumbering* both mean sleeping.

11. **a.** To *banish* and to *exile* both mean to force to leave.

12. **d.** To *tailor* and to *alter* both mean to make something fit.

13. **b.** To *waive* and to *relinquish* both mean to give up.

14. **b.** *Evade* means to *avoid*.

15. **a.** *Eternal* and *timeless* both mean without end.

16. **a.** *Timid* means *shy* or lacking boldness.

17. **a.** To *stow* and to *pack* both mean to store away.

18. **d.** *Revoke* means to take back or *annul*.

19. **b.** *Covert* means *hidden*.

20. **c.** *Falter* means to *stumble*.

Practice 4

1. **c.** *Inferior* is *lower* in rank, quality, or importance.

2. **a.** *Curt* means in a rude or *gruff* manner.

3. **a.** *Perilous* means hazardous or *dangerous*.

4. **b.** *Precise* means *exact*.

5. **a.** *Commence* means *begin*.

6. **d.** Someone who is *humble* is *unassertive*.

7. **b.** *Jubilant* means *joyful*.

8. **d.** A *replica* is a close reproduction; a *copy* or duplicate.

9. **a.** *Temperate* means not extreme or excessive; *moderate* means avoiding extremes of behavior or expression.

10. **a.** *Destitute* means lacking possessions and resources.

11. **b.** *Agile* means marked by ready ability to move with quick and easy grace; *nimble* means quick and light in motion.

12. **a.** *Brazenly* means marked by contemptuous boldness.

13. **c.** *Unique* means being the only one of its kind; *unparalleled* means unequaled.

14. **d.** To be a *prerequisite* is to be required; to be *required* is to be needed.

15. **a.** To *alleviate* is to make more bearable; to *ease* is to minimize difficulty.

16. **c.** *Ample* means *generous* or more than adequate.

17. **a.** *Unanimous* means in complete assent or agreement; *uniform* means unvarying or the same as another or others.

18. **d.** To be *proficient* is to be expert or adept at something; to be *skilled* is to show ability or expertness.

19. **d.** *Obstinately* means refractory or stubborn; *stubbornly* means unduly determined, not easily persuaded.

20. **a.** To *rectify* is to set something right; to *correct* is to remove errors from something.

Practice 5

1. **a.** *Expedite* means *accelerate* the process; to speed up.

2. **b.** *Fictitious* means *imaginary*.

3. **c.** To *absolve* means to exonerate or *forgive*; to free from blame or responsibility.

4. **d.** *Hoist* means to *raise*.

5. **a.** *Disrupt* means to *interrupt* or to disturb.

6. c. To *sustain* means to *support*.

7. d. *Simmering* means barely controlled; *seething*.

8. b. To *initiate* means to *begin* or cause to begin.

9. c. *Ravenous* means *voracious*, all-consuming.

10. b. *Uninhabitable* implies conditions are so terrible that life cannot be sustained there.

11. b. *Suppressed* means held in, repressed, not expressed outwardly.

12. b. To be *immersed* means to be absorbed, engrossed, or involved in profoundly.

13. d. *Detract* means to diminish the importance of something.

14. a. *Haggle* means to bargain.

15. d. A *palpable* tension is so intense it almost seems to be a physical, tangible presence.

16. b. *Solemn* means serious.

17. c. One meaning of *sprawl* is haphazard growth of a city, usually outward toward the suburbs.

18. c. *Ingenious* means original or clever.

19. d. To *meander* means to follow a winding course.

20. b. *Precarious* means dangerous.

Practice 6

1. a. *Unity* means harmony or compatibility; *discord* means a lack of harmony.

2. d. *Detest* means to feel hostility toward, to strongly dislike; the opposite of detest is *admire*.

3. b. *Valiant* means acting with bravery or boldness; *cowardly* is the opposite.

4. d. *Lenient* means permissive, tolerant, or easygoing; *domineering* means exercising overbearing control.

5. c. *Tarnish* means to destroy the luster of; *shine* means to make bright by polishing.

6. d. *Credible* means *believable*; choice **d** is the opposite.

7. c. *Yield* means to submit; *resist* is the opposite.

8. d. *Commence* means to begin; *terminate* means to end.

9. a. *Conscientious* means careful, cautious, and thoughtful; *careless* means not showing care.

10. b. *Deficient* means lacking some necessary quality; *complete* means having all necessary parts.

11. c. *Clarify* means to make clear; *obscure* means to make dark, dim, or indistinct.

12. a. To *grant* is to permit; to *deny* is to refuse to permit.

13. d. *Lucid* means clear.

14. b. *Impartial* means not partial or biased; *prejudiced* means biased.

15. c. *Judicious* means wise or prudent; *imprudent* means not prudent.

16. a. *Shallow* means having very little depth of feeling; *profound* is the opposite.

17. a. *Erudite* means learned or possessing knowledge; *uneducated* means to lack training or knowledge.

18. c. *Amiable* means friendly; the opposite of friendly is *aloof*.

19. c. *Competent* means having adequate abilities; *inept* means incapable or not competent.

20. b. To *promote* is to advance someone to a higher rank or to advocate something; to *curtail* is to cut something short.

Practice 7

1. d. *Deplete* means to lessen; *add* is the opposite.

2. a. To *irritate* means to annoy; to *soothe* means to calm.

3. a. *Deceitful* means deceptive; *honest* is the opposite.

4. c. *Virtue* means a moral goodness; *vice* means a moral failing.

5. d. *Harmony* means agreement; *discord* means disagreement.

6. a. An *insult* is a gross indignity; a *compliment* is an admiring remark.

7. b. *Thrive* means to succeed; *fail* is the opposite.

8. c. *Serene* means calm; *chaotic* is the opposite.

9. **b.** *Diligent* means painstaking; *sloppy* is the opposite.

10. **c.** To *demolish* means to tear apart; to *create* means to build.

11. **d.** *Notable* means unusual; *ordinary* means usual.

12. **d.** *Berate* means to scold; *compliment* is the opposite.

13. **b.** *Prosperous* means rich or affluent; *destitute* means very poor.

14. **a.** *Convene* means to gather; *scatter* is the opposite.

15. **d.** To be *critical* is to be important or vital to something; to be *trivial* is to be unimportant.

16. **b.** *Nimble* means quick and light in motion; *sluggish* means slow or inactive.

17. **a.** *Tranquil* means peaceful; *agitated* means disturbed or excited.

18. **c.** *Sprightly* means lively; *dully* suggests a lack or loss of keenness or zest.

19. **c.** *Generate* means to produce; *destroy* is the opposite.

20. **d.** To be *impulsive* is to be swayed by emotion or to make rash decisions; to be *cautious* is to show forethought.

Practice 8

1. **a.** To be *prudent* is to exercise good judgment; to be *hasty* is to show a lack of thought.

2. **b.** To *retain* is to keep or hold; to *release* is to let go.

3. **c.** *Scant* is meager; *copious* is abundant.

4. **c.** *Knowledgeable* means intelligent; *ignorant* is the opposite.

5. **b.** To be *stringent* is to be rigorous or severe; to be *lax* is to be lacking in rigor or strictness.

6. **b.** *Commonplace* means normal or typical; *mysterious* is the opposite.

7. **d.** To be *succinct* is to be concise; to be *verbose* is to be wordy.

8. **a.** To be *tiresome* is to be boring; to be *stimulating* is to be exciting.

9. **b.** To be *uniform* is to be consistent or the same as another or others; to be *diverse* is to have variety.

10. **d.** To be *wary* is to be on guard or watchful; *careless* is the opposite of watchful.

11. **d.** The adjective *novel* means new or not representing something formerly known; the adjective *old* means having lived or existed for a long time.

12. **a.** A *fallacy* is a false or mistaken idea, or trickery; a *truth* is something which conforms to the facts.

13. **c.** *Permanent* means everlasting; *fleeting* is the opposite.

14. **d.** *Subsequent* means coming after or following; *previous* means coming before.

15. **c.** To be *nonchalant* means to have an air of easy indifference; to be *concerned* means to be interested and involved.

16. **b.** To *excise* means to remove; to *retain* means to keep.

17. **a.** To *disperse* means to scatter; to *gather* means to collect in one place.

18. **b.** *Pressing* means urgent; *unimportant* is the opposite.

19. **b.** *Mirth* means merriment; *solemnity* means seriousness.

20. **a.** *Sensible* means reasonable; *foolhardy* is the opposite.

Practice 9

1. **a.** To *orient* means to adjust to; to *confuse* means to mix-up.

2. **d.** To *levitate* means to rise and float; to *sink* means to go under the surface.

3. **c.** To *pacify* means to calm; to *excite* means to stir up.

4. **c.** To be *plausible* is to be likely; to be *unbelievable* is to be unlikely.

5. **b.** *Avidly* means characterized by enthusiasm and vigorous pursuit.

6. **c.** *Meekly* means not violent or strong; *forcefully* means powerfully.

7. **a.** *Complacent* means self-satisfied or unconcerned.

8. **b.** To be *ambiguous* is to be equivocal or obscure; to be *certain* is to be definite or fixed.

9. **d.** *Spontaneous* means impulsive or without planning; *prepared* is the opposite.

10. **c.** To be *eloquent* is to be fluent; to be *inarticulate* is to be unable to speak with clarity.

11. **a.** A *deterrent* prevents or discourages; *encouragement* inspires or heartens.

12. **d.** *Entangle* means to twist together; *separate* is the opposite.

13. **d.** Someone who is *impertinent* is rude; someone who is *polite* is courteous.

14. **c.** To be *ludicrous* is to be absurd; to be *reasonable* is to be rational.

15. **b.** To be *archaic* is to be ancient or outdated; to be *modern* is to be up to date.

16. **d.** *Sullen* means gloomy or dismal; *jovial* means very happy.

17. **a.** To be in *awe* of something is to admire it; to have *contempt* for something is to consider it worthless.

18. **b.** *Taut* means extremely tight; *relaxed* means not tense.

19. **a.** To *rile* is to upset; to *appease* is to pacify or satisfy.

20. **d.** To *mar* is to damage or deface; to *repair* is to restore or fix.

Practice 10

1. **d.** An *intrepid* person approaches a challenge without fear, which is the opposite of *fearful*.

2. **a.** *Methodical* means careful or in a planned manner; *erratic* means having no fixed course.

3. **d.** *Latent* means present but not active; *active* is the opposite.

4. **a.** *Affable* means pleasant and at ease; agreeable.

5. **c.** *Trepidation* means fear; the opposite would be *fearlessness*.

6. **a.** *Auspicious* means something taken as a sign promising success; the opposite is *unpromising*.

7. **c.** *Idle* means inactive; *busy* is the opposite.

8. **b.** *Furtively* means done stealthily or secretively.

9. **d.** *Entice* means to attract by arousing hope; *repel* means to drive away.

10. **a.** *Ornate* means highly decorated; *simple* is the opposite.

11. **b.** To be *ostentatious* is to be showy and boastful; the opposite would be *humble*.

12. **a.** *Endorse* means to approve; *condemn* means to disapprove.

13. **c.** *Accede* means to express approval or give consent; *disapprove* means to express disapproval.

14. **b.** *Frail* means weak; *hardy* is the opposite.

15. **b.** *Ambivalence* is uncertainty as to which approach to follow; *decisiveness* is having the power or quality of deciding.

16. **b.** *Divergent* means differing from a standard; *identical* means being the same.

17. **d.** *Pensive* means sadly thoughtful; *thoughtless* means lacking concern for others, careless, or devoid of thought.

18. **a.** One definition of *discernible* is visible, so the opposite would be *invisible*.

19. **b.** *Blemished* means having marks or flaws; *flawless* is the opposite.

20. **c.** *Abhor* means to regard with repugnance; *desire* means to long for or hope for.

Using the codes below, you'll be able to log in and access additional online materials!

WITHDRAWN

Your free online practice access code is:
FVEL267QP7HZEMC628PO

Follow these simple steps to redeem your codes:

- Go to **www.learningexpresshub.com/affiliate** and have your access codes handy.

If you're a new user:
- Click the **New user? Register here** button and complete the registration form to create your account and access your products.
- Be sure to enter your unique access codes only once. If you have multiple acess codes, you can enter them all—just use a comma to separate each code.
- The next time you visit, simply click the **Returning user? Sign in** button and enter your username and password.
- Do not re-enter previously redeemed access codes. Any products you previously accessed are saved in the **My Account** section on the site. Entering a previously redeemed access code will result in an error message.

If you're a returning user:
- Click the **Returning user? Sign in** button, enter your username and password, and click **Sign In**.
- You will automatically be brought to the **My Account** page to access your products.
- Do not re-enter previously redeemed access codes. Any products you previously accessed are saved in the **My Account** section on the site. Entering a previously redeemed access code will result in an error message.

If you're a returning user w
- Click the **Returning use** and new access codes, and click **Sign In**.
- If you have multiple ac to separate each code.
- Do not re-enter previ eviously accessed are saved in the **My Acco** emed access code will result in an error messa

If you have any questions, t at LXHub@Learning ExpressHub.com. All inquiri g our normal business hours: 9:00 A.M.–5:00 P.M. Ea

17.95   9/14/15.

LONGWOOD PUBLIC LIBRARY
800 Middle Country Road
Middle Island, NY 11953
(631) 924-6400
longwoodlibrary.org

LIBRARY HOURS

Monday-Friday	9:30 a.m. - 9:00 p.m.
Saturday	9:30 a.m. - 5:00 p.m.
Sunday (Sept-June)	1:00 p.m. - 5:00 p.m.